NEW ACCENTS

General Editor: TERENCE HAWKES

Re-Reading English

IN THE SAME SERIES

Re-Reading English

Edited by
PETER WIDDOWSON

METHUEN
London and New York

First published in 1982 by
Methuen & Co. Ltd
11 New Fetter Lane, London EC4P 4EE
Published in the USA by
Methuen & Co.
in association with Methuen, Inc.
733 Third Avenue, New York, NY 10017

Printed in Great Britain by
Richard Clay (The Chaucer Press) Ltd, Bungay, Suffolk

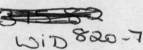

British Library Cataloguing in Publication Data

Re-reading English.—(New accents)
1. English literature—Study and teaching (Higher)
—Great Britain
I. Widdowson, Peter   II. Series
820'.7'1142   PR51.G7

ISBN 0-416-74700-0
ISBN 0-416-31150-4 Pbk

Library of Congress Cataloging in Publication Data

Re-reading English.

(New accents)
Bibliography: p.
Includes index.
1. English literature—History and criticism—
Addresses, essays, lectures.   2. Criticism—Great
Britain—Addresses, essays, lectures.   3. Criticism
—United States—Addresses, essays, lectures.
4. Politics and literature—Addresses, essays, lectures.
I. Widdowson, Peter.   II. Series: New accents
(Methuen)
PR67.R4   1982   820'.9   81-18864
ISBN 0-416-74700-0
ISBN 0-416-31150-4 (pbk.)   AACR2

Contents

General editor's preface

It is easy to see that we are living in a time of rapid and radical social change. It is much less easy to grasp the fact that such change will inevitably affect the nature of those disciplines that both reflect our society and help to shape it.

Yet this is nowhere more apparent than in the central field of what may, in general terms, be called literary studies. Here, among large numbers of students at all levels of education, the erosion of the assumptions and presuppositions that support the literary disciplines in their conventional form has proved fundamental. Modes and categories inherited from the past no longer seem to fit the reality experienced by a new generation.

New Accents is intended as a positive response to the initiative offered by such a situation. Each volume in the series will seek to encourage rather than resist the process of change. To stretch rather than reinforce the boundaries that currently define literature and its academic study.

Some important areas of interest immediately present themselves. In various parts of the world, new methods of analysis have been developed whose conclusions reveal the limitations of the Anglo-American outlook we inherit. New concepts of literary forms and modes have been proposed: new notions of the nature of literature itself, and of how it communicates are current: new views of literature's role in relation to society flourish. *New Accents* will aim to expound and comment upon the most notable of these.

In the broad field of the study of human communication, more and more emphasis has been placed upon the nature and function of the new electronic media. *New Accents* will try to identify and discuss the challenge these offer to our traditional modes of critical response.

The same interest in communication suggests that the series should also concern itself with those wider anthropological and sociological areas of investigation which have begun to involve scrutiny of the nature of art itself and of its relation to our whole way of life. And this will ultimately require attention to be focused on some of those activities which in our society have hitherto been excluded from the prestigious realms of Culture. The disturbing realignment of values involved and the disconcerting nature of the pressures that work to bring it about both constitute areas that *New Accents* will seek to explore.

Finally, as its title suggests, one aspect of *New Accents* will be firmly located in contemporary approaches to language, and a continuing concern of the series will be to examine the extent to which relevant branches of linguistic studies can illuminate specific literary areas. The volumes with this particular interest will nevertheless presume no prior technical knowledge on the part of their readers, and will aim to rehearse the linguistics appropriate to the matter in hand, rather than to embark on general theoretical matters.

Each volume in the series will attempt an objective exposition of significant developments in its field up to the present as well as an account of its author's own views of the matter. Each will culminate in an informative bibliography as a guide to further study. And while each will be primarily concerned with matters relevant to its own specific interests, we can hope that a kind of conversation will be heard to develop between them; one whose accents may perhaps suggest the distinctive discourse of the future.

TERENCE HAWKES

List of contributors

Catherine Belsey: lecturer in English, University College, Cardiff
Tony Bennett: course chairman for Popular Culture, Faculty of
    Arts, The Open University
Peter Brooker: senior lecturer in English, School of Humanities,
    Thames Polytechnic, London
David Craig: senior lecturer (non-departmental), University of
    Lancaster
Tony Davies: lecturer in English, University of Birmingham
Brian Doyle: research student, School of Humanities, Thames
    Polytechnic, London
Antony Easthope: senior lecturer in English, Manchester
    Polytechnic
Michael Egan: professor of English, University of Massachusetts
Michael Green: senior lecturer, Centre for Contemporary Cul-
    tural Studies, University of Birmingham
John Hoyles: lecturer in English, University of Hull
Peter Humm: senior lecturer in English, School of Humanities,
    Thames Polytechnic, London
Derek Longhurst: senior lecturer in English, School of
    Humanities, Thames Polytechnic, London
Graham Martin: professor of English, Faculty of Arts, The Open
    University
Wendy Mulford: senior lecturer in English, School of Humanities,
    Thames Polytechnic, London

John Oakley: principal lecturer in Literature and Sociology, Portsmouth Polytechnic

Elizabeth Owen: principal lecturer in Literature, Portsmouth Polytechnic

Carole Snee: community education worker, Lee Centre Education Project, Goldsmiths' College, University of London

Peter Widdowson: principal lecturer in English, School of Humanities, Thames Polytechnic, London

1

Introduction: The crisis in English studies

PETER WIDDOWSON

I

This book is an attempt to take stock of the current state of that area in higher education traditionally referred to as 'English' or 'Literary Studies', and to redirect it in response to pressing social and political needs. An increasing number of people teaching and studying in this field are aware that their subject is in the midst of some kind of crisis. At the moment of writing, in early 1981, there is a bitter debate in the University of Cambridge English faculty about what should constitute an 'English' syllabus, and this, which even *The Guardian* recognised as 'partly political, partly intellectual' (17.1.81, p. 1), is front-page news in the 'quality' press at least, and has air-space on the other media. In 1980, a similar debate, almost exclusively (and significantly) instituted by the students, was under way at Oxford. But it is also worth noting that just as Oxford and Cambridge were relatively late on the scene in establishing schools of English, so too are they now belatedly confronting issues which have been on the agenda for some years elsewhere – arguably, most productively in the public sector of higher education. They simply were not front-page news until they came of age in Cambridge.

There is a quaint irony, then, in Professor Christopher Ricks's recent remark, quoted in the same issue of *The Guardian*, that 'it is our job to teach and uphold the canon of English literature', because that is exactly what is in question. In recent years in Britain (as in America and elsewhere), there has been a growing debate amongst radical critics about the value of 'Literature'; about the principles by which we evaluate different literary productions; and, indeed, about the validity of the category 'Literature' itself." The causes of this are complex and wide-ranging, but we can remark, as one immediate instance, the exposure of 'Literature' and 'Criticism' to the glare of other subjects' methodologies and interrogations within the interdisciplinary courses developing in some institutions of higher education. 'Why', the historian or the sociologist asks, 'is "major" Text A so much more valuable for an understanding of society than "minor" Text B? And in any case, who decided it was "major", and on what grounds?' Any answer to such questions based exclusively on formalistic criteria is no answer at all. And any critic who acknowledges the force of those questions must begin to suspect and analyse the received tradition of 'great' literary works (designated 'Literature' here, as distinct from the older, generic, term literature which subsumes, in one of Raymond Williams's 'keywords', 'the whole body of books and writing'); to scrutinise the premises on which Criticism has operated; and to ask how far Criticism has itself *created* 'Literature' by way of its pre-selections, evaluations and tacit assumptions as to what constitutes 'literary value'. In other words, received notions of the whole 'discipline' of Literary Studies are fundamentally challenged. Equally, the development of alternative, but contiguous areas of study (such as Cultural or Communications Studies), which engage with other 'popular' forms of communication ('low-brow' fiction, for example, or television and film), challenge the hierarchical and élitist conceptions of Literature and Criticism, both in the range of material made available for serious study (culture not Culture) and in the theoretical and methodological models they bring to it.

It is, however, this last point which signals the dominant cause of the accelerating critique of Literary Studies. In the wake of the past ten years' marxist-structuralist debate – particularly about Ideology – there has developed a body of theory concerned to produce a fully-articulated marxist aesthetics. These theoretical positions (often engendered by Althusserian structuralism) have sharply focused those questions about Literature and Criticism which were already being formulated independently. The focus – predictably, perhaps – has been on the ideological space which literature as a specific category occupies (whether it has a 'relative autonomy', and what, by virtue of this, its value may be), and on the exposure of Criticism as an ideological practice. 'Literature' is, in effect, being recognised as the construct of a criticism which, while assuming and proclaiming its 'descriptiveness', its 'disinterestedness', its ideological innocence, has so constituted Literature as to reproduce and naturalise bourgeois ideology as 'literary value'. Literary value, therefore, as perceived by criticism in the 'great tradition' of master works or 'classic' texts, correlates closely with the values of liberal individualism in general, and substantially helps to underpin them.

This process is focused most exactly and concretely by the way it has been institutionalised and reinforced – at least in Britain and America – as a central element within the educational system. The significance of Matthew Arnold's conceptions of Culture and Education, as capitalism attempted to consolidate itself in nineteenth-century England, cannot be overestimated, nor can his influence on later, formative, critics like T. S. Eliot and F. R. Leavis, both of whom have been profoundly instrumental in making (forging?) a 'Literature' and a 'Tradition' for study and criticism in the twentieth century. Equally significant, perhaps, was the development, at another critical moment for bourgeois society (the years immediately after the First World War), of professional criticism, and the concurrent rise of 'English' in Britain and America as an important factor in the higher education curriculum. The reciprocal relationship between the construction of Literature by modern criticism, and the establishment of that criticism as 'English' in higher education is a nexus of great importance in the sustaining of liberal ideology. What students do, in fact, if they are 'reading English' in sixth form, university or polytechnic, is to spend most of their time 'approaching' or 'understanding' Literature by way of listening to criticism (lectures) and reading criticism (books and articles) in order to make criticism (seminar discussions, essays, etc.) and to become passable critics themselves (this in effect, is what is being assessed in the final examinations). Two related assumptions underlie and are fostered by this. One is that there is something called Literature – given, and of great value – which criticism addresses itself to, explains and approves; it assumes, that is, that Literature exists independently of criticism, not that the literature actually studied is itself constituted for the student by the critical attention paid to it. The other assumption is that the common purpose and function of criticism is the fuller understanding of Literature, and that, therefore, criticism exists as a largely undifferentiated corpus of scholarship – undoubtedly representing many different individual 'views' of literary texts, but innocent of other ulterior design or motive. Such criticism thus suppresses any sense of its informing 'approaches' which carry in their train tacit attitudes to the nature and value of Literature, to how Literature should be read, to criticism's own status and function in relation to Literature, and ultimately to the notions of social order which underlie it. Both Literature and Criticism, in other words, are naturalised by the process, floating free of any ideological determinants. The primary focus of the current critique of Literary Criticism has been, quite simply, a questioning of the assumption that there is a *given* Literature of inherent value by which, if we can learn to 'read' it properly (and it is Criticism's job to teach us how), we can all be nourished. It is on the demystification of this myth of 'literary value' as a universal and immanent category, that the debate pivots.

I should make it clear at once, however, that this debate is by no means as widespread or as potent in Literature Departments in British and American institutions of higher education as it should be, nor, despite the barrage of finely-honed theoretical work aimed at their destruction, are those departments reeling as they might be. The power and resistance of such a vested interest is not so easily shaken. A bland empiricism, congenitally inimical to theory, a profound belief in a Literature replete with 'value' and in a Criticism which has not yet been proved, point for point, to be other than 'impartial', oppose such a catastrophe. That this is so is confirmed by the reiteration, in the Cambridge English debate, of the centrality of the 'canon' and the need ultimately to dispense with the distractions of history and theory in order to return to the unproblematic *reality* of the 'literary works themselves'. The fact that history and theory may have called into question that very reality is, of course, why they must be finally ignored or rejected. And it is noteworthy, too, that in 1980 a large publisher (Routledge & Kegan Paul), whose list includes several examples of radical critical theory, produced a book entitled *The Anatomy of Literary Studies*, by Marjorie Boulton, which is clearly aimed at those going on to read English in higher education, and in which 'good literature' is regarded much as it was by Matthew Arnold and by the Newbolt Report of 1921 on *The Teaching of English in England*: that is, as a humanist surrogate for religion. That the process does not always work, Boulton concedes, and offers us, with pained incredulity, the case of William Joyce ('Lord Haw Haw') who took a first in English at London University and who, even 'knowing some of the things he must have known to achieve this' (p. 7), could still go on to be a Nazi traitor. But this, we infer, is an aberration. Normally literature in its revelation of 'universals' – 'its main business is to show us some of the more permanent mysteries and multiplicities of our human nature and social relations' (p. 45) – is a 'civilizing' influence, and the study of it the privileged access to its 'mysteries'. If this is 'Literary Studies' in the 1980s, it is indeed trapped in a time-warp of its own making. But such attitudes remain a dominant force in the educational-political field of 'English'. It is therefore imperative, if literature (past and contemporary) remains a massively consumed product in society, and if the study of it widely persists, that a criticism be mobilised which can positively engage with them. The theoretical work of the last decade had made the space for this, but it has not, in itself, filled it.

The immediate pragmatic consideration is the largely unshaken dominance of conventional criticism, precisely within its principal arena of activity – secondary and tertiary education. Such a criticism is predicated on empirical practice, on the study of 'texts', and heavily reinforced by the publishing industry, both in its large investment in Literary Criticism – even, increasingly and significantly, versions of marxist criticism – and in its publication of 'Libraries' of 'classic texts' and 'student editions'. Theory, articulated at a high level of abstraction, in fact has little material purchase here. Now I do not wish to identify myself with a crude 'new empiricism', opposed to Theory in principle. I recognise that the major advances beyond a poverty-stricken literary criticism have been made possible only by the production of a sustained theoretical critique and that a rupture with the empiricism, the questions, discourse, and hence the assumptions, of bourgeois criticism was fundamental to the development of a marxist criticism. But the result has been, in effect, that marxist criticism now means 'critical theory'.

Here a danger emerges: marxist criticism (i.e. Theory) has vacated – or at least can too easily and opportunistically be seen as having done so – the domain of the *practice* of the criticism of literature. In other words, it becomes (or is regarded as) 'something else', a 'different', autonomous, self-generating intellectual field, tending to leave the empirical field of study (Criticism) clear for the continuing operations of literary critical practice. At least, I should say, it does this within the untransformed education system of a still powerfully entrenched bourgeois culture. And it does so in two main ways – the second more serious than the first. First, pathetically but damagingly, it enables the established critics/teachers of higher education to dismiss or ignore such 'theoreticist absurdities' with mocking disdain: the wild young persons (they would say men) of the Left striking despairingly at the immanent phenomena of Literature and Criticism, when we can all see (can't we?) that the texts are solidly *there* (in attractive covers on the shelves of the university bookshops), are there to be 'understood', and when understood to be 'valued' – as students join (by the *rites de passage* of Finals) the serried and historical ranks of common(-sense) readers. Second, it allows little or no operational space to those who are not primarily theoreticians, but who wish to occupy the new spaces created by the theoretical work, and who are still teaching Literature in schools, colleges, polytechnics and universities. They are trapped: on the one hand by existing courses, by course-validating bodies, by students' expectations of what Literature courses are, and by their academic opponents; on the other, by the existence of a body of abstract, often abstruse, theoretical work which is inaccessible to their students and so easily dismissed by precisely those academic opponents. This predicament results in teacher/critics abandoning the field to establishment criticism. They may actually leave it for other, more 'progressive', studies (Cultural and Communication studies, for example) – which amounts to saying 'Here is a problem to which we theoretically know the answer but cannot resolve, let us discard it and take on another'. Or they develop an intellectual schizophrenia whereby they teach within English or Literary Studies, knowing all the while that their real practice should be an application of those theoretical models which they possess but cannot deploy.

This situation is explained, I think, by the very rapid developments of the last ten years or so. It has meant that certain theoretical positions and perceptions have not had the space fully to realise themselves before being superseded by others. In particular, the fear of being cast as an 'empiricist' has led to positions being abandoned (often to the opposition) before any substantial work has been done. And it has meant that teacher/critics have not been able to fight their daily battles with a body of substantive empirical work to hand, that would enable them to controvert the achieved (and hence proprietorial) enterprises of literary criticism. This is not to imply, of course, that there should be a moratorium on Theory. What it *does* imply is the need for critical work to be produced which challenges the assumptions and practices of conventional criticism, not in the form of theory, but as a detailed rebuttal of them in practice and as a substantive replacement for them which teachers at all levels may draw on and refer to in their classes and courses. It implies a criticism which must reveal, identify and describe the value it discerns in whatever literature it elects to address, according to precise criteria which it explicitly propounds. Such a criticism must offer both a sharply conscious explanation of *what* is being criticised, *why*, in what conditions and to what end, and an exact accountability to the text-for-study and to the reader of the analysis offered. This is essential if a materialist criticism is to develop the tools, as well as the models, to penetrate the special space occupied by literature in the social process.

II

The 'crisis' in English, then, is no longer a debate between criticisms as to which 'approach' is best. Nor is it directly, yet, a question of English Departments being closed down along with other economically unproductive (and ideologically unsound) areas – although in Thatcherite Britain that is all too real a possibility. Rather it is a question, posed from within, as to what English *is*, where it has got to, whether it has a future, whether it *should* have a future as a discrete discipline, and if it does, in what ways it might be reconstituted. This is the situation in which this book has developed and seeks to intervene. The business of making one's own academic discipline itself the object of scrutiny, of deconstructing and/or reconstructing it, has not been commonly undertaken, and certainly not for English. Such seemingly simple questions as: when did English begin to occupy a crucial position in the higher education curriculum, and why? what are its relations with certain schools of criticism? who or what determined the formation

of a normative 'English Literature'? and what is the genesis of the
present crisis in English? – reveal themselves, in this context,
as new, difficult and disquieting. They do so precisely because the
answers are not there for the taking.

The aim of this book is two-fold – as is witnessed by its structure.
First, it assembles the information which is wanting in order to
understand and answer the questions about English and its present
situation. To this end, it presents essays on the history of the rise of
English as an academic discipline; on the dominant critical practice
which has sustained it; on the critical theories which are challenging and deconstructing it; and on certain institutions which have
both hastened and accommodated this challenge. Second, it offers
a collection of 'instances' of empirical projects which may help to
occupy the space created between a moribund literary criticism
and the pioneering theoretical work which has made that space
available. These instances may, indeed, prove to be only too easily
and rapidly incorporated by the dominant latitudinarianism of
English Studies in higher education. But they are, nevertheless,
examples of a materialist criticism in progress, which acknowledges its conception in theory and yet is applicable in critical and
educational practice.

The first essay in Part I, by Brian Doyle, shows how, over a very
long period of time, English evolves from complex and changing
ensembles of cultural and ideological pressures into the academic
discipline of the twentieth century. This is not a 'history of English
Studies', but an explanation of why the 'national Language and
Literature' finds its place as the ideological centre of the bourgeois
educational curriculum. It is particularly interesting both in its
exposure of the determinants which 'produce' a seemingly innocent academic discipline and in its insistence that the study of a
subject should include that subject's own history – a point which is
later taken up by John Oakley and Elizabeth Owen. The 'texts-
for-study', in other words, are meaningless without some account
of the material processes which place them there. The following
essay, by Tony Davies, complements this by suggesting how silently
and spontaneously the practice of teaching Literature in higher
education naturalises the subject and the critical presuppositions
on which it is based. Criticism, and particularly its expression in the
seminar room, represents a common-sense philosophy which finds
its legitimation in the literature it selects, and in the modes of

discourse it employs to teach and assess its students. Catherine Belsey and Antony Easthope later extend this perception to the written literary criticism which they discuss, whilst Michael Green and Derek Longhurst confirm Davies's highlighting of pedagogic practice as the vehicle of ideological transmission.

John Hoyles and Peter Brooker, in different ways, critically survey the theoretical developments which have challenged the established aesthetic and critical premises of English Studies, indicating very clearly how insular the Englishness of English has been, and how the incursion of European schools of thought has proved instrumental in exposing the theoretical vacuum at the centre of its empiricism. Hoyles takes the longer perspective of marxist and structuralist theories, whilst Brooker concentrates more closely on post-structuralist and 'deconstructionist' critics and their role in making 'the text' – that central element in the bourgeois critical project – so problematic that it cannot survive as a substantive concept. What is important about both these essays is that they are not merely 'surveys', which finally endorse the latest theoretical positions, but are critical analyses of them, revealing their weaknesses and limitations and proposing ways in which a materialist criticism may go beyond them.

The last three essays in Part I form a small section in themselves, and a word of explanation is necessary. The challenge to conventional conceptions of English has not solely been by way of European theory. Certain developments in educational practice in institutions in Great Britain have played some part – if not always unambiguously. The Centre for Contemporary Cultural Studies (CCCS) at Birmingham University, the Open University (OU) and the Council for National Academic Awards (CNAA) seem an oddly assorted trio; and where, one might expect to be asked, is the work of the established university departments represented here? My answer has to be that in their different ways these three institutions have contributed more to a radical reassessment of English and the teaching of it in the last two decades in Britain than any other institutions – however unfair that may be to individuals and even individual departments within the universities. There is no question that the CCCS has over that period acted as the lonely and crucial focus in Britain for new ideas, theories and practices, and has been profoundly instrumental in challenging English with Cultural Studies, Michael Green maps that contribution, indicating how an intellectual history is at once a political history, and how Cultural Studies, if it is to retain its force, must remain a set of critiques or challenges within the historical process and not itself become an academic discipline. Green's essay also, and significantly, focuses on pedagogic practices, not merely the syllabus, as a central factor in transforming education. The OU, in itself a radical development in British higher educational methods, has constantly placed English or 'Literature' within a broader conspectus of disciplines, and has, as Graham Martin shows, forced its course teams to confront questions about the nature and place of Literature in interdisciplinary units. What Martin reveals, however, are the institutional and academic pressures working against major departures from the conventions of 'the subject' and, perhaps more importantly, the real difficulties involved in achieving a more than gestural interdisciplinarity in undergraduate courses. He identifies the problems of 'Period Studies' – which is significant in the light of a number of essays in Part II of this book – and suggests how often interdisciplinarity is, in effect, *multi*disciplinarity, how a true interdisciplinarity means a radical dissolution of the disciplinary boundaries – something which is only gradually emerging in such new fields as Cultural Studies. The CNAA, the largest degree-awarding body in Great Britain, has also fostered interdisciplinarity in many of its colleges and polytechnics, and English has increasingly found itself a component of Humanities courses. As Elizabeth Owen and John Oakley point out, this is not an unequivocally radicalising process, nor is it the result of radical policy initiatives within the Council. But they also point to the way CNAA validation procedures force staff-groups, even on single-subject courses, continuously to review the nature of their subject and ways of teaching it. This, they propose, is the result in particular of having to *write about* the subject in the process of producing a submission document for validation. Owen's and Oakley's essay, like the preceding two, also concludes that within Cultural Studies the artificiality of subject divisions is brought into consciousness, and that a fuller interdisciplinarity may occur there. Finally, what is apparent from the essays on the OU and the CNAA – both of which are pioneering accounts of these institutions' effects on English – is how ambivalent, even contradictorily conservative, new institutional departures can still be. Nevertheless, in the present situation, such large 'public' institutions are most active in encouraging change and, in the Humanities and Social Science areas at least, in calling into question the dominant orthodoxies of 'the subject' and its pedagogic practices – which may go some way towards explaining why the 'public sector' is in the front-line for government cuts in higher education expenditure.[1]

While the essays in Part I offer an empirical analysis of the constitution of English as an institution and as a discursive practice, those in Part II are intended as case studies (we would not claim 'models') of alternative critical work. They should not, however, be regarded as just another set of eclectic 'approaches'. Within the general project of a realigned study of history and culture, they indicate rather some of the possible directions and terrains of study. Nor should it be assumed that they simply jettison the canon of English Literature and substitute some other 'text' in its place. In fact, the essays cover a number of the main periods and genres of English Studies, while also going beyond them. But in the process, the canonic texts are placed in different sets of relations to those of the literary tradition, ceasing to be 'Literature' in becoming literary texts in history.

Catherine Belsey's essay shows how necessary it is to 'read' the constitutive criticism of the classic texts, in order to see how it produces meanings on those texts while purporting objectively to display their 'inherent' meanings, and how complicit in values and method are this critical project and the texts it canonises. In the light of this she reclaims a 'great tradition' text by consciously producing its contemporary (feminist) meaning. Antony East-hope, deploying modes of analysis derived from structuralism in the close reading of a sonnet by Sidney, also shows how consonant bourgeois critical ideology is with the humanist individualism of the literature it favours and elevates, and thus why it occludes other ('popular') forms of poetry from the canon. Derek Long-hurst, focusing on Shakespeare as the keystone of English Litera-ture and of the critical tradition, confirms this (together with Doyle's and Davies's representation of the nationalistic and naturalising functions of Literature) by analysing how Shakes-peare has been put to use by educationalists and critics in the twentieth century. He also suggests how Shakespeare may be studied within history (both Jacobean and modern), rather than being idolised as the eternal national/literary genius. In this, his essay relates to Carole Snee's (and Wendy Mulford's) emphasis on the 'period study' as the proper mode of study – where the *issues* of a period are the primary focus, and where literary texts, although not necessarily the canon, may find their appropriate place. What is especially interesting about Snee's essay, however, is the unexpected reversal involved in employing the now often denigrated techniques of 'close-reading' on a text which is emphatically non-literary. In a sense, this essay might appear just as appropriately in a book attempting a similar reappraisal of the discipline of History. Wendy Mulford's essay supports a conception of the 'period study', but from the particular perspective of socialist-feminism. Mulford argues for the rediscovery of work which has been 'hidden from history' by the dual alliance of bourgeois literary criticism and a male-dominated sexual politics. It is important to see here that a suppressed or 'forgotten' literary text, ignored by the critical tradition as 'ephemeral', is reconstituted by a modern feminist reading as a work of striking immediacy: that it is to be *understood* by way both of its historical moment of production and of its present historical moment of reading. Peter Humm's essay – focusing on a field which radical criticism has itself tended to ignore, post-modernist 'New Fiction' – also proposes a form of 'period study', albeit here in a contemporary context, by placing the literary text in another set of relations, that of the visual media and especially television. Humm's argument is that one of the major material determinations of 'New Fiction' is television, that it is impossible to understand it without inserting it into that context – the 'play' between the two forms now being integral to each – and that the idea of the discrete literary text as object-for-study does not, here, make sense. The question many of the essays are asking is: does it anywhere? David Craig and Michael Egan, from a rather different perspective, would answer 'No', because they see the crucial function and value of literature as dramatic witness of human experience in history. Literature is produced in history and read in history and can only be significant, therefore, in an engaged understanding of the historical process. They would claim, however, that some literary texts are more significant than others; that there is a dialectical relationship between their accuracy as witness and their quality as literature; and that it is for a materialist criticism to discriminate those texts, and to reveal by close textual analysis the specific features of their superior significance.

The final essay by Tony Bennett, whilst an independent contribution, offers a synoptic conclusion to the book as a whole, drawing together several of its salient ideas. In the light of the recent theoretical work discussed in Part I, Bennett points again to the problematic nature of 'the text' and to conceptions of it as receptacle of inherent meanings. He argues that marxist theory (like bourgeois criticism) has over-emphasised this by concentrating on the historical moment of the text's production, and that greater attention should now be given to the moment when the text is consumed, and so 'produced', in the reading: to the sets of social relations which determine its 'reading' and its 'meaning' in contemporary history. A truly historical sense of the text means recognising its historically variable meanings and a truly materialist criticism will, therefore, recognise that it can put *its* readings to use in the social process.

Re-Reading English, then, is a structured collection of essays – or perhaps chapters, since it is one book by several hands. We would not claim that the politics of all the contributors are by any means identical, although they are all broadly socialist; nor that the 'case studies' in Part II necessarily exemplify the theoretical positions dicussed in Part I, although they follow from them; nor again, that all the contributors would agree in detail as to the directions a reconstituted English should take. Part II clearly offers a plurality of kinds of study – although, once more, each commonly implies a breaking-down of disciplinary barriers, a re-situating of literature within the broader ambit of the study of history and cultural production. Nevertheless, the essays have certain common features and concerns which should be clearly understood before they are dismissed outright by the theoretically or politically pure in heart.

Each of them explicitly enunciates from the outset its theoretical premises and its methodological procedure, and each is written in as clear and accessible a language as its subject will permit. Indeed, this is central to our attempt to break out of the new academicism and to circulate ideas beyond a privileged élite. Equally central is the brevity of the essays; none purports to be definitive. No doubt there are many books to be written here, but that is not the point. The essays *had* to be short if all the material were to be brought together in one volume, and an immediate and collective intervention made. This sense of a need for direct engagement with critical and educational practice is one of a number of recurrent themes in the essays. It is not fortuitous, in this context, that several of them point to the example of feminism, at least in passing, as an active radical practice which directly challenges the dominant ideology in its specific social forms and relations. What is most insistently stressed is the need for a thoroughgoing analysis of the constitution of academic disciplines such as English, and for the inclusion of that analysis in any course of study; for a continuous fore-grounding of Criticism as the discourse in which leterary texts are produced and reproduced; for a simultaneous questioning of the status of 'the text' as the primary material of 'English' and as the ultimate source of 'meaning' and 'value'; for the introduction onto the syllabus of other forms of writing and cultural production than the canon of Literature; for a resiting of literature in history – both past and contemporary – as one specific discourse in the general study of culture; and for a full understanding of the place and function of 'reading' and 'criticism' in present society.

But what all the essays proclaim is the need to occupy that space in the higher education curriculum which English has hitherto held and which, in the present situation, we cannot afford to lose. We cannot afford to lose it because it is a space, within the crucial institution of education, in which intellectual work can go on in the struggle to reappropriate that institution. And it is a space which will be quickly claimed by even more regressive educational tendencies if radical teachers vacate it. Most importantly, then, what these essays recognise is that all education is a *political* activity, and that the teaching of English is especially so. Some of them reveal the extent to which this has always been the case in the traditional modes and practices – although a fundamental tenet of liberal ideology has been precisely to deny that. But they all emphasise that if English is necessarily a site on which social meanings are constructed, and that if this has been the case within and on behalf of the dominant ideology, then let it now become such for a materialist politics.

Note
1   This was written before the University Grants Committee initiative of the summer of 1981 when universities themselves became the victims of Thatcherite policy.

PART I:

History, theory, institutions

2

The hidden history
of English studies

BRIAN DOYLE

I

How and why did English become a major subject in higher education? Within disciplines such as sociology, history and philosophy
the question of the significance of a discipline's own past for a
reflexive understanding of its present operations has to some
extent been posed: not so within English.[1] Yet, as anticipated by the
1921 Report of the Board of Education, *The Teaching of English in
England* (Newbolt Report), English has since been consolidated as a
central feature of the curriculum at all levels of education; and, in
this process, become the object of concern regarding its efficacy by
teachers, educationists, politicians and others. Unlike the comparable case in France,[2] such concern has failed to generate any
extensive understanding of the ways in which the teaching of a
'national' language and literature operates as a key feature in
reproducing the cultural relations within what is usually called
'our' society. English (as 'our' language and literature) within education is thus not normally recognised as a significant influence
over commonly acquired senses of self, class, gender, family and
nationality.

Such accounts of the history of English in education as have been
written[3] are posited on an easy sense of its self-evident value as an
educational subject: 'English' and 'education' in these accounts are

not seen as disturbed or disturbing terms; except, in recent years, at that 'chalk-face' which is the urban school in crisis. It is evident, as I hope to show, that English and education both tend to carry the sense of an unproblematic national cultural heritage, to which (in the liberal versions) all citizens should in principle be accorded equal access. Thus 'the English language' and 'the national literature', in dominant definitions, represent ratifications of a selective sense of culture and history, or comfortable affirmations of certain structures and forms of cultural authority. "

Up to a point, everyone knows that 'the language' and 'the literature', by virtue of their very restrictions of access, embody forms of cultural authority. We know it in our felt relations to everyday uses of literature and language in the school and in the media – in the common exchanges of power that we call 'communication'.[4] But selective uses of English as a language and a literature have also been of great importance in mediating power relations between classes and other groups in British society. The emphases within the academic study of English, however, upon 'appreciation' and 'communication' have provided little understanding of this history. Thus they are of little help, either, in translating into articulated forms of knowledge ordinary senses of the present-day power relations of language and literature in education or elsewhere. One object of this essay is to assist in such work of translation.[5]

Another obstacle which must be overcome is the tendency to reduce all events prior to the establishment of English at Oxbridge to the level of a pre-history, an ideological husk discarded by English in its advance to the status of an academic discipline.[6] I want to show that the move since the first quarter of the present century within English towards a state of professional respectability and systematisation cannot be adequately explained in terms of a shift from a pre-paradigm (or pre-historic) stage to one fully formulated in intellectual and practical styles. Such formalistic discriptions tend to evacuate the political and cultural significances of the shift (which was real). The accepted focus upon Oxbridge also misses the key fact that institutional initiatives there were *responses* to a 'well-founded national demand' for English in education (to use a phrase characteristic of the late nineteenth-century debate on this matter).[7] I shall examine, in turn, the long history which led to this demand; the radically altered nature of the English language and literature as used in nineteenth-century education compared to anything that had gone before;" and (up to now least noticed of all)" the ways in which English and education were articulated as devices for altering the gender relations of the 'national family'."

II

It needs to be noted immediately that 'the English language and literature', as a field of semantic and practical activity, did not simply arrive on the scene from nowhere, full and complete. It had to be worked for, constructed, forged out of struggles between differing lived meanings and cultural forms. And this means real people and classes. It was out of such struggles, for example, that in the Middle Ages forms of English ousted French as the linguistic ensemble most suited to facilitate intimacy amongst what was not yet a truly national ruling class.[8] At first little part was played in the process of generating cultural homogeneity at this level by written forms; the spoken language was the true national vehicle of discursive power.[9] The great local magnates could employ clerks for such writing tasks as were necessary, considering their seal to be of greater significance than their signature.[10] Written, and later printed forms, really belonged to a Church whose allegiance was to Rome and to Latin.[11] 'Culture', it is interesting to observe, carried the sense of 'worship', which it was only to lose in the massive transformations of the sixteenth century under the Tudor monarchy.[12]

The Tudor process of 'assimilation to the dominant national patterns'[13] was also the one which gave to written and printed forms a truly national currency among the nobility and gentry, and facilitated the spread of a novel set of cultural relations now mediated by *status* in addition to the more direct exercises of power.[14] The question of the precedence of a (classical) literary education over arms was for the first time a centre of discussion among the nation's rulers.[15] Thereby also arose forms of 'private' education which extended the existing modes for inculcating courtly manners to include more 'modern' subjects such as geography, history and English, using the services of a home tutor or 'governor'.[16] Public education such as was provided in the petty and grammar schools and the universities was firmly shaped, in contrast, to the needs of clerical vocation and, as such, was dominated by the study of Latin.[17] What happened during the post-Reformation process of Tudor assimilation was that these public forms came under private pressure as the sons of rich laymen began to flood into the universities.[18] Already under Henry VIII an essential uniformity had been established within education (nationally directed by forces mostly antagonistic to Rome), which seems to have been a necessary precondition for the establishment in turn of a culturally homogeneous ruling gentry and nobility.[19] Such homogenising tendencies generated the first truly 'national' sense of country and tongue, and thus the first attempts at gathering together written vernacular productions, or 'literature', in the role of 'hand-maidens' of the 'national tongue'.[20]

Cultural uniformity, in so far as it was related to the vernacular language, called for the establishment of standardised linguistic forms on the 'fixed' model of Latin (and to some extent Greek), and these, under the influence of courtly humanism, were to have an increasing presence in both public and private education in the course of the sixteenth century.[21] The attempt was to construct an acceptably *classical* ensemble of linguistic and literary practices, that is to establish a 'ruled' language or classical vernacular.[22] Of course such work of construction necessitated ruling certain forms *out* as well; Milton's attack upon 'common rhymers', in his essay on education, is a later example of this process.[23] However, by the time of Milton's attack, the first great challenge to dominant forms of education and learning had also been mounted. Much of the revolutionary agitation and pamphleteering was directed against the existing 'learned ministry' and favoured a local or 'gathered' religious formation rather than a national one. The challenge was anti-classical, biblical, and vernacular in nature, and supported by an imagination and enthusiasm which rocked the basis upon which the ruling cultural relations had been built since the Reformation.[24]

When the moment came, with the Restoration, for constructing a new cultural synthesis, the Anglican ruling groups were able to call upon, among other forms, those developed within the universities. These had substantially altered the relation between English and education from early on in the seventeenth century.[25] Within the universities the increased lay presence had caused greater attention to be given to 'culture' in education in a sense which was of relatively recent origin. Instead of 'worship', with its exclusively clerical vocational orientation, 'culture' now meant a process of personal 'cultivation', by transfer from the sense of cultivating plants and livestock. If letters had by now achieved at least some precedence over arms, concern over personal 'merit' was causing a revaluation of the social role of 'blood'.[26] 'Merit', here, was something more amenable to systematic cultivation than had been exclusively aristocratic blood, although it had not yet taken on its later dominant sense as 'measurable intelligence'. Cultivation involved something other than the 'heavy breeding' of scholarship. In the universities, it was becoming the 'extra-statutory' role of English and other modern subjects to provide the 'lighter breeding' which private education had formerly established as necessary to the complete gentleman.[27]

The Restoration synthesis drew upon such developments rather than the vernacular enthusiasms of the left-wing puritans. But, in learning the dangers of upheaval from below which the unprecedented challenge of the period of revolutionary agitation had taught them, supporters of the new Restoration order also instituted major interventions at all levels of education as part of the more highly policed cultural ensemble which was now constructed.[28] One such measure, paradoxically of particular significance for the development of English, was the systematic exclusion of Dissenting groups from public education. This resulted in the growth of autonomous Dissenting Academies which, in marked distinction to continuing university practices, increasingly taught through the medium of English and eventually took English itself as one of their subjects of study.[29] In this they were influenced by educational developments in Scotland, where, following the political and economic union with England of the early eighteenth century, educational practices were evolved which were intended to facilitate forms of cultural union; thus the great concern with measures to educate what may be called the 'abstract gentleman'.[30] Hume, for example, whose main concern was with abstract human nature, continued to speak Scots while intellectualising in written metropolitan English, and, together with such contemporaries as Kames and Smith, was concerned to connect, according to a systematically abstracted model, standards of English discourse and scientifically-grounded public 'taste'. It was within the Scottish universities and out of such cultural concerns, that pedagogic forms developed which were recognisable as akin to what later became 'English' (they were called 'English Rhetoric' or 'Belles Lettres').[31]

If the new rhetoric can be seen largely as an outcome of the cultural synthesis of the Restoration, developments in the teaching of reading and writing within eighteenth-century charity schools are a direct consequence of measures also instituted at the same time: measures intended systematically to police the 'morality' and 'criminal' tendencies of the lower orders as a result of lessons learned during the revolutionary ferment.[32] Much of the tradition of English teaching in the elementary schools of the nineteenth century and beyond should be traced, in its disciplinary force, to the latter tendency.

III

The eighteenth century also saw the production of a considerable literature on female education.[33] These writings were dominated by the notion of a greater natural endowment among women for modern languages as compared to classics and mathematics. Such little formal provision as was made for female education carried a similar emphasis. Although this provision was small, it was none the less significant for the future, since it provides the earliest evidence of an educational sense of the special 'fittedness' of women for English. The private boarding schools which were developed during the late eighteenth century to complement the home education of (upper-class) women reflect this same sense of fittedness. A gradual shaping and articulation of this 'fit' can be traced in the course of the following century, to the point at which it becomes of central importance to the functions of the teaching of English at all 'higher' levels of the national system of education. The interests of educationalists in female education during the eighteenth century may have been peripheral, but it gave way over the next hundred years to the institution of a fully national system of schooling in which the staffing was predominantly female. And the new profession of teacher was constituted to a great extent around a conception of women in the national culture which was radically new and intimately attuned to the development of 'personal' characteristics – itself becoming associated with 'the national literature'.

'We must put a stop to this', said Admiral Fairfax of his daughter's interest in mathematics, 'or we shall have Mary in a straitjacket one of these days.'[34] This characteristic late eighteenth-century upper-class attitude was a far cry from proclamations a century later on the need for a new breed of women to mother the nation's children through education. The change can be traced to a number of contributory forces, not least of which were the new attitudes to marriage and the family which developed among the middle classes from early on in the new century. The eighteenth-century conception of the 'blessing' which accompanied early marriage and a large family was, by the 1830s, being replaced by a concern among the middle classes for the achievement of a 'prudent' union. Marriage should be postponed until it could be afforded; and an 'imprudent' marriage in this sense was seen as both unwise and immoral.[35] In fact, by the middle of the century, with the tendency of middle-class men to marry late or not at all, and with the general demographic trends of the time, considerable worry over the 'surplus' of women in society was being expressed. The Census of 1851 revealed that this surplus included 876,290 women who were neither wives nor mothers, 24,770 of whom were employed as governesses.[36] In the event, the impetus towards a conception of a national culture seen in terms of an organically unified whole national way of life, promoted a related view of education as a central mechanism for the reproduction of this national culture, and in a sense helped to 'solve' the problem of the surplus. The dominant conception of woman as homemaker and the notion of women as potentially and acceptably employed in professions were absorbed into a quasi-professional and at the same time quasi-maternal composite function whereby women educated the children of the national 'corporate body'.[37]

But this necessitated the education of women into their new role. Here the foundation of the Governesses' Benevolent Institution, Queen's College, London, and of the multiplicity of schools and training colleges and other institutions of female instruction during the second half of the century was crucial. And within this new general formation the role of English was to be central. Charles Kingsley, for example, in his introductory lecture as Professor of English at Queen's College, London, clearly stated the objective at which women students should aim. In his view the reading of English Literature (to include modern works) would help towards an understanding of the 'English spirit', thus counteracting the notion that 'the minds of young women are becoming un-English'.[38] And the study of history (intimately connected with the study of English as both a language and a literature at this time) would play its part, by helping to 'quicken women's inborn *personal interest* in the actors of this life-drama, and be quickened by it in return, as indeed it ought: for it is thus that God intended woman to look instinctively at the world'.[39] The full force of this new movement in education began to be evident from the time of James Stuart's course of university extension lectures under the auspices of the North of England Council for Promoting the Higher Education of Women in 1867.[40] It is difficult to decide whether the extension movement or female education in general was the more powerful factor. What is certain is that each developed in concert with the other, and together played a major part in establishing a formal system of education which would support the framework of cultural relations appropriate to a fully national organism. After 1870 the huge demand for schoolteachers who had a higher education led to a dramatic rise in the number of women so employed, causing female students at Oxford, for example, to skip the intermediate examinations and read for honours as directly as possible. Indeed up to the First World War teaching was the most common occupation of women graduates.[41]

However, at Oxford the study of English had found little favour despite its support by a Royal Commission in the 1850s.[42] But in 1873 English was included in the examinations for a Pass Degree; and, following a major public campaign during the 1880s, a final Honours School of English Language and Literature was founded in 1893.[43] For a long time this remained largely a women's course, English being considered a 'women's subject' unsuited to the masculine intelligence. As late as the Great War, 'English' still carried such connotations, symbolised by being commonly referred to as 'pink sunsets'.[44]

The nature of the 'national demand' for English during the late Victorian period may now be evident. It was really a key element in a more general demand to school the 'nation's children', predominantly using personnel of a certain kind (the mother-teacher). Some time later, within the secondary schools, this was reinforced by a disciplinary ensemble known as the 'English subjects'[45] (English language and literature, geography, history and perhaps some science, which were only gradually specialised to their component parts). At 'higher' levels of education the demand was expressed as a call for the 'nationalisation' of the ancient universities, which in effect meant greater support by these institutions for a National Extension Movement increasingly directed to the production of teachers educated to university level and to female education.[46] In the newer civic and local university colleges it was precisely the pressure of grant-aided student teachers which made possible developments in education in the English subjects and the arts in general.[47]

However, even such a limited development in the education of middle- and upper-class women constituted a continued challenge to the idea that 'masculine' academic studies[48] (i.e. intellectual studies in general, but especially classics and mathematics: 'English' as an artistic accomplishment was always equivocal in this respect) were unsuitable for the future mothers of 'the race'. In the event a dual solution emerged: the higher education of women by means of English remained in the hands of a predominantly male teaching profession (as it continues to be today), while the subject became gradually transformed into a 'masculine' academic discipline by concentration on a specific set of objects (the 'texts') and developing a strict 'scientific' method of understanding these objects (cf. I. A. Richards and 'practical criticism').[49] These were, however, developments predominantly of the twentieth century, and involved a number of transformations away from nineteenth-century conceptions of English as simply an element in a study of the *national* culture, i.e. of those features characteristic of the national organism or body. The study of English in the nineteenth-century curriculum meant committing to memory the components of a historical map of the National Literature and Language,[50] while the work of scholarship was largely directed towards the production of a suitably detailed and documented chart of the English cultural tradition. Ironically, the term 'Cultural Studies' would more accurately describe 'English' at this stage. In their major working directions such cultural studies moved towards large-scale syndicated projects, to which the New (later 'Oxford') English Dictionary and the Cambridge History of English Literature stand as monuments.[51] Such 'ordnance surveys' of the national culture provided the base from which the mission of propagating Culture through English was launched, a mission to which both the government funding of the Dictionary and, later, the foundation by the Board of Education of a commission to report on 'The Teaching of English in England' gave the final stamp of official governmental approval.

IV

One can further identify the transformation of modern subjects from being handmaidens of the abstract gentlemanly character to studies of the national culture or 'national character', by looking at some institutional developments early in the nineteenth century. The earliest instruction in the English language and literature was provided at University College, London from the 1820s. This – despite the new title – was similar to eighteenth-century Scottish Rhetoric and Belles Lettres.[52] What was perhaps new, though, was an emphasis upon the use of literature as a vehicle for moral instruction,[53] and as a liberal counterweight to the principles of pure utilitarianism upon which the new London foundation was based. The continuity with eighteenth-century approaches is more apparent at the new Anglican university in Durham where, while instruction was firmly based on the classical models of the ancient English universities, allowance was none the less made during the 1830s for the 'lighter breeding' in the form of a readership in 'History and Polite Literature'.[54] More significant for future developments was the emergence at King's College, London during the same decade, of a professorial subject called 'English and History' (a pattern which was later followed at Leeds, Liverpool, Sheffield and the Queen's Colleges at Belfast, Cork and Galway). However, it would be inaccurate to characterise this as an example of an 'academic discipline', since the term tended to function as a catch-all for what would later become specialised into English Literature, Modern History, Philology, English Language, and even – in some developments – Geography, Economics and Social Studies. In the post-elementary schooling sector, as we have seen, an equivalent formation was developing as what was normally called the 'English subjects'.[55] More recognisably modern disciplinary developments were presaged, from the middle of the century, at Manchester where the academic structures and practices which were to challenge, and to a great extent supersede, the collegiate and classical system of the ancient universities began to be formulated. These included, as well as the disciplinary structure, a concern with research and a sense of professional expertise, supported by a hierarchical system of administrative organisation and an academically autonomous professoriat.[56] From the 1860s such modernising forces started to be felt even at Oxbridge (albeit to produce little institutional effect until much later in the century) in the battles which began to be staged between the collegiate and professorial systems.[57] But a formation called the 'English Language and Literature' is more characteristic of this moment, when professorial subjects under that heading were instituted at Trinity College, Dublin, Glasgow, Edinburgh, Birmingham and Newcastle.

At the same time that the work of scholarly syndication mentioned above was taking place, history – most notably under the influence of Tout at Manchester – was staking its claim for disciplinary autonomy on the basis of a singular 'methodological' approach to its subject matter.[58] English now began to be affected by two tendencies: a further specialisation from the 'English Language and Literature' to the separate professorial institutionalisation of 'Language' and 'Literature', and a 'methodological' or 'scientific' posture of its own. Within the domain of literature the new specialising tendency was represented by a view of English as a study which involved the kind of personal growth appropriate to properly balanced citizens.[59] The Cambridge Tripos of the 1920s stands as a monument to this tendency.[60]

In the meantime, following the 1902 Education Act, the national system of education was beginning to be reconstructed on the principle of stages (primary, secondary, tertiary, rather than the autonomous 'elementary' and 'higher' sectors as previously) mediated by examinations between the various levels. In this context a move was begun to install the English subjects, and later 'English' as such, as the core element of the curriculum and the one subject absolutely essential for students at all levels of what was becoming a fully 'national' system. The move was supported by the Board of Education from early in the twentieth century, and reinforced by the 1921 Report and by the life-long campaign of Denys Thompson and his associates on the journals *Scrutiny* and *The Use of English*.[61]

As part of these processes of specialisation and professionalisation the status of the 'text' became increasingly important, and from the 1920s onwards was enshrined as the central and supposedly objective element in the study of literature within higher education, supported by the equally objective-looking notion of 'literary value'.[62] At this moment, and from this perspective only, English literature as a discipline in higher education shook off much of what had previously been its role (as one aspect of the study of the 'national character') and emerged as an autonomous academic domain almost exclusively concerned with the study of its own texts. None the less, its past (despite dismissal as a 'pre-history' by historians of the fully-fledged 'discipline') has continued to reassert itself from time to time, even if in somewhat altered forms. Whether as 'Culture and Environment Studies' or as versions of cultural and social studies, that residual past has opposed the dominant practices of the profession of English.[53]

But as long as the discipline-based structure holds, the texts will be with us, together with all the problems for teachers of English which flow from what is ultimately a professional conception of a specific set of teaching practices.[64] What then is a teacher to do today about this problem of the 'texts'? I want to make it clear that my major object has been to bring into view the dominant force of 'English Language and Literature' as a practical and definitional process involving historically a series of gatherings and reinscribings of actual written works. It must, however, be recognised that 'English' normally tends to nullify the possibility of any substantial understanding of either the social forces which have brought such writings about, or their later, selective and variable use and appropriation. It must be doubted, therefore, whether those dominant ideological forces which have generated a sense of 'English' as an integrated set of manifestations of the national character, and then as a casebook of literary value, can be counteracted *within* the ambit of a literary education as presently constituted. Other contributors to the present collection have proposed a variety of alternative uses to which these writings may be put within the processes of higher education. I want to urge the necessity of including under any 'English' rubric a course which retrieves the hidden history which I have outlined, if only to show that apparently 'personal' responses to 'self-evidently' literary works are much more than the innocent responses to pleasure that they are normally made out to be; and that a more rewarding pleasure is to be found in discovering and understanding the social forces at work in and around 'the English Language and Literature'.

Notes

Throughout the book, unless otherwise indicated, place of publication is London.

1   On sociology see Goran Therborn, *Science, Class and Society* (New Left Books, 1976); on history C.J.W. Parker, 'Academic history: paradigms and dialectic', *Literature and History*, 5, 2 (Autumn 1979), 165–82; on philosophy Jonathan Rée, 'Philosophy as an academic discipline: the changing place of philosophy in an arts education', *Studies in Higher Education*, 3, 1, 5–23. See also note 4 below.

2   I have in mind here particularly the work of Renée Balibar and Pierre Bourdieu. The following are the most accessible examples of such work in English translation: Renée Balibar, 'An example of literary work in France' in Francis Barker *et al.* (eds), *1848: The Sociology of Literature* (Colchester: University of Essex Press, 1978), pp. 27–46; Pierre Macherey and Etienne Balibar, 'Literature as an ideological form', *Oxford Literary Review*, 3, 1 (1978), 4–12; Pierre Bourdieu and J.-C. Passeron, *Reproduction in Education, Culture and Society* (1977). An application to British education can be found in Tony Davies, 'Education, ideology and literature', *Red Letters*, 7 (n.d.), 4–15.

3   Stephen Potter, *The Muse in Chains* (Jonathan Cape, 1937); E.M.W. Tillyard, *The Muse Unchained* (Bowes & Bowes, 1958); D.J. Palmer, *The Rise of English Studies* (Oxford University Press, 1965); J.M. Newton, 'English literature at the university: a historical enquiry', unpublished thesis (University of Cambridge, 1963). For a more extensive treatment of English and cultural transmission see Brian Doyle, 'The tyranny of the past', *Red Letters*, 10 (n.d.), 23–33.

4   See Ray Holland, *Self and Social Context* (Macmillan, 1977), for a useful discussion of the problems of a 'self-reflexive' understanding and its relation to what he calls the 'pathological' rigidity of the divisions between academic disciplines.

5   See also R. Fowler *et al.* (eds), *Language and Control* (Routledge & Kegan Paul, 1979).

6   J.M. Newton, for example, speaks of the 'bad old days' before Cambridge English and expresses an expectation that the reader may be surprised to learn of the 'social' emphasis given during this earlier period to the value of a literary education. Newton, op. cit., pp. 1, 42.

7   The phrase is attributed to Henry Nettleship (1887) by C.H. Firth in his 1909 Oxford pamphlet *The School of English Language and Literature* (Oxford: Blackwell).

8   Raymond Williams, *The Long Revolution* (Chatto & Windus, 1961), p. 239.

9   I.e. those aspects of social power relations most directly mediated by means of linguistic exchanges ('discourses'). See also note 5 above.

10 John Lawson and Harold Silver, *A Social History of Education in England*, (Methuen, 1973), p. 35.

11 Irene Parker, *Dissenting Academies in England* (Cambridge: Cambridge University Press, 1914), p. 3.

30   Re-Reading English

12 Raymond Williams, *Keywords* (Fontana/Croom Helm, 1976), and the *OED*.

13 See Christopher Hill, *Reformation to Industrial Revolution* (Weidenfeld & Nicolson, 1967), p. 15.

14 Hugh Kearney, *Scholars and Gentlemen* (Faber, 1970), p. 26.

15 Foster Watson, *The Beginnings of the Teaching of Modern Subjects in England* (Pitman, 1909), p. xxiv.

16 Ibid., p. xxix.

17 T.W. Baldwin, *William Shakespeare's Small Latine and Lesse Greeke* (Urbana, Illinois: University of Urbana Press, 1944), p. 182, vol. 1.

18 M. Curtis, *Oxford and Cambridge in Transition, 1558–1642* (Oxford University Press, 1961), p. 54.

19 Baldwin, op. cit., p. 183.

20 Palmer, op. cit., p. 2.

21 R.F. Jones, *The Triumph of the English Language* (Stanford: Stanford University Press, 1953), p. 71.

22 Ibid., p. 286.

23 John Milton, 'Treatise on Education' (1644) in *Selected Prose* (Harmondsworth: Penguin, 1974).

24 Kearney, op. cit., p. 75; R.F. Jones, 'The humanistic defence of learning in the mid-seventeenth century' in J.A. Mazzeo (ed.), *Reason and Imagination* (Routledge & Kegan Paul, 1962), pp. 71–92; R.L. Greaves, 'Gerrard Winstanley and educational reform in puritan England', *British Journal of Educational Studies*, XVII, 166–76.

25 J.J. O'Brien, 'Commonwealth schemes for the advancement of learning', *British Journal of Educational Studies*, XVI, 30–42; Jones, op. cit. (1962).

26 Watson, op. cit., p. xxix.

27 Curtis, op. cit., pp. 131–2.

28 Jones, op. cit. (1962).

29 See Parker, op. cit. and H. Maclachlan, *English Education under the Test Acts* (Manchester: University of Manchester Press, 1931).

30 Newton, op. cit., pp. 63ff.

31 ibid., pp. 81–91.

32 D.W. Sylvester, *Educational Documents, 800–1816* (Methuen, 1970), p. 176.

33 Lawson and Silver, op. cit., p. 208.

34 Quoted in C.S. Bremner, *Education of Girls and Women in Great Britain* (Swan Sonnenschein, 1897), p. 10.

35 J.F.C. Harrison, *Learning and Living, 1790–1960* (Routledge & Kegan Paul, 1961), pp. 84–5.

36 Vera Brittain, *The Women at Oxford* (Harrap, 1960), p. 25; Elaine Kaye, *A History of Queen's College, London, 1848–1972* (Chatto & Windus, 1972), p. 14.

37 Kaye, op. cit., p. 47.

38 Palmer, op. cit., p. 39.

39 Bremner, op. cit., pp. 92–3.

40 Brittain, op. cit., p. 32; M. Sanderson (ed.), *The Universities in the Nineteenth Century* (Routledge & Kegan Paul, 1975), p. 16.

41 Brittain, op. cit., p. 40.
42 Ibid.
43 Firth, op. cit.
44 Brittain, op. cit., p. 40n.
45 I.A. Gordon, *The Teaching of England* (Oxford University Press, 1947), p. 7.
46 Bremner, op. cit., p. 162.
47 W.H.G. Armytage, *Civic Universities* (Ernest Benn, 1955), p. 256.
48 Sheldon Rothblatt, *The Revolution of the Dons* (Faber, 1968), p. 192.
49 I.A. Richards, *The Principles of Literary Criticism* (1924), (repr. Routledge & Kegan Paul, 1976).
50 Newton, op. cit., p. 154.
51 Ibid., p. 103. The fact that the government was prepared to grant financial aid to J.A.H. Murray to assist in the preparation of the *OED* was used by Henry Nettleship in 1877 as an argument for the foundation of an English School at Oxford (Palmer, op. cit., p. 106).
52 Palmer, op. cit., p. 18.
53 H.H. Bellot, *University College, London, 1826–1926* (The Athlone Press, 1929).
54 C.E. Whiting, *The University of Durham, 1832–1932* (Sheldon Press, 1932), p. 48.
55 Gordon, op. cit. See also note 36 above.
56 H.B. Charlton, *Portrait of a University, 1851–1951* (Manchester: Manchester University Press, 1951).
57 A.I. Tillyard, *A History of University Reform* (Cambridge: Heffer, 1913), pp. 160–1.
58 Charlton, op. cit., pp. 85–95.
59 Newton, op. cit., p. 152. This approach is best exemplified in I.A. Richards's theory of poetry as a means of achieving psychological balance between otherwise unstable 'impulses'. Richards, op. cit.
60 E.M.W. Tillyard, *The Muse Unchained* (Bowes & Bowes, 1958), provides a suitably 'intimate' account of this moment.
61 For a more detailed account of the development of English within the national schooling system at this time see Brian Doyle, *Some Uses of English* (1981) (available from the Centre for Contemporary Cultural Studies, University of Birmingham).
62 Newton's account of Bradley's notion of 'intrinsic value' is useful for an understanding of this development.
63 See note 61 above.
64 See Francis Mulhern, *The Moment of 'Scrutiny'* (New Left Books, 1979), pp. 309–20.

3
Common sense and critical practice: teaching literature

TONY DAVIES

I

What does it mean, to 'read English'? There has been a good deal of discussion in recent years about the history, nature and purpose of literary criticism, ranging from complacent self-admiration through uneasy introspection to polemic and summary dismissal. Literary criticism has itself been, from the outset, a notably reflexive and self-conscious activity, repeatedly posing, through its chosen texts and traditions, the question of its own sufficiency. There has been, too, a proliferating meta-discourse of 'criticising the critic': 'readers' on criticism, undergraduate courses on the history of criticism, postgraduate seminars on 'critical theory'. But 'reading English'? That is a separate or at least a separable issue.

I would guess that most people who teach Literature in higher education will have had some experience of the problematic discrepancy, for their students, between 'reading' and 'criticism'. It's not uncommon, I've found, for a student to linger after a tutorial to ask, in a worried way, whether 'her own ideas' about a text are enough, or whether she should be 'reading some criticism'. These same students attend a lecture course on critical 'methods', but generally find it not very helpful when it actually comes to 'reading the texts'. The uncertainty is easily understandable. Of course there is no such thing as 'reading the texts', with a kind of unmedi-

ated purity of response. But few first-year students are in a position, given the dominant pedagogies of sixth-form English, to
recognise the extent to which their simple 'reading' has itself been
constructed by and around a powerful and habitual (powerful
because habitual) literary-critical practice. Many, indeed, have been
told to 'avoid criticism' by teachers whose every judgement, whose
very position, carries the force of a latent critical mode, an invisible
theory about the nature of Literature, the composition of the
canon, the preferred procedures of reading and response.

A Gramscian distinction is useful here, between the conscious
and systematic 'philosophy of the intellectuals' and that 'spontaneous philosophy' engrained imperceptibly in language, in practical
activity, in the operative conceptions and intuitions of everyday life
(Gramsci, 1971, pp. 323, 331). Gramsci emphasises the integral
relationship between the two, arguing that 'everyone is a
philosopher' and attacking the 'widespread prejudice that
philosophy is a strange and difficult thing'. But few people regard
themselves spontaneously as 'philosophers', and the difference
between philosophy and common sense is not simply a matter of
prejudice. Nor is it only a question of language, of degree of
elaboration, or of practical function. It is, as Gramsci insists, a
question of *politics*: of linguistic and social power ('the relationship
between common sense and the upper level of philosophy is
assured by "politics".' (ibid., p. 331)). The uncertainty of the university student torn between 'reading the texts' and 'reading criticism', between the seemingly natural, immediate response and
elaborated 'method', points to the systemic ambiguity of the
undergraduate position itself, intermediate and transitional between the 'reading' of school and the assured 'criticism' (still more,
the 'theory') of the postgraduate and the tenured academic.

This is crude, of course, in its suggestion of a smooth transition
from a common-sense practice of reading in the schoolroom to an
incrementally articulate practice of criticism in the seminar and
common room. It may go some way to explain the distinctive
ambivalence of undergraduate education, an ambivalence experienced by many students and perhaps underlying the strange social
atmosphere of English departments, with their odd mixtures of
deference, matiness and resentment, their uncertainty about
modes of address, their curious little rituals of recognition and
evasion. But such a characterisation of the structure of the

literary-critical career, in which the teacher appears as the incarnation of discursive authority, suffers, from the point of view of those who engage in it, from a certain unreality. Being a university or polytechnic lecturer doesn't actually *feel* much like that. Whatever I may write or think, however pure, rigorous and systematic my discourse may be on such occasions, when once again I sit down to a tutorial or seminar, with *Lycidas* or *Middlemarch* open in front of me, and turn, in that expectant pause, to the surrounding faces, what comes out of my mouth then is likely to sound, by the highest standards of discursive rigour, decidedly limp: 'Well, what do you think of this, then?'

The limpness of that question, repeated in its various inflections – aggressive, conciliatory, pleading or plain desperate – a thousand times a day, is my subject: the limpness, and the hidden coercions. Not Literary Criticism, the literary 'philosophy of the intellectuals', but Literature teaching. Or rather, the ways in which the teaching of Literature in higher education carries embedded within it, in often unconscious or half-conscious ways, a certain common sense, a 'disjointed and episodic' philosophy of literary critical practice (Gramsci, op. cit., p. 323). I want to argue that though the varied and competing criticisms – neo-formalist, post-structuralist or whatever – have the greater clarity and glamour, it is in the humdrum, everyday and generally quite 'untheoretical' activity of English teaching that the real effectivity of 'Literature' as a practice is to be found; an activity within which those criticisms appear, if at all, as half-concealed traces, modal inflections of question and answer, a fluid and contradictory debris of discursive fragments.

It will be as well to acknowledge a difficulty at the outset. Gramsci insisted that although a transformative practice (of philosophy, of politics) 'cannot but present itself at the outset in a polemical and critical guise', as a scientific revolution, a new mode of thought, 'it is not a question of introducing from scratch a scientific form of thought into everyone's individual life, but of renovating and making "critical" an already existing activity' (ibid., pp. 330–1). But how to know, in a properly distanced and critical fashion, what an 'already existing activity' is – especially one rather stubbornly unselfconscious and practised between consenting adults in private? There is a vast literature on the techniques and ideologies of the classroom. Schoolteachers are trained, assessed, supervised. Lecturers in higher education are untaught and unsupervised. For Gramsci, the 'lack of documentary material' meant that the history of 'common sense' would have to be reconstructed from the history of philosophy. But the absence of documentary and ethnographic information about the routines of Literature teaching in higher education will hardly be supplied, without a futile circularity of self-confirming hypotheses, by mere assumptions about the diffusion and 'sedimentation' of literary theory in the practical activity of classrooms. So any account must be admittedly limited and personal.

II

Introducing in 1970 a representative collection of contemporary 'criticisms', Malcolm Bradbury observed that:

> all criticism, whether empirical or not, contains a poetics – which is to say a mode of analysis based on assumptions about the relevant object of attention in criticism, and the relevant procedures or modes of talking that can be brought to bear upon it. (Bradbury and Palmer (eds), 1970, pp. 34–7)

The problem, he argues, lies in the provenance of those assumptions. In the two dominant modes of postwar criticism they derive either from the text itself (a paradoxical kind of extreme formalism, as in some 'New Criticism') or, in what Bradbury sweepingly calls 'historicism', from outside the text altogether ('science, or sociology, or politics, or anthropology, or linguistics'):

> On the one hand, then, criticism seems to have capitalized on its resources to deal with those problems of a literary text which derive from linguistic recurrences, syntactical features, tones and registers; and, on the other, to deal with large-range problems about literature's relationship to cultural typologies and myths.

What it has lost, he suggests, is its traditional capacity

> to deal with those middle-range problems which used to be the essential preserve of criticism . . . those of analysing, describing and evaluating the features of structure, design and organisation that are the essential constituents of any recognition of the complexity both of aesthetic and of experience which gives us our sense of the texture and quality of major art.

The summary analysis of critical formations is useful, if familiar. Much more interesting, and quite widely symptomatic in recent metacriticism, is the linguistic and discursive slippage. In the space of a page we slide from hard analytic talk of 'recurrences', 'registers', 'typologies' to the opacity, the gestural invocation of 'experience', 'sense', 'texture and quality', 'major art'. At this point objectivity goes overboard. 'Historicism' reappears briefly as 'a predetermined set of hypotheses' (the balancing formalism has vanished)' and the cool language of analytic survey flounders helplessly against the incoming tide of experiential indeterminacy:

> a poetics derived in the first instance from literature itself . . . responsive to its particular organisation . . . its feel, its way of persuasion . . . capable of making hypotheses in sympathetic relation to the works that it is reading [in their] essential existence and essential independence.

Only in these terms will literary criticism be able 'to support its claim to be a genuinely worthwhile mode of knowledge'.

The desperation and confusion of all this need no comment. Some may feel, indeed, that the price – in consistency, in sheer self-respect – of salvaging the legitimacy of an activity for whose status as 'a genuinely worthwhile mode of knowledge' we have rarely had more than its own word, is too great. And admirers of *The History Man* (1975) will relish the poignancy of the scene, as the frail and virginal figure of Literary Criticism struggles vainly to resist the repulsive but overpowering importunities of History. It is not, however, for its predictable politics that I quote the passage, nor for the sweet disorder of its arguments, but in order to acknowledge its familiarity. For I, and others too, I know, have felt myself caught on innumerable occasions in the same slippage, in the strong undertow of literary common sense. On that fatal page, you might say, Bradbury declines from a critic to a teacher; and if his language teeters from a smile to a frown, from the bullying to the plaintive, are not those the very lineaments, the authentic discourse of the honest pedagogue?

It would be very difficult, within the liberal mode of English teaching, not to be caught at every turn in those and similar confusions and contradictions; difficult, that is, without reverting to an oppressive authoritarianism. For while the empirical and unreflective character of Literature teaching owes something to

the strong persistence in English departments of critical notions –
realist, reflectionist, intentionalist – whose deconstruction in
theory has scarcely damaged their practical effectiveness, it derives
at least as much from the pedagogic forms themselves: the tutorial
and the seminar. Those forms represent something that cannot
simply be cast aside: the development, in place of the older, more
intransitive modes of 'discipline', of kinds of instruction more
flexible, responsive and humane. (The comparison with similar
transformations in other institutions – psychiatry, the prison 'service' – is striking. There, too, authoritarian modes of surveillance
and management have been partially superseded by more liberal
and 'interpersonal' styles.) The oppressive statement gives way to
the tactful, sympathetic inquiry ('This is so, is it not?' (see Leavis,
1962, p. 213)); the authoritative monologue to the open-ended
conversation.

These newer modes, evolved within the struggle of an emergent
liberal English Studies to disengage itself from older traditions of
classical pedagogy, obviously represent a real, if ambiguous,
advantage. Few English teachers would wish to return to the tedi-
ous monolithic lecture, the mechanical dictation of parts of speech
and figures of rhetoric, the imposition of narrow orthodoxies of
taste. They may indeed require, in the immediate future, a spirited
defence, as policy and material scarcity conspire to press for a more
'rational' and cost-effective pedagogy. But such immediate urgen-
cies should not obscure the recognition that the relative informal-
ity and openness of Literature teaching, its disinclination to impose
judgements or dictate pre-given conclusions, itself constitutes a
determinate discursive regime, constrained by its own rules, limits
and positionalities: a regime that can be characterised as 'liberal' in
so far as it imposes itself not by insisting on the positional authority
of the teacher, nor by compelling assent to a given and explicit
curriculum of knowledge, but by inviting a voluntary recognition
of the existence, purpose and value of a 'subject': Literature itself.
That subject is powerful but (perhaps *because*) elusive: not to be
defined territorially in relation to other subjects; epistemologically
bashful, but when pushed, self-validating; not reducible to its
constituent texts, though everywhere present in them; not a function of its pedagogic relations of production, though those relations encode and reproduce its central values; an ethical as much as
an intellectual activity, which invites its practitioners to view it not

as a specific discourse or domain of mental production but as a seamless continuation – in some accounts, the indispensable centre – of an essential humanism, an extension of 'living' (see Richards, 1929, pp. 348–51).

Hence the importance, and the specially charged inflection, of the interrogative mode. The appeal to the implicit values of the 'common pursuit', in the heuristic question that opens the tutorial, in the examination paper that invites 'discussion', that is 'open' in the sense that no 'correct answer' exists. But it is decidedly 'closed' by the train of tacit assumptions and evaluations which the question motivates, and which are not themselves up for discussion or judgement. The most fundamental of these is Literature itself. But Literature appears, in the practical state, not as a conceptual category, still less as a formal or historical problem, but in the dispersed, contingent, common-sense form of texts and authors. It remains the case that, however energetically both 'texts' and 'authors' have been theoretically problematised, it is extraordinarily difficult to imagine, still more to imagine *teaching*, a Literature syllabus whose nodal points of reference and intelligibility are not textual and authorial. To shift the emphasis decisively – towards, say, those other histories that determine and enclose the history of Literature, or towards cognitive and cultural questions of reading – would be to break out of the subject, and to cut adrift into a kind of interdisciplinary limbo: a move with serious implications for students and teachers whose identities and futures are enlisted in quite concrete ways (degrees, promotions) to the existing curricular economy.

This is not to deny that the subject allows, *en route*, a good deal of latitude, a vaunted pluralism in teaching, research and publication to which this book is itself an ironic testimony. That genial ecumenicalism looks now considerably less secure than it did ten or even five years since. But even before the onset of the recent ominous chill in the political atmosphere (known once as 'the Gould Report' but going about lately under the name of 'Canon' Christopher Ricks), students – many of them articulately aware of the ambiguities and limitations, as well as the pleasures, of the day-to-day practice of Literature – have found the boundaries of legitimacy brought into sharp focus for them by their final examinations. In those 'momentous decisions of the will' for which, in I.A. Richards's seminal formulation,[1] only the reading of Literature can prepare us ('good reading, in the end, is the whole secret of "good judgement" ' (Richards, 1929, p. 305)), the unstated thematics of a three-year apprenticeship in 'judgement' and 'discrimination' are drawn to a point in the gnomic pronouncements of the examination paper: ' "In the postwar period, we find many good writers and no great ones." Discuss.' This question, from a recent (1980) final paper on modern literature, is fairly typical in my experience. The form, a 'quotation' (generally invented by the examiner) followed by an invitation (actually an instruction) to 'discuss', is widely current, and encodes that conception of Literature not as an authoritative knowledge but as an inexhaustible opportunity for the exchange of views. But the verbal form is revealingly at odds with the practical occasion. The author of the 'quotation', with its affable bland neutrality ('What do *you* think?'), is also the author of the question, whose peremptory mode admits of no refusal. The required 'discussion', seemingly no more than an extension in writing of the friendly open-ended dialogue of the tutorial, is in fact a monologue in which the student, to 'cover the question', is obliged both to reply 'in his or her own words' and to assume the position ('*we* find . . .') of the absent but watchful questioner. Given the complex intertextualities that have gone to produce a student's 'own words', the writing of a simple examination essay becomes a feat of multiple and simultaneous impersonation beside which *The Waste Land* looks like the performance of an amateur impressionist. Few will truly succeed, across the whole range of papers. Those that do may go on, in time, to ask such 'questions' themselves.

As for the substantive 'question' (most examination questions are in fact assertions and commands), it only acquires meaning when it is decoded as the conjuncture of a number of specific discursive and practical contexts, none of which is itself open to discussion: a national-historical discourse of 'periods', with their own transparent literary-historical unity (enforced, this, by the periodisation of the paper itself); a literary-critical discourse of 'writers' (not, evidently, of philosophy, advertising copy or lavatorial graffiti); an ethical-aesthetic discourse of the 'good' and the 'great', with their implicit antonyms; and a pedagogic discourse of 'discussion'. Not the least surprising thing about this conspiracy of assumptions is that few teachers of Literature would admit to an unreserved conviction about any one of them, except perhaps the last. The form, with its own substantive content, imposes itself as it were *unconsciously*. The *parole* of Literature teaching changes with the seasons (I find it hard to believe that anyone actually still teaches contemporary literature in terms of 'good' and 'great' writers). But the *langue* endures like the rock beneath.

If examinations are the dreams of teaching, revealing something of the deep structure of the practice, they can also afford a glimpse of some of its anxieties. Consider the following, all taken from the same paper (in 1978):

> 'One theme saturates Tennyson's verse: the idea that the poet is hopelessly caught between the urge to retreat from society and the urge to serve it.' Discuss.

> 'Arnold expresses the dilemma of the modern intellectual, who can find satisfaction neither as a recluse in a cloister nor as a participant in public affairs.' Discuss.

> 'How can an artist respond to the immediate crisis of his time and yet remain true to his art? This was the essential aesthetic question for writers in the thirties.' Discuss.

Fortunate, perhaps, that the injunction to students to avoid repetition does not apply to their examiners. For here, surely, the 'mirror held up to nature' faithfully returns, in case after case, the image of the questioner. The recurrent oppositions (retreat and service, private and public life, art and time) palpably derive their pertinence, and their note of panic ('hopelessly caught', 'immediate crisis'), less from the texts and authors onto which they are rather clumsily projected, than from the predicament of the liberal academic in the late seventies. It would be interesting to try to compose a set of final examination papers consisting entirely of variations on a single question, and to see whether anyone *noticed*. ('In this, then, lies the enduring greatness/charm/relevance of Chaucer/Shakespeare/middle-English alliterative romance/practically anything: that he/she/it brings alive the eternal conflict between private happiness and public duty.' Discuss.)

There is an engaging piquancy about this, reminiscent of Woody Allen at his most soulful. Inside the wigs, corsets and imposing beards of the literary Great can be discerned, time after time, the unmistakable outline, the characteristic timbre, of our old acquaintance – the 'modern intellectual'. In a brilliant invention, David

Lodge has his redbrick protagonist Philip Swallow toy with the idea of publishing his examination papers:

> a critical work of totally revolutionary form, a concise, comprehensive survey of English Literature consisting entirely of questions, elegantly printed with acres of white paper between them, questions that would be miracles of condensation, eloquence and thoughtfulness, questions to read and re-read, questions to brood over, as pregnant and enigmatic as *haikus*, as memorable as proverbs, questions that would, so to speak, contain within themselves the ghostly, subtly suggested embryos of their own answers. *Collected Literary Questions*, by Philip Swallow. (Lodge, 1975, p. 12)

This is a good joke, because a serious one. Swallow is the paradigmatic teacher, as his counterpart Morris Zapp ('Any damn fool, he maintained, could think of questions; it was *answers* that separated the men from the boys') is the archetypal professional critic, assertive, peremptory, terroristic:

> The idea was to be utterly exhaustive, to examine the novels from every conceivable angle, historical, biographical, rhetorical, mythical, Freudian, existentialist, Marxist, structuralist, Christian-allegorical, ethical, exponential, linguistic, phenomenological, archetypal, you name it; so that when each commentary was written there would be simply nothing further to say about the novel in question. (ibid., p. 35)

The two modes coexist in the novel, as in the practice of most of us who teach and write about Literature. In the closing pages Swallow draws them together in terms reminiscent of the examination questions quoted earlier, and looks forward, in another familiar and recurrent formulation, to the death of Literature:

> I think it revolves around this public/private thing. Our generation – we subscribe to the old liberal doctrine of the inviolate self. It's the great tradition of realistic fiction, it's what novels are all about. The private life in the foreground, history a distant rumble of gunfire, somewhere offstage. . . . Well, the novel is dying, and us with it. (ibid., p. 232)

The prognosis is premature, no doubt; more interesting for its *mood* than for its historical accuracy. But the passage brings out very clearly the mutual interdependence of Literature and of those who teach it, so that it can seem to express by its very existence the perplexities of an intellectual generation, the cultural identity of a class, the central values of a whole 'civilisation'. This has got nothing whatever to do with what the texts actually 'say' – though they can usually be found, or selected, to confirm it. It has everything to do with the maintenance, within the academic division of labour and the overall discursive economy, or the opposition between public and private life. The modes of reading, discussion, teaching, even examination (notionally 'public' as it is) that constitute Literature as a practice are all modes of *privacy*: intimate, colloquial, inward-looking, domestic. Literature, we might say, is the family life of the discursive economy. Work, politics, history happen somewhere else, outside the window, if at all. And just as the production of material life requires, under present arrangements, that ambiguous private space called the family, so the 'two cultures' of scientific-technical knowledge and literary-ethical value depend on one another in an uneasy détente of mutual necessities.

This is no more than an analogy. But it may serve as a background against which to observe the remarkable resilience and autonomy of Literature, its ability first to devour its parents and then to excrete them as its own offspring. Bradbury calls for 'a poetics derived in the first instance from literature itself'. But 'literature' would not exist without a 'poetics' (however loosely conceived) to constitute it as an object of knowledge. Christopher Ricks assures us that 'the essential context' (of literary texts) 'may be the other texts' (1970, p. 10); as if to say: 'this train may be nothing but the passengers', or, more pertinently: 'this English Faculty may be nothing but myself; not a structure, nor a history, but simply *me*.' For these apparently harmless epistemological monsters, nourished in the bosom of a liberal and empirical discipline, have taken to exhibiting some very dogmatic and illiberal expressions lately: and the famous Cambridge question – this is so, is it not? – is showing a tendency to lose its second, interrogative phrase. Liberal English Studies, a generous conception at its best, may yet need tactically to be defended against the 'liberals' themselves. What strategic transformations may follow, in the struggles that will inevitably ensue, is another question altogether.

References

Bradbury, M. and Palmer, D. (eds) (1970), *Contemporary Criticism*, Edward Arnold.
Gramsci, A. (1971), *Selections from the Prison Notebooks*, Lawrence & Wishart.
Leavis, F.R. (1962), 'Criticism and philosophy' in *The Common Pursuit*, Peregrine.
Lodge, D. (1975), *Changing Places*, Secker & Warburg.
Richards, I.A. (1929), *Practical Criticism*, repr. Routledge & Kegan Paul, 1970.
Ricks, C. (1970), in *Sphere History of English Literature*, vol. 2, Sphere.

4

Radical critical theory and English

JOHN HOYLES

Recent radical critical theory owes most to the traditions of marxism (all fifty-seven varieties of them). Some historical perspective may be gained by sampling contributions from Plekhanov at the turn of this century down to Vaneigem and Kristeva around 1968. Radical developments within English proper take a new turn in the 1960s with the work of Raymond Williams and Terry Eagleton. Emergent radicalism has, however, to confront the pervasive influence within the British and American academy of the dominant traditions (residual belles-lettrism, conformist Anglo-American New Criticism, nonconformist Leavisism). No new theory can break with the dominant ideological and institutional mode without taking it seriously and analysing it. Since the 1960s radical theory has oscillated uncertainly between 'a critical structuralism often in confusing association with an objectivist form of Marxism,'[1] (cf. Althusser and the post-Althusserians), and a libertarian tradition in perhaps no less confusing association with a subjectivist form of marxism (cf. E. P. Thompson and John Fekete). Perhaps one way out of this impasse lies in a reworking of sociological poetics following the example of the Bakhtin school; for it was this school (notably Volosinov, Medvedev and Bakhtin) who in the twenties provided the first serious marxist critique of the Russian formalists and paved the way for a theory and practice of textual politics whereby literary criticism would avoid the twin reductionisms of formalist poetics and vulgar marxist sociology. I shall return in more detail to the work of the Bakhtin school towards the end of this essay. Recent studies by Pierre Zima in France and Tony Bennett in Britain suggest that the dialogue between marxism and formalism has been productive, is unfinished and may yet prove fruitful.

In this essay I have attempted to do justice to the debates and trends outlined above, but I make no pretence to be objective. The alert reader will have his own sympathies and antipathies and will easily detect my own bias which claims a place within marxism for a libertarian and humanist perspective. At the risk of reducing this perspective to a contentious and programmatic viewpoint, let me declare that my own position which informs this chapter is not far removed from that put forward with exemplary clarity by Herbert Marcuse:

> In contrast to orthodox Marxist aesthetics I see the political potential of art in art itself, in the aesthetic form as such. Furthermore I argue that by virtue of its aesthetic form, art is largely autonomous vis à vis the given social relations. In its autonomy art both protests these relations and at the same time transcends them. Thereby art subverts the dominant consciousness, the ordinary experience.[2]

Against 'the reified objectivity of established social relations', Marcuse sets 'the rebellious subjectivity' of art; of course art has 'its affirmative-ideological features', but it 'remains a dissenting force'; 'only as estrangement does art fulfil a cognitive function'; and, in a formula which conventional marxism and sophisticated neo-marxism overlook at their peril, 'art fights reification by making the petrified world speak, sing, perhaps dance'.[3] This libertarian humanist revision of orthodox marxism (originally developed by Marcuse's Frankfurt school colleague Theodor Adorno) remains for me an indispensable corrective to those tendencies within radical theory which have sought a prematurely scientific (e.g. structuralist) solution to the aesthetic question.

Historical perspectives

George Steiner is subtle enough to distinguish between the 'genuine marxist critic' and the 'Zhdanovite censor',[4] and generous enough to acknowledge that 'the dread gravity of the Marxist view of literature' is 'neither academic in the manner of some of the New Criticism practised in America, nor provincial, as is so much of current English criticism'. Already in Georgei Plekhanov (1856–1918), a leading theoretician among the first generation of Russian Social Democrats, the central problem of marxist aesthetics is adumbrated. On the one hand, the tendency towards reductionism leads directly to the Zhdanovite censor ('When an artist leans towards symbolism it is an infallible sign that his thinking does not dare penetrate the reality which lies before his eyes'[5]). On the other hand, a recognition of literature's specificity and autonomy prefigures Adorno's formulation that 'art is the negative knowledge of the actual world' ('The tendency of artists towards art for art's sake arises when they are in hopeless disaccord with the social environment in which they live'[6]). After the Russian Revolution these contradictory trends exploded into quarrels about 'pure art' and 'art with a tendency', but it was in vain that Trotsky declared that such quarrels 'took place between liberals and populists' and that 'materialistic dialectics are above this',[7] because, although the Bakhtin school did attempt to rise above such sterile polemics, what actually happened on the ground was the rigorous elimination of 'liberal' formalism by a 'populist' socialist realism.

For Radek under Stalin the choice was simple: either James Joyce or socialist realism.[8] For Trotsky and oppositional communism there was the dialogue with surrealism. Revolt was now divorced from the official revolution, and surrealist theory, with its slogans 'Change the world said Marx, change life said Rimbaud' and 'We must dream said Lenin, we must act said Goethe',[9] resurrected the challenge of the formalists by juxtaposing avant-garde literary practice and revolutionary politics. The surrealist breakthrough certainly opened up a space for radical theory. It inspired the writings of Herbert Read whose anarchist aesthetics led him to declare that the 'true revolutionary artist today is not any artist with a Marxist ideology; it is the good artist with a revolutionary technique' (Picasso and the Marxists', 1934); and that 'when work is a perpetual and exquisitely timed palsy, then art, which is the only freedom left the invalid, must expand its savage liberty' ('The social significance of abstract art', 1960).[10] Read reminds us that libertarian marxism keeps alive the formalist challenge so effectively suppressed by official marxism.

The surrealist breakthrough was no mere episode. It anticipates, amongst other initiatives, E. P. Thompson's attempts to recuperate the revolt of Romanticism for the Left,[11] Vaneigem's work in the 1960s (see below, p. 48), *Tel Quel's* theory of the avant-garde, and Adorno's championing of modernism against Lukács. Symptomatic of this whole libertarian tendency is Fredric Jameson's juxtaposition of Mallarmé and Lenin, and his reference to Schiller's remark in 1793 that 'it is precisely the path through the aesthetic question that we are obliged to take in any ultimate solution of the political question'.[12] In *Marxism and Form* (1971), *The Prison-House of Language* (1972) and other subsequent interventions, Jameson extends the insights of the Frankfurt school of marxism and in particular Adorno's polemics against Lukács.

'The Lukács line' was 'a highly sophisticated version of Soviet critical orthodoxy'.[13] In Lukács the Zhdanovite censor is never far away, and yet a residue of radical theoretical space remains. His positions can still be debated. He has a point when he argues that 'the broad mass of the people can learn nothing from avant-garde literature' which 'foists onto its readers a narrow and subjectivist attitude to life' and which in turn is 'analogous to a sectarian point of view in political terms'.[14] And a recent editor can legitimately suggest that Adorno's work is 'not so much a Marxist defence of Modernism as the expression of a distinctly modernist Marxism'.[15] It may well be that neither realism nor the avant-garde is 'intrinsically progressive';[16] nevertheless, in the course of polemicising this issue, both Adorno, and to a lesser extent Lukács, raise issues which cannot yet be eliminated from the purview of radical theory.

Adorno mediates the challenge of formalism in terms which adumbrate a theory of sociological poetics:

> I know of no better materialistic programme than that statement by Mallarmé in which he defines works of literature as something not inspired but made out of words; and the greatest figures of reaction . . . have this explosive power in their innermost cells.[17]
>
> Kafka's prose and Beckett's plays have an effect by comparison with which officially committed works look like pantomimes.[18]

Adorno also raises the question of the pleasure principle in aesthetics. At the risk of being identified as a decadent bourgeois, he

argues that 'petty-bourgeois hatred of sex' is the 'common ground
of Western moralists and the ideologists of Socialist Realism':

> No moral terror can prevent the side the work of art shows its
> beholder from giving him pleasure, even if only in the formal
> fact of temporary freedom from the compulsion of practical
> goals. Thomas Mann called this quality of art 'high spirits', a
> notion intolerable to people with morals.[19]

In the Marcusean 1960s, Adorno's theories with their emphasis on
the ludic (literature as play, cf. Roland Barthes's analogous highlighting of the pleasure of the text) were more influential in the
apparently desublimated west than were those of Lukács, pursued
as he was by those totalitarian pressures which had in 1956 and
1968 stifled movement in Budapest and Prague. In this context
Adorno leads straight on to Raoul Vaneigem and Julia Kristeva.

For Vaneigem 'the spirit of play is the best guarantee against the
sclerosis of authority'; 'poetic language is bound up with radical
theory'; and 'no poetic sign is ever definitively recuperated by
ideology'.[20] And for Kristeva and the *Tel Quel* school the avant-
garde texts of high modernism remind us that revolution contains
a dimension of liberating pleasure, of *jouissance*, and that rupture is
not without its rapture.[21] By a perhaps circuitous route, which
from the vantage point of the Lukács position may seem contaminated by advanced bourgeois decadence, the inheritors of the
surrealist breakthrough remind us of the autonomy and ultimate
independence of form, along lines that are not irreconcilable with
Bakhtin's concept of 'carnivalisation' and the Bakhtin school's project of relating the semiotic, the ideological and the class struggle in
the reading of a given literary text.[22]

English starting points

Until fairly recently 'English' in British universities has remained
so impervious to the trends outlined above, that one may be forgi-
ven for supposing that E. P. Thompson's 1965 essay on 'The
Peculiarities of the English'[23] conveyed some special revelation. In
some ways it did, and it was not long before Perry Anderson, in
'Components of the National Culture' (1968),[24] although apparently writing from a diametrically opposed position (the classic
xenophilia of the left-wing intellectual, as diagnosed by Orwell),

confirmed these peculiarities with specific reference to the various disciplines of the British academy and with special attention to Leavis and English studies. While these essays retain considerable force, the conditions they describe and analyse have not gone unchallenged. In a sustained series of interventions, Raymond Williams (from *Culture and Society* (1958) to *Marxism and Literature* (1977)) and Terry Eagleton (from *Shakespeare and Society* (1966) to *Criticism and Ideology* (1976)) have placed radical critical theory on the agenda in the 'English' academy. Both Williams and Eagleton have concisely, if summarily, defined their concerns in a liberal-pluralist anthology entitled *Contemporary Approaches to English Studies* (1977). The following points culled from these essays are germane to my present purpose.

Williams's sequence of interventions can be described as blazing a trail from the cul-de-sac of Left-Leavisism to the high-road of continental marxism. Some would argue that this trail was too personal and arduous to be easily followed. What nevertheless stands out from the undergrowth, in the developing course of Williams's project, is a concern with the inseparability of the linguistic and the social in the structure of discourse: 'Now if I were asked to suggest a definition by which the practice of discourse in writing could be recognised in social terms, I would suggest communication.'[25] Anglo-American New Criticism (and contemporary structuralist criticism) is taken to task for 'abstracting the substance of communication to such a degree that it deals only in isolated works'; for treating the practice of writing as an object and readers as consumers of objects; and for ignoring 'questions of the relations between writers and readers and of the relations between writers' social experiences and other social experiences'.[26] The Bakhtin school took Russian formalism to task on similar grounds. It is probable also that Williams's obstinate commitment to the term 'structure of feeling'[27] (so often castigated by pure hard marxists as an indelible sign that Williams has never escaped the Left-Leavisite cul-de-sac) corresponds to the Bakhtin school's emphasis on the way ideology is *generated* (as diachronic process) rather than *given* (as synchronic monolith).

For Eagleton, 'the aim of Marxist criticism is to expose the ideological tendentiousness implicit in that familiar narrowing of the social to a question of cotton-mills and bread-riots' on the grounds that 'all imaginative production is social production': 'The social is never merely one particular term to be casually equalised with others, say mythological, sexual, personal, political. It is the matrix within which all other terms are fleshed and shaped.' It follows that the 'correlation of literary and social . . . must involve some concept of structure'. This has been provided by the neo-Hegelian tradition of marxist criticism from Lukács, through the Frankfurt school, to Sartre and Williams. This critical tradition, Eagleton says, 'promises to root literature in social conditions without reducing it to them'. Its project is 'to grasp the dialectics whereby Marxist historical logic can be "read" in the formal structures of literary works', and 'that grasp is, naturally, an *evaluative* one'.[28] Like Williams, Eagleton in his basic formulations is arguing for a sociological poetics akin to that originally called for by the Bakhtin school.

It may be that this is too premature an account of the dissolution of the peculiarities of the English. From the depths of provincial Wales the voice of a militant Leavisite (one Garry Watson) can still be heard, reminding us of E. P. Thompson's 1961 judgement that although Williams conducts 'an oblique running argument with Marxism, in another sense Marx is never confronted at all'.[29] There is some justice in this; Williams's trail largely post-dates Thompson's assessment. But the outlawed Leavisite voice will not be stilled, for did not Eagleton himself, and as late as 1976, dub his mentor with the equivocal title 'major exemplar . . . of Left-Leavisism'?[30] And, with a nice flourish of subversive rhetoric, our Leavisite friend reveals his hand: 'But I intend to show that while in one sense Raymond Williams's work can be seen as an oblique running argument with the Leavises, in another, the Leavises are not confronted at all.'[31] One may detect here the jealousy of an erstwhile oppositional movement towards an emergent radical theory. But it is worth considering that Left-Leavisism might be just as substantial as is Left-Labourism, and that Leavisism itself, like Anglo-American New Criticism, will not go away by being ignored. If thinking people can support these causes in considerable numbers, then radical theory cannot advance without initially analysing their ideological structure. In other words, to go *beyond* them means to go *through* them.[32]

'Beyond' means 'through'

John Fekete's analysis of New Criticism in *The Critical Twilight* (1978) and Francis Mulhern's analysis of Leavisism in *The Moment of 'Scrutiny'* (1979), like the Bakhtin school's analysis of Russian formalism, provide tools to prise open the dominant practices of English; dialectically, to get *beyond* means to work *through*. For Volosinov, 'the truth is not to be found in the golden mean and is not a matter of compromise between thesis and antithesis, but lies over and beyond them, constituting a dialectical synthesis'.[33] The question arises whether New Criticism and Leavisism (like formalism) can be used by radical theory to set up new perspectives, as opposed to simply being demolished. The Bakhtin school did not so much reject formalism as use it, and by using it change it. Can a similar dialectical use be made of New Criticism and Leavisism in order to bridge the perilous disjuncture between 'holistic Marxist theory and concrete analysis'?[34]

In his foreword to Fekete's book Raymond Williams calls attention to a similar disjuncture between New Critical theory (discourse about social life) and practice (attention to the words on the page). This disjuncture is part of the strategy of New Criticism from the 1920s to the 1960s; in spite of appearances, 'what has been called, in English, Literary Criticism has in this major period always fundamentally been something more than the specialised practice the term seems to indicate'. For Williams, as for Fekete, structuralism (even when enmeshed with an 'objectivist form of Marxism') merely perpetuates the 'continuing dominance of critical formalism'.[35]

For Fekete, 'New Critical close reading . . . like econometry or other technologies . . . is never innocent of the determinations of the conceptual systems which implicitly or explicitly control it'. On the other hand, New Criticism constitutes 'a genuine advance' over all earlier methodologies 'by asserting the ontological status of art as aesthetic'. Finally, however, the New Critics fail to locate art as 'a moment of the historical practice of the social formation'.[36] Fekete's close analysis of New Criticism, from Eliot and Richards, through Ransom and Frye, to McLuhan, provides an informed perspective against which radical theory can measure itself.

Mulhern's *The Moment of 'Scrutiny'* goes some way towards explaining why there are still voices in the wilderness claiming that 'neither the Marxist nor the French New Critical options constitute anything remotely like the challenge to ruling literary culture that is made by the Leavises'.[37] Mulhern gives us a sociology of Leavisism as an oppositional movement ('to mediate the large-scale entry of a new social layer into the national intelligentsia'); identifies the educational problematic at the heart of *Scrutiny's* project ('the belief that education, a potentially "humanising activity", was at present complicit with "the economic process"; that it should be reformed as a centre of opposition to the latter; and that in this effort, the role of literary training was paramount'); and argues persuasively that the Leavisite revolution *in* the discipline was also a revolution *of* literary criticism against the palsied cultural regime of post-war England'. Hence *'Scrutiny's* hegemony in English criticism'; hence *'Scrutiny's* quite constant appeal for the Left over nearly fifty years'.[38] The message is clear: in Britain at least, radical theory cannot bypass Left-Leavisism.

For Mulhern, the work of *Scrutiny* 'opened up an educational space within which the cultural institutions of bourgeois-democratic capitalism could be subjected to critical analysis . . . a space which was to be utilised to remarkable effect, most notably by Raymond Williams and the Centre for Contemporary Cultural Studies'.[39] On the other hand, Leavisism has ensured that 'literary criticism as it is mainly practised in England' constitutes 'the focal activity of a discourse whose foremost general cultural function is the repression of politics'.[40] Mulhern provides no easy solution to this dilemma and concludes that something of the 'peerless militancy' of Leavisism 'will have to be discovered by the Left before the moment of *Scrutiny* can at last be ended'.[41] It follows that the task of radical theory is not to hit Leavisism in the back, but to 'meet it face to face'. Only then will marxist criticism be able to discover how far Leavisism is a 'good opponent' and how far a 'poor ally'.[42]

Culturalism versus structuralism

How far does the confusing association of structuralism and marxism take us beyond either Fekete's critical twilight or Mulhern's moment of *Scrutiny*? Not very far, I suspect, unless one takes seriously the important opposition (analogous to the confrontation between E. P. Thompson and the Althusserians[43]) between libertarian, 'Romantic', '68-ish, 'humanist' marxism and the more fashionable avent-garde high theory of post-structuralist marxism (to be found in the journals *Tel Quel* in France and *Screen* in England).[44] Is Fekete's critique of New Criticism/structuralism also applicable to the various projects of the post-Althusserians?[45] How widespread (and incorrect) is this objectivist marxism, to whose

> theoretical consciousness the world appears given to us not as the ground of historical praxis and the field of goals, needs and efforts, but as an object of knowledge, a system of formal signs . . . which renounces the projects around which society is built and sees everything, from literature to social relations . . . as forms of signification?[46]

How does the post-Althusserian 'elegant but quite unholy Trinity'[47] of Lacanian psychoanalysis, semiotics and Marxism measure up to the libertarian critique?

The problems inherent in both structuralism and the theory of the subject can be resolved by the traditional marxist formula:

> Marxism conceives at once of a subject who is produced by society and of a subject who acts to support or to change that society.[48]
>
> Man in a period of exploitation is at once both the product of his own product and a historical agent who can under no circumstances be taken as a product.[49]

But this formula is not easily fulfilled in practice, and it may not be immediately clear whether Althusser and E. P. Thompson, for example, avoid the pitfalls of objectivist and subjectivist heresy respectively. What is clear is that the libertarian critique of 'a structuralist version of Marxism'[50] needs to be seriously examined.

In *Au-delà du structuralisme* (1971), an anthology of essays dating back to 'Le romantisme révolutionnaire' (1957), Henri Lefebvre confronts what he calls the 'New Eleaticism' (Althusser's structuralist version of marxism) which values immobility above Heraclitean movement.[51] These terms taken from opposed philosophical schools in ancient Greece correspond in some measure to the opposition between the objectivist and subjectivist 'heresies' within marxism and to recent debates among left-wing historians between structuralist and culturalist tendencies. For Lefebvre, structuralism and its neo-marxist variants are trapped within the ideology of neo-capitalist consumerist society;[52] official marxism disguises its political failures and retreats into scientism and epistemology;[53] with pendantic asceticism it eschews sensibility, sensuality, emotion and experience; space is fetishised at the expense of time; science and ideology are hypostasised into 'theoretical practice' while the actual ideological situation and the actual conditions of scientific knowledge are bracketed off.[54]

Some of these points find an echo in a Centre for Contemporary Cultural Studies document of 1974:

> By putting between brackets or simply failing to acknowledge the material conditions of the practices they examine, and treating them and society solely as a sign system, structuralism and semiotics have remained caught in the very ideology they claim to have exposed.[55]

Fredric Jameson (1977) argues that Lacan's 'programmatic demonstration of the primacy of the signifier furnishes powerful ammunition for . . . the ideology of structuralism', and that the 'Althusserian emphasis on science' constitutes an 'extreme over-reaction, leaving no place for . . . the phenomenology of everyday life'.[56] The Centre for Contemporary Cultural Studies and Jameson represent a trend within radical theory which has not abandoned the possibility of working within post-Althusserian categories, but which nevertheless remains on its guard against the worst excesses of eleaticism (structuralism). For the full Heraclitean (culturalist) position as adumbrated by Lefebvre, we have to look at Fekete's *The Critical Twilight* and at *One-Dimensional Marxism* (1980).

Fekete takes up Lefebvre's argument that 'since the early preparatory stages of neocapitalism' there has been 'a decline in referentials' and 'an uncoupling of signifier and signified within the sign'.[57] Structuralism co-operates in this process, seeking to 'suppress the categories of alienation and praxis' which characterise the 'Marxist philosophy of liberation'; and 'the French versions in particular recapitulate the Comtean obsession with invariances and stabilities in the context of the worst excesses of dogmatic rationalism'.[58] Against Lacan, who 'eternalises the elimination of the subject from the centre', he argues that this is a 'historical not a categorical problem', and that 'the subject, today displaced from the centre by the reification of social relations, can in fact be centred'.[59] Libertarian humanist marxism, following Adorno and

Marcuse, concludes that there is 'a rich contradiction between the position of the intelligentsia as an ideological agency of hegemonic domination and their situation as oppressed alienated labour', and that in the last resort 'art cannot solve the subject/object problem for us': 'What art does is to question the extent to which our world is human and tailored to our humanity. Criticism must make this question conscious as art makes it sensible'.[60] To the Althusserian charge that 'humanism' is a word 'exploited by an ideology which uses it to kill another word . . . class struggle',[61] and that therefore marxism is not a humanism, Fekete answers that there is a world of difference between a marxist humanism which believes in the class struggle and 'the modern humanists' obscene complacency at having found a comfortable specialty far from the madding crowd, where they can serve . . . as the official pessimists or the official consciences of a permanently established order'.[62]

One-Dimensional Marxism addresses a spirited Thompsonian blast against Althusserian eleaticism. *A propos* words and the class struggle, Althusser 'is unable to understand that the same word can have very different meanings in different practices', and 'cannot see that the revolutionary concept of humanity emerges as the expression of a political struggle not against the *word* of bourgeois humanism, but against its *practice*'.[63] Second-generation semiotics or radical structuralism of the *Tel Quel/Screen* variety also comes in for some rough treatment for claiming (Kristeva) 'to give theoretical access to *all* social practices' and (Derrida) 'that the relation between signifier and signified is the basis upon which Western metaphysical discourse is based'.[64] Such 'empty formalism, which sees language as the decentred play of signifiers – no longer having any referential relation to the real world – has led to its easy absorption as a radical bourgeois theory'.[65] As for the Lacano-Althusserian theory of language, it is part of the problem, not part of the solution:

> The Lacano-Althusserian theory of language is a thoroughly alienated conception which replicates at the level of theory that alienation of language and meaning which has increasingly come to characterise late bourgeois societies, which seek to extend the domination of capital to the subjective sphere itself. . . . Language, like capital, imposes itself on subjects, 'bearers' who are now playthings not of the Gods, but of the Signifier(s).[66]

For readers subject to chronic structuralist constipation a dose of culturalist Heraclitism is highly recommended; it works wonders.

Sociological poetics revisited

At this point, with radical theory in the 1960s and 1970s oscillating dizzily between objectivist and subjectivist heresies, it is time to wonder whether in the 1980s it can attain a dialectical programme for its future development and not collapse into the inertia of compromise. A recent issue of the *Oxford Literary Review* juxtaposes Medvedev (1928) and Tony Bennett (1979). Referring to 'the effective silencing of the debate between Formalism and Marxism through half a century of Zhdanovite and Neo-Hegelian (or Left-Leavisite) hegemony', the reviewer argues that in Medvedev's book 'Marxist reductionism and Formalist isolationism of the literary are equally opposed and the literary is defined by a double orientation'.[67] It is to be hoped that the project of sociological poetics inaugurated by the Bakhtin school will now receive wider critical attention as a matrix from which radical theory may fruitfully develop.

The Bakhtin school does not ignore the hard kernel of formalism contained in Shklovsky's slogan 'Things replaced by words do not exist'.[68] But the 'double orientation' is clear.[69] For Volosinov, 'without signs there is no ideology'; 'consciousness becomes consciousness only once it has been filled with ideological (semiotic) content, consequently only in the process of social interaction'; 'it is not experience that organises expression, but the other way round'; 'sign becomes an arena of the class struggle'; and, in a central formulation:

> A word is not an expression of inner personality; rather inner personality is an expressed or inwardly impelled word. And the word is an expression of social intercourse, of the social interaction of material personalities, of producers.[70]

Medvedev/Bakhtin agree that 'ideological creation . . . is not within us, but between us', that 'social evaluations' are 'lodged' in words, that the literary work 'enters life . . . between people organised in some way', and, crucially, that 'the work cannot be understood nor can even one of its functions be studied outside of the organised interrelationships of the people between whom the work is situated as the ideological body of their intercourse'.[71] In other words the contribution of formalism is taken up and transformed to constitute a radical critical theory. Can the same be said to have been done with New Criticism and Leavisism in Britain?

Pierre Zima (1978) and Tony Bennett (1979) have taken up the challenge of the Bakhtin school in an attempt to forge a new synthesis out of the 'long interrupted dialogue'[72] between marxism and formalism. Zima uses Adorno's dialectical perspective to identify the double nature of the text, arguing that the specificity of literary texts lies in their resistance to conceptual thought, and that this resistance has at the same time a social sense. The autonomy of the text is guaranteed by its polysemanticity, and this is itself a social phenomenon which can be neither reduced nor isolated without distortion.[73]

Bennett sticks closer to the texts of the Bakhtin school. Whereas Saussure, 'by failing to deal with the theoretical consequences of the polysemanticity of the word ... exiled the mechanisms of change from the heartland of language, Volosinov by contrast views the use of the word as part of a primarily class-based struggle for the terms in which reality is to be signified'.[74] Bennett joins elements of the libertarian critique of Althusser with his reworking of the Bakhtin school's formulations, to conclude (in a tone closer to E. P. Thompson than to Althusser):

> It is *we* who do the condemning; *we* who do the preferring, and on grounds that have to be argued and struggled for. There neither is nor can be a science of value. Value is something that must be produced. . . . To neglect this is to reify the text as the source of its own value. . . . The text is not the issuing source of meaning. It is a site on which the production of meaning – of variable meanings – takes place. The social process of culture takes place not within texts but between texts, and between texts and readers.[75]

It does *not* go without saying, however, (witness this my final sentence, which is by no means innocent of an ideologically inbred sexist tokenism), that recent developments in feminist criticism, as revealed for example in two separate essays entitled 'Towards a Feminist Poetics'[76], have already brought about a substantive modification/subversion of the *'we'* (*pace* Bennett) whose radical theory produces meanings on the *'site'* of the text.

58   Re-Reading English

Notes

1 Raymond Williams, 'Foreword' in John Fekete, *The Critical Twilight: Explorations in the Ideology of Anglo-American Literary Theory from Eliot to McLuhan* (Routledge & Kegan Paul, 1978), p. xiv.
2 Herbert Marcuse, *The Aesthetic Dimension* (Macmillan, 1979), p. ix.
3 Ibid., pp. 7, 8, 10, 73.
4 George Steiner, 'Marxism and the literary critic' (1958), repr. in *Language and Silence* (Faber, 1967), p. 290. A. A. Zhdanov laid down the official party line to writers in the USSR in the immediate postwar period. For an example of his methods see his 1947 attack on Zoshchenko and Akhmatova in David Craig (ed.), *Marxists on Literature. An Anthology* (Harmondsworth: Penguin, 1975), pp. 514–26.
5 Plekhanov, *Ibsen*, quoted in Fredric Jameson, *Marxism and Form* (Princeton: Princeton University Press, 1971), p. 337.
6 Plekhanov, *Art and Social Life*, quoted in Jameson, op. cit., p. 386. For Adorno's formulation, see 'Reconciliation under duress' (1961) in Ernst Bloch *et al.*, *Aesthetics and Politics* (New Left Books, 1977), p. 160.
7 Trotsky, 'Literature and revolution' (1923) in *On Literature and Art* (New York: Pathfinder Press, 2nd edn. 1972), pp. 29–30.
8 See Lee Baxandall (ed.), *Marxism and Aesthetics* (New York: Humanities Press, 1973), p. 144.
9 André Breton, *Position politique du surréalisme* (Paris: Denoël/Gonthier, 1972), pp. 95, 84. (First published in 1935).
10 See Baxandall, op. cit., pp. 78–9.
11 See in particular E.P. Thompson on Blake in *The Making of the English Working Class* (1963; Harmondsworth: Penguin, 1968), and more generally on Romanticism in *William Morris, Romantic to Revolutionary* (1955; New York: Pantheon, 1978).
12 Jameson, op. cit., p. 86.
13 See Tony Bennett, *Formalism and Marxism* (Methuen, 1979), p. 37.
14 Lukács, 'Realism in the balance' (1938) in Bloch *et al.*, op. cit., p. 57.
15 Bloch *et al.*, op. cit., p. 149.
16 Bennett, op. cit., p. 136.
17 Adorno, 'Letter to Benjamin' (March 1936), in Bloch *et al.*, op. cit., p. 122.
18 Adorno, 'Commitment' (1965), ibid., p. 191.
19 Adorno, 'Commitment' (1965), ibid., p. 193.
20 Raoul Vaneigem, *Traité de savoir-vivre à l'usage des jeunes générations* (Paris: Gallimard, 1967), pp. 272, 103.
21 Julia Kristeva, *La Révolution du langage poétique* (Paris: Seuil, 1974), quoted in my contribution to Francis Barker *et al.* (eds), *1936 The Sociology of Literature, Vol. 1, The Politics of Modernism* (Colchester: University of Essex Press, 1979), pp. 123–4.
22 M. Bakhtin, *Rabelais and His World* (Cambridge, Mass.: MIT Press, 1968), p. 273 and *passim*. (Written 1940, first published 1965.)
23 This essay originally appeared in *The Socialist Register*, and has been reprinted with 'editorial cuts restored' in E.P. Thompson, *The Poverty of Theory and Other Essays* (Merlin Press, 1978), pp. 35–91.
24 *New Left Review*, 50.

25 Raymond Williams, 'Literature *in* society' in Hilda Schiff (ed.) *Contemporary Approaches to English Studies* (Heinemann, 1977), p. 28.
26 Ibid., pp. 29–30.
27 Ibid., pp. 36–7.
28 Terry Eagleton, 'Marxist literary criticism', ibid., pp. 95–7, 102.
29 Quoted in Garry Watson, *The Leavises, the 'Social' and the Left* (Swansea: Brynmill, 1977), p. 3. Cf. *New Left Review* (1961).
30 Quoted in Watson, op. cit., p. 3. Cf. *New Left Review* (1976).
31 Watson, op. cit., p. 3.
32 Cf. Bennett, op. cit., p. 75.
33 V. Volosinov, *Marxism and the Philosophy of Language* (New York: Seminar Press, 1973), p. 82. (First published in 1929.)
34 I.R. Titunik, 'The formal method and the sociological method (Bakhtin, Medvedev, Volosinov) in Russian theory and study of literature' in Volosinov, op. cit., pp. 177–8.
35 Fekete, op. cit., pp. xii–xiv.
36 Ibid., pp. 101–2.
37 Watson, op. cit., p. 205.
38 Francis Mulhern, *The Moment of 'Scrutiny'* (New Left Books, 1979), pp. 318, 101, 28, 329.
39 Ibid., p. 329.
40 Ibid., p. 331.
41 Ibid.
42 P.N. Medvedev/M.M. Bakhtin, *The Formal Method in Literary Scholarship* (Baltimore: Johns Hopkins University Press, 1978), p. 174. (First published in 1928.)
43 See Thompson, op. cit., (1978).
44 Cf. Rosalind Coward and John Ellis, *Language and Materialism* (Routledge & Kegan Paul, 1977); Colin MacCabe, *James Joyce and the Revolution of the Word* (Macmillan, 1978); and the debate between Stanley Mitchell and Peter Wollen (1971–2) reprinted in John Ellis (ed.), *Screen Reader I, Cinema/Ideology/Politics* (SEFT, 1977), pp. 380–93.
45 On the post-Althusserians, see Bennett, op. cit., pp. 143–68. Bennett relies heavily on Pierre Macherey, *A Theory of Literary Production* (Routledge & Kegan Paul, 1978). Macherey's French text dates back to 1966.
46 Fekete, op. cit., p. 197.
47 Kevin McDonnell and Kevin Robins, 'Marxist cultural theory: the Althusserian smokescreen' in Simon Clarke *et al., One-Dimensional Marxism* (Allison & Busby, 1980), p. 197.
48 Coward and Ellis, op. cit., p. 61.
49 Sartre, *Search for a Method* (1960), quoted in Fekete, op. cit., p. 180.
50 Henri Lefebvre, 'Claude Lévi-Strauss et le nouvel Éléatisme' (1966) in *Au-delà du structuralisme* (Paris: Anthropos, 1971), p. 280.
51 Ibid.
52 Ibid., p. 282.
53 'Préface', ibid., pp. 21–2.
54 'Les paradoxes d'Althusser' (1969), ibid., pp. 391, 416, 380.
55 Iain Chambers, 'Roland Barthes: structuralism/semiotics' in *Cultural Studies* 6 (Autumn 1974), 50.

56 Fredric Jameson, 'Imaginary and symbolic in Lacan: marxism, psychoanalytic criticism and the problem of the subject', *Yale French Studies*, 55/6 (1977), 374, 392.
57 Fekete, op. cit., p. 248.
58 Ibid., p. 195.
59 Ibid., p. 197.
60 Ibid., pp. 201–2.
61 L. Althusser, 'Interview on philosophy' (Feb. 1968), in *Lenin and Philosophy and Other Essays* (New Left Books, 1971) p. 24.
62 Fekete, op. cit., p. xxi.
63 Simon Clarke, 'Althusserian marxism' in Clarke *et al.*, op. cit., p. 76.
64 McDonnell and Robins, in Clarke *et al.*, op. cit., p. 187.
65 Ibid., p. 189.
66 Ibid., pp. 222–3.
67 Graham Pechey, 'Formalism and marxism', *Oxford Literary Review*, 4, 2 (1980), 72, 76.
68 V. Shklovsky, *Khod konia* (1923), quoted in Richard Sheldon, 'The formalist poetics of Viktor Shklovsky', *Russian Literature Triquarterly*, 2 (Winter 1972), 352.
69 Cf. Pierre Zima, 'Le caractère double du texte' (1975), *Pour une sociologie du texte littéraire* (Paris: Union générale d'éditions, 1978), pp. 23ff.
70 Volosinov, op. cit., pp. 9, 11, 85, 23, 153.
71 Medvedev/Bakhtin, op. cit., pp. 8, 123, 131, 153.
72 Pechey, op. cit., p. 72.
73 Zima, op. cit., pp. 46, 48–9, 159.
74 Bennett, op. cit., p. 80.
75 Ibid., pp. 173–4.
76 By Elaine Showalter in Mary Jacobus (ed.), *Women Writing and Writing About Women* (Croom Helm, 1979), and by Sandra Gilbert and Susan Gubar in *The Madwoman in the Attic* (New Haven, Conn.: Yale University Press, 1979).

5

Post-structuralism, reading and the crisis in English

PETER BROOKER

I

'Examine the relevance of post-structuralist theory to the teaching of English.' In a future where essay topics and examinations still exist, this question may look like a doddle. At least it might do so to a candidate like the regurgitating mechanical Bitzer in Dickens's *Hard Times*:

> *Post-structuralist theorists*: Louis Althusser, Pierre Macherey, Jacques Derrida, Jacques Lacan, Michel Foucault (amongst others).

> *Leading concepts*: overdetermination, problematic, relative autonomy, levels of the social formation, deconstruction, inscription, *differance*, interpellation, decentred human subject, etc.

> *Influence and reaction*: cf. Terry Eagleton, Hindess and Hirst, Jonathan Culler, Colin MacCabe, E. P. Thompson, Denis Donoghue, Christopher Ricks; *New Left Books, New Accents, Working Papers in Cultural Studies, Oxford Literary Review, Radical Philosophy, Screen;* the 'Cambridge Crisis' (in England, to begin with).

Sissy Jupe from the same novel, but now a teacher of English in higher education threatened with redundancy, and herself responsible for the question, might find it as difficult to give a straight answer as she did when asked to define a horse. In that instance her answer was written by the social novelist Dickens, himself inscribed, as we know, in an ideological conjuncture whose main feature was the internal confrontation of middle-class romantic humanism and utilitarianism. And the text's resolution of this conflict, we also know, has been rewritten by generations of readers and critics, including F. R. Leavis, whose verdict of 'masterpiece' helped give this fictional examination of the ideology of Education a place within a reformation of that ideology, constituted through criticism, syllabuses, teaching, essays, and of course, examination questions. Where Bitzer shoots from his seat at the press of a button, Sissy is dumbfounded before her own question and any assistance from outsiders – social novelists, social historians, Leavisites, Left-Leavisites, post-structuralists – turns out to be part of the question.

My own answer is no exception; it falls between Bitzer and Sissy Jupe and has accordingly two aspects. The first lies in the mixed implications for English of the intrinsic concepts and procedures which have emerged from within 'discourse theory', theories of ideology and of the human subject *in so far* as these have informed or prompted ways of reading which might have a strategic, oppositional effect upon the practices which have served as a linch-pin in the critical and pedagogic routines of English teaching. To this end I offer a conspectus, an abbreviated critical exposition, of the work of Althusser, Macherey, Derrida, Foucault and Lacan.

As many will understand, such an exercise is riddled with problems. Even to broach it, as part of the present short chapter, in a book determined to be empirical and accessible, smacks of lunacy. How is it possible to avoid emptying this work of its proper depth; how avoid trampling over the spreading tendrils of complex arguments, treading on the toes of aficionados, tripping over the booby traps of abstruse jargon, or sinking into a morass of theoreticism? The last is certainly a horrible fate, and while the others, though more or less serious, are not fatal, the undertaking requires some justification. My own lies in the contention that it is vital to develop a socialist pedagogy; that this demands a challenging and shifting of orthodoxies, a re-articulation of the working ideologies of English as an academic discipline and therefore of its insertion within the educational system and, indeed, the national culture. What pass as the commonsensical practices and assumptions of reading – an unproblematic relation between the isolated text and the individual, sensitised, reader; the authority of the author as creator of his/her text; the assembly of both authors and texts in a hierarchised, selective tradition – are one important front on which this re-articulation might be pursued, and one to which post-structuralism has manifestly contributed. For this reason alone it demands a familiarity. I suggest, however, that the more pressing, practical and political need is to develop a materialist criticism and socialist pedagogy, and that it is in terms of this priority that the post-structuralist contribution ought to be judged. It is in these terms too, then, that the survey which follows is a critique as well as a review.

The second aspect of an answer to the opening question I have already indicated. This is less a matter of relevance than of influence, or rather of how the question of either in relation to post-structuralism comes to be asked at all. It concerns movements over the past decade within intellectual culture and their social and economic explanation, the relation of post-structuralism to developments within marxism, the circumstances of the uneven publication of key texts in this theory, and its assimilation and rebuttal. That post-structuralism has presented itself as a sometimes firm and sometimes treacherous landscape; that positions of discipleship, casual acquaintance, apostasy and enmity have become familiar in most self-respecting English Departments, and even in the public representation of academic life, are themselves features of the crisis this book takes as its subject. Clearly this requires more than a theoretical exposition and critique, and more than the strategic appropriation of certain concepts to English, though they may have a particular application there. Here I can do no more than re-affirm the need others must also have felt for a cultural history which would accurately chart the broad, but undulating contours in recent British intellectual-political culture. Its particular object I suggest should be the nature and political function of intellectual work, an issue given some attention in this period, notably through the published writings of Antonio Gramsci, but one which remains undefined and at the heart of uncertainties which mark the sense of crisis.

Clearly this is to propose an exceedingly strenuous and difficult task. It is worth recalling, however, the precedent and initiative towards it provided by Perry Anderson's two seminal essays:

'Origins of the present crisis' (1964) and 'Components of the national culture' (1968). In these essays Anderson identified in turn the double absence of any serious comprehensive history of recent British society, and of a native tradition of classical sociology or marxism. In 'Components', which is particularly relevant to present concerns, Anderson drew already on Althusser in conceiving of education as a political target, since it is here Althusser had concluded, in the dissemination of knowledge, that we find 'the number one strategic point of the actions of the dominant class'; here 'that the bourgeoisie exerts its greatest control' (quoted Anderson, 1969, p. 214). On this premise Anderson had offered, as an assistance to the emergence of a militant student movement, to open 'a direct attack on the reactionary and mystifying culture inculcated in universities and colleges' (ibid.), concluding that 'a revolutionary practice within culture is possible and necessary today' (ibid, p. 277). The intervening analysis is of course well-known: in the absence of a national marxism or bourgeois sociology, the totalising conception of English society found, uniquely in Europe, a displaced home in the literary criticism of F. R. Leavis. The political and intellectual terrain has of course shifted dramatically since the late 1960s, as have positions within it, not least Anderson's own.[1] The introduction nevertheless, under Anderson's direction, of the texts of 'western marxism' through New Left Books (enriched by a spate of radical journals and publications through the 1970s) has constituted a remarkable remedial intervention in British intellectual culture, which has helped orchestrate the sense of crisis and stimulated a process of vital politicisation. The contemporary developments in marxist history, cultural studies and marxist criticism, particularly as the latter has sought to re-occupy and redistribute the ground claimed, by default, by the Leavisite tradition, may be seen still as related responses to the early conditions diagnosed by Anderson. His essay remains, then, a valuable point of entry.

In retrospect, however, one can see that British intellectual culture sagged and gaped not from one, but from three important absences, signalled schematically by the names Saussure, Marx and Freud. The effects upon the production of knowledge within English and higher education generally, have followed, one can also see, from the recovery, assimilation and refusal of these three sometimes overlapping, sometimes antagonistic, theoretical traditions. It is in this way also that the writers examined below have become involved in the cat's cradle of recent intellectual fashion, confusion and advance. I have referred to these writers as post-structuralist. This, it should be admitted, is a journalistic label, only useful, first, in distinguishing them from structuralists as such (Todorov, Lévi-Strauss, the early Roland Barthes) whose work has more explicitly depended on the linguistic theory of F. de Saussure; and second, as expressing their often critical debt to certain of Saussure's concepts, or as suggesting a general concern with discourse initiated within linguistic theory.[2] None of the theory discussed here, it should also be clear, is directly concerned with criticism or literature. Its intellectual bearings are variously situated in philosophy, linguistics, psychoanalysis and marxism. Of the affinities and differences this gives rise to, I suggest the relations with marxism are of most interest and importance. I try to keep this in view, together with the situation of English and the question of reading practices, in the very cursory exposition which follows, before returning to these main themes more directly in the final section.

II

Derrida's early essays in 'deconstruction' expose the persistence, largely in philosophy, but also in Saussure, Freud and his own contemporaries, Lacan, Lévi-Strauss, Foucault, of what he terms a 'metaphysics of presence'. They disclose, that is to say, a lingering assumption that there are pre-existent, fixed origins; first causes, essences, or ideal transcendent norms.[3] Saussure, for example, as Derrida shows, relegates 'writing' to the position of a second-order representation of a pure spoken original, and Lévi-Strauss, in his use of the distinction nature/culture, reveals a nostalgia for the first as a privileged realm of supposedly untainted origin. Both are victims, as it might otherwise be termed, of the fallacy of representation, and the first step in Derrida's deconstructive reading is to prise apart and reverse the hierarchical orderings such as speech/writing, nature/culture, essence/appearance, on which representation depends. The second step is 'displacement'. In his discussion of Saussure, for example, Derrida argues first that speech is in effect a form of writing, and then further that both are instances of the condition of all language, marked by what he calls '*differance*', a neologism which splices the senses of difference and deferral suggested by the French '*différer*':

> on the one hand, it indicates difference as distinction, inequality, or discernibility; on the other, it expresses the interposition of delay, the interval of a *spacing* and *temporalizing* that puts off until 'later' what is presently denied, the possible that is presently impossible. (Derrida, 1973, p. 129)

The difficulty here is that '*differance*' appears to be a concession in Derrida's thinking to a transcendent origin, or presence. Derrida insists otherwise, implying that 'the possible that is presently impossible' is in fact never possible, but he allows also that a residual 'metaphysics of presence' is inescapable, since one must 'operate according to the vocabulary of the very thing that one delimits'. The test, then, of the 'quality and fecundity' of discourse, commonly implicated in a frustrated desire for presence, is

> the critical vigour with which this relationship to the history of metaphysics and to inherited concepts is thought. . . . It is a question of posing expressly and systematically the problem of the status of a discourse which borrows from a heritage the resources necessary for the deconstruction of that heritage itself. A problem of *economy* and *strategy*. (Derrida, 1978, p. 282)

This is important, and clearly relevant to the ways in which English might remove itself by a process of critical re-appropriation from within bourgeois ideology. The crucial question, however, concerns the 'status' of this critical removal, both philosophically and politically.

Michel Foucault raises this same question in a passage of self-interrogation at the close of *The Archaeology of Knowledge*:

> for the moment, and as far ahead as I can see, my discourse, far from determining the locus in which it speaks, is avoiding the ground on which it could find support. It is a discourse about discourses . . . it is trying to deploy a dispersion that can never be reduced to a single system of differences, a scattering that can never be reduced to absolute axes of reference, it is trying to operate a decentring that leaves no privilege to any centre . . . its task is to *make* differences . . . it is continually making *differentiations*, it is a *diagnosis*. (Foucault, 1974*a*, pp. 205–6)

Clearly this evades rather than answers the question of status or legitimacy. For his part, Derrida's successive critiques are held within philosophy, while they are themselves philosophically disengaged; they have a bearing upon common sense and the theme of authority, but are politically unfocused. His thinking, moreover, is patently unmaterialist, his conception of history is confined to the history of western philosophy, and his deconstructive procedure, if subversive, is incompletely dialectical, offering no guarantees of progressive acceleration and transformation. Furthermore, the manoeuvre of displacement, expressed in the series of terms *'differance'*, 'trace', 'dissemination', etc., appears as a rhetorical evasion of the 'presence' which would ground not only his own, but all discourse in a reference and object outside itself. In short, it signifies a refusal of the problems of determination and real change.

Foucault's early texts are studies of the mutations in institutions, disciplines and discourses which have given rise to the modern biology, linguistics and economics. As his remarks above suggest, to give his writing at this stage an authorial face or intellectual location would be precisely to impose the conditions (of the 'history of ideas' or the sovereignty of the subject, for example) which he wishes to purge or evade. An alternative 'legitimacy' has appeared, however, and with it the most cogent aspects of Foucault's thought, in his discovery of the pivotal theme of the relation of discourse to power.

'When I think back now,' said Foucault after May 1968, 'I say to myself what could I have been speaking about in *Madness and Civilisation* and *Birth of the Clinic* if not power?' (quoted in Gordon, 1977, p. 18). Foucault's theme is explicitly announced in the prospective essay 'The discourse on language' and then dramatically developed in *Discipline and Punish* and *The History of Sexuality*. His thesis in these texts upsets his own earlier, and the common juridical, understanding of power as a negatively repressive, unitary force. The operation of power, he writes, 'is not ensured by right but by technique, not by law but by normalisation, not by punishment but by control, methods which are employed on all levels and forms that go beyond the state and its apparatus' (Foucault, 1979, p. 89). Power, Foucault argues, is immanent in social, economic and knowledge relationships, and from these there are built up, from below, major alignments, convergencies, cleavages and hegemonic dominations. It follows also that resistance is likewise immanent, fluid and ubiquitous in power relationships; their 'strategic codification', Foucault adds, makes revolution possible.

This is, of course, generally relevant to education, and particularly so since one point of resistance, Foucault suggests elsewhere (1977b), lies with a newer type of 'specific' intellectual, whose features are attributed to class position, professional conditions and, most importantly, the 'politics of truth': the types of discourse and accompanying mechanisms and representatives by which it obtains and sanctions its statements of truth. The regime of truth, says Foucault, 'has been a condition of the formation and development of capitalism', and it is the political function of the intellectual to know it is possible to constitute a new regime, detaching the power of truth from present hegemonic forms. Here, sketching the political 'ground' of his own intellectual work upon the 'will to truth', Foucault offers an initial means by which we might judge his 'status' and 'right to speak' and also our own, as producers of knowledge, in education. It is a cryptic recipe, but a considerable advance upon a 'discourse about discourses'. For orthodox marxism also, the questions Foucault asks of 'the conditions of possibility' of discourse, and its supportive reproduction of power relations and of received truth, offer a serious initiative and challenge which has yet to be met.

Louis Althusser has been received into British intellectual culture like a heart transplant after difficult surgery, only to be repulsed as a foreign body. It is hard now that the charge of idealism and Stalinism, aimed at the 'status' of Althusserian 'theoretical practice', has become a virtual reflex action, to see anything like this whole process, and clearly it would be the task of a cultural history to follow its twists and turns.

Althusser's theory of reading is derived from his reading of Marx and is built upon two components. First, a theory of science and ideology which would 'prove' the antagonism between marxism and bourgeois ideology in terms of Marx's 'epistemological break' in *Capital* from classical political economy. And second, a theoretical practice and method of reading derived from dialectical materialism and turned upon *Capital* itself, so as to disclose the conceptual limits, or 'problematic', out of which the science of historical materialism emerged. Such a strategy of reading and its use in English is opposed to the fallacy of humanist interpretation which assumes a text's transparency, and aims, instead, to reconstruct the internal theory or 'problematic' which produces a text, *'the objective internal reference system of its particular* themes, the system of questions commanding the *answers* given' (Althusser, 1969, p. 67n). Thus emerges Althusser's 'symptomatic reading', alive to the contradictions, gaps, silences which are 'symptoms' of a text's latent constraints, a reading which 'divulges the undivulged event in the text it reads, and in the same movement relates it to a *different text*, present as a necessary absence of the first' (1971, p. 28).[4]

The 'status' of Althusser's marxist-structuralism raises many difficulties which cannot be pursued here. His theory of ideology, however, for good or ill, clearly helped rewrite the agenda for British marxist criticism, alerting critics and teachers to the inherent ideology of the concept literature and the systems of British education,[5] and giving currency to a vocabulary of terms (such as 'problematic', 'overdetermination', 'relative autonomy', etc.) which has had an uneasy but abrasive career in our criticism. The chief weakness in Althusser's work, of which he has rightly, if hysterically, been accused, lies in its theoreticist limitation; the reduction, for example, of historical conditions and change to a conceptual or 'epistemological break' in his reading of Marx. The problem lies then, as it does in other ways with Derrida and Foucault, in the unarticulated relationship between discourse and the non-discursive facts of material history.

Pierre Macherey's elaboration of a 'scientific criticism' in *A Theory of Literary Production* (1978) proposes a 'double reading' in dealing with this problem: a first which respects the specificity of the literary text, not as a totality, but as an uneven and incomplete response to ideological conditions, offering to reveal what the text *cannot* say; and a second which aims to explain the text's silences and 'determinate absence' in terms of ideology's own false resolution of historical contradictions (pp. 90–5). There is, says Macherey, a triple dialectic: within the work in its internal encounter with ideology; within the historical process; and in the relation between the two (p. 129). Historical contradictions produce ideology which contrives to efface them, but this is then itself displaced and exposed, as ideology, by the contradictions within the literary work; thus,

the text explores ideology . . . puts it to the test of the written word. . . . Implicitly, the work contributes to an exposure of ideology, or at least to a definition of it; thus the absurdity of all attempts to 'demystify' literary works, which are defined precisely by their enterprise of demystification. (pp. 128, 133)

This is already a complex theory and reading procedure, but there are several questions it does not address. Is it the 'natural' condition of literature to expose or demystify ideology, or are some works more demystifying than others, and if so, how are they distinguished? Does literature's self-critique offer a unique access to ideology as such, or to historical conditions; if not, what is to save the reading of literature from a disabling redundancy? More importantly perhaps, Macherey does not perceive that the dialectical configurations of text, ideology and history (the determination of 'the real contradictions of a historical period' is one he passes over) move through complex mutations on all fronts. Literature's 'critique of the ideological' is subject to successive readings which occlude or produce it, not in the Derridian sense that these successive readings entirely constitute or reconstitute the text, but according to their relation to ideology and historical change.

Jacques Lacan's psychoanalytic theory and its application to literature has been pursued by Julia Kristeva and the *Tel Quel* group in France, and in England principally through Coward and Ellis's *Language and Materialism* (1977). Lacan reads Freud's theory of the psyche in terms of an anti-rationalist theory of language, parallel to Derrida's critique of Saussure. But whereas Derrida dislodges the notion of a homogeneous unified subject, Lacan offers to theorise the constitution of this subject. Reclaiming the importance of the unconscious (and its governing mechanisms of condensation and displacement, which he equates with metaphor and metonymy), Lacan comes to assert that the 'unconscious is structured like a language', and that the subject is constituted in contradictory positions, including pre-eminently sexual difference, through unconscious processes at the point of entry into the social order, via the 'symbolic', i.e. primarily through language. As advanced by Coward and Ellis, Lacanian theory fills a theoretically and politically disabling absence in orthodox marxism. To Althusser's addition of the 'relative autonomy' of ideology to the economic and political levels of the social formation, they propose the further level of 'signification': a theory of language and the human subject, and offer thence to conduct Lacanian theory, via the work of Kristeva, towards a materialist theory of language and ideology. This remains crucial. At present the reservations on psychoanalytic theory and its compatibility with marxism, as outlined notably by Stuart Hall (1980, p. 6), are, however, powerful and cogent. The theory is universalist rather than historically or socially specific; it collapses the levels of the social formation under the domination of 'signification' and the explanatory power of Lacanian psychoanalytic theory; and its idea of the resolution of the Oedipal complex in favour of patriarchal ideology at the point of entry into language, confines psychosexual development within that ideology. Moreover since Lacan's 'desire', like Derrida's *'dif‐ ferance'*, is never satisfied but continually deferred, the theory denies the possibilities of struggle and change. These are serious reservations, but they should not obscure the importance of unconscious processes and the constitution of the subject for an understanding of literary language and the positions of writer and reader. In this connection the most profitable lead is suggested in the concept of 'interpellation' (the 'hailing' of the subject into certain positions), derived from Lacan but applied by Althusser and others to the positioning of the subject in ideological discourse.[6] In this, a debt to psychoanalytic theory might unite with ideological analysis, and also with Foucault's broadly historical analysis of the possible subject positions within discursive terrains and their integral power relations. A mutually enriching connection with historical materialism, however – if in prospect – is still at some distance.[7]

III

What are the gains and weaknesses of this theory? A question that must be asked if it cannot be readily answered. First what I have loosely called post-structuralism is commonly opposed to the bourgeois humanist assumption of an unchanging identity or individual human subject. The subject is seen rather as 'decentred' and as contradictorily 'inserted' within discourse or ideology. From this anti-essentialist premise much follows, but chiefly a radical scepticism (though it takes different forms) towards the assumed existence of the single, isolated text, with a single, transparent meaning, and towards the presumed authority of the author over his/her text. Post-structuralism would argue, therefore, that 'literature' cannot be adequately read through the varieties of 'practical' or 'new' or 'structuralist' criticism (which invoke an 'ideal' text), or through humanist interpretation (which looks behind a text for its author), or through commentary (which produces a simulacrum of the text). Instead the text is to be understood as produced within discursive and/or ideological constraints, as opened (for Derrida, Lacan and in some measure Foucault) to the intertextual play of a differentiated discourse, yielding an extending, unrepressed plurality of meanings (here Foucault would seem to part company from the rest), produced not by the intentions or creativity of the author, but *reproduced* through a succession of readings which themselves constitute the texts.

In immediate terms, the reading of texts is directed, with all due rigour and ingenuity, towards their internally latent, or marginalised, contradictions which announce a complicity in a 'metaphysics of presence' (for Derrida); a pre- or anti-symbolic language of desire (for Lacan); the 'conditions of possibility' in relation to power and the governing discourses of truth (for Foucault); or the boundaries which circumscribe but do not contain their relation to ideology (for Althusser and Macherey). The differences here arise from, for one thing, the relative emphases given to the constraining processes of production and the liberating, or critical, processes of reproduction, and are, in other terms, at the basis of the uneasy alliance between marxism and the structuralist heritage. If however, from this conflicting and overlapping set of ideas and procedures, we can appropriate (chiefly from discourse theory and psychoanalysis) the concepts of a decentred human subject, of an internally riven text, of the intertextuality of discourse, of contradictory and changing subject positions for writers and readers, then we would at once free literary writing from a literary enclosure and question the bulk of written criticism and English courses, founded alike on assumptions of a fixed subject, and strung by distinctions of genre upon single authors and texts in a loose chronology drawn from the received tradition.

In some ways this would seem to offer a more immediately subversive set of procedures than the more recognisably marxist interest in ideology, which if it has surpassed (but has it?) the detection of homologous literary and ideological forms, is too often confined to the nexus of author-text-social class and a derivative historical background. Even with the introduction of the concept of hegemony and a principled silence on authorial creativity, marxist criticism still pays undue and unexamined deference to the privileged, discrete text. But neither of these two broad approaches is in these forms sufficient. To open canonic texts to the intertextuality of discourse would valuably expose them to relations of difference and antagonism, with criticism itself, and with the subordinated, ignored, or silenced forms of 'popular' literature, historical documents, autobiography, women's writing, black literature, song, TV and film. Deconstructive or symptomatic readings could in this way have a tactical, reformist effect in X-raying and dismantling the supportive structures of bourgeois criticism and the received tradition. But even so, if we are adequately to 'read' and explain the full contradictions within and across discursive and socio-economic formations, the field of discourse itself must be opened to the specific and changing patterns of ideological struggle in which criticism and teaching are implicated, and which occur in a material history. To this end, the 'legitimacy' referred to earlier of these ways of thinking, the use of concepts such as 'problematic' and 'conditions of possibility', even when understood quite crucially in relation to power, need to be radicalised in a tradition of dialectical and historical materialism, itself alert to its own lapses into a reductive economism. And this is necessary not for any reasons of philosophical purity, but because marxism is a philosophy of change, because change in education, as elsewhere, will proceed, inevitably, at the level of ideology – 'where men become aware of their struggle and fight it out' – and because discourse theory, even at its most politically responsible in Foucault, retreats from this prospect.

Furthermore, if English teaching, as a form of intellectual work engaged in the production of knowledge, is to be recognised as a meaningful site for political change, it will need to co-ordinate radicalised textual deconstruction and a critique of the ideology of 'literature' with an argued challenge and socialist alternative to conventional pedagogy: to the construction, imperatives, validation and assessment of English courses, and to their complicity in the institutional mechanisms of control and authority which serve bourgeois hegemony. In this, it will need to join, across discipline boundaries, with similarly directed efforts in other neighbouring subject areas. In other words, if it is to move positively out of the present crisis, English will need to find and confirm a changed place within a changed Humanities, or, in spite of problems of definition, within 'Cultural Studies', which has itself been experiencing and supervising this change. The name, however, counts less than the reason for it. Literary works have been produced and reproduced in a changing cultural history as have the forms of English teaching, criticism and theory. Both the forms of writing, the texts, and the discipline itself, require a study equal to their different, blurred but blended histories. But English has also been shaped by attempts to occupy the role of moral educator, to rule over the Humanities, and in fact to read and instruct the very culture and history of which it has been part. A definition of cultural studies is required, therefore, which will not simply offer to study literary discourse and English in their histories, but of necessity intervene in the second so as to reappropriate and re-articulate the literary and puncture English's pretensions to cultural centrality.

There are glaring theoretical and practical problems involved in this. And what real chance is there, after all, in universities and polytechnics of such a proposal being seriously considered? What can it mean to the day-to-day, term-by-term teaching of English which is pummelled by cuts and looking to keep what it has got? Jobs do come first. But what, we should still ask, comes next? What might be achieved even in the conventional arrangement of an English lecture and seminar series? Is a post-structuralist or marxist-structuralist reading of *Hard Times*, for example, possible? (Of course it is, but it is significant that it doesn't exist to point to.) How then might it be introduced in an undergraduate seminar, and to what effect? My own view is that it is more than feasible to think of *Hard Times*, and to think of teaching it, as historically produced and reproduced, in relation, say, to Carlyle, Ruskin, Leavis and its TV serialisation. I do not rate the chances so highly, however, of the suggestion that 'authors' are not responsible for the texts associated with their names, that Leavis, ITV, me, you or we, not Dickens, have 'written' *Hard Times*, and that outside our readings, which are rewritings, it does not exist. Against this view there stands a wall of common sense, composed of reading practices, motivations of personal interest and pleasure, and criteria of value, which are worked out in a supposed dialogue between the individual reader, text and author. Much more needs to be known about these assumptions and expectations (which do *not* derive, I suggest, from F. R. Leavis or *Scrutiny*) and about how they are inculcated and reinforced prior to and within higher education. A first task, then, might be to inspect their legitimacy and implications. Whatever else, however, these assumptions are common and they do appear to make sense; they provide reasons for reading literature and for 'doing English'. What different reasons, we can ask, which will gain consent, are given by post-structuralism or marxism, or their cross-breeds? The question 'why read?', therefore, clearly assumes priority over the question 'how read?' It has also, willy-nilly, a political answer.

Notes

1 Cf. P. Anderson, *Considerations on Western Marxism* (New Left Books, 1976) and *Arguments Within English Marxism* (New Left Books, 1980). For an examination of the history and politics of *New Left Review*, see Ian Birchall, 'The autonomy of theory', *International Socialism*, 2, 10 (1980/1), 51–91.

2 For two recent examinations of post-structuralist theory see the essays in John Sturrock (ed.), *Structuralism and Since* (Oxford University Press, 1979) and Frank Lentricchia, *After the New Criticism* (The Athlone Press, 1980).

3 This critique runs especially through the early texts, written in 1967, and translated as *Writing and Difference* (Chicago: Chicago University Press, 1978), *Speech and Phenomena* (Evanston: Northwestern University Press, 1973) and *Of Grammatology* (Baltimore: Johns Hopkins University Press, 1977). The dramatically uneven dates of publication here are a common feature of the work under review, and ought to have some place in a full explanation of its assimilation into English thought. As introductory reading on Derrida, see the essays 'Differance' and 'Structure, sign and play' in *Speech and Phenomena* and *Writing and Difference* respectively, and the interview 'Positions', translated in *Diacritics*, II, 4 (1972) and III, 1 (1973). Derrida's 'deconstruction' of Saussure appears in *Of Grammatology*.

4 For Althusser's discussion of relations between art and ideology, which there is no space to examine here, see the essays 'The "Piccolo Teatro", Bertolazzi and Brecht' in *For Marx* (Harmondsworth: Allen Lane, 1969), pp. 131–51; 'A letter on art in reply to André Daspre' and 'Cremonini, painter of the abstract' in *Lenin and Philosophy* (New Left Books, 1971), pp. 203–8 and 209–20, respectively. For a useful discussion of these essays see Francis Barker, 'Althusser and Art', *Red Letters*, 4 (1977), 7–12.

5 Cf. Althusser's 'Ideology and ideological state apparatuses' in *Lenin and Philosophy* (New Left Books, 1971), pp. 121–73; Renée Balibar, *Les Français Fictifs* (Paris: Hachette, 1974); Balibar and Laporte, *Le Français National* (Paris: Hachette, 1974); Balibar and Macherey, 'On literature

as an ideological form: some marxist propositions', *Oxford Literary Review* **3**, 1 (1978). See also T. Davies, 'Education, ideology and literature', *Red Letters*, 7 (1977), 4–15, and T. Bennett, *Formalism and Marxism* (Methuen, 1979), pp. 156–68.
6 Cf. Althusser's 'Ideology and ideological state apparatuses' in *Lenin and Philosophy* (New Left Books, 1971); Ernesto Laclau, *Politics and Ideology in Marxist Theory* (New Left Books, 1977); the discussion in Dave Morley, 'Texts, readers, subjects' in S. Hall *et al.* (eds), *Culture, Media, Language* (Hutchinson, 1980), pp. 163–73; and Colin Mercer 'Culture and ideology in Gramsci', *Red Letters*, 8 (1977), 30–8.
7 In a succinct discussion Andrew Collier suggests how Freud is closer to Marx than Lacan, 'Lacan, psychoanalysis and the left', *International Socialism*, 7 (1980), 51–71. For background reading on Lacan see the two *Yale French Studies*, 'French Freud', 48 (1972), and 'Literature and psychoanalysis', 55/6 (1977).

References

Althusser, L. (1969), *For Marx*, Harmondsworth: Allen Lane.
—— (1971), *Lenin and Philosophy and other Essays*, New Left Books.
Anderson, P. (1964), 'Origins of the present crisis', *New Left Review*, 23, reprinted in P. Anderson and R. Blackburn (eds) (1965), *Towards Socialism*, Fontana.
—— (1968), 'Components of the national culture', *New Left Review*, 50, reprinted in A. Cockburn and R. Blackburn (eds) (1969), *Student Power*, Penguin. References in the text are to this publication.
Coward, R. and Ellis, J. (1977), *Language and Materialism*, Routledge & Kegan Paul.
Derrida, J. (1973), *Speech and Phenomena*, Evanston, Illinois: Northwestern University Press.
—— (1978), *Writing and Difference*, Chicago: Chicago University Press.
Foucault, M. (1974a), *The Archaeology of Knowledge*, Tavistock.
—— (1974b), 'The discourse on language', appendix in 1974a, Tavistock.
—— (1977a), *Discipline and Punish*, Harmondsworth: Allen Lane.
—— (1977b), 'The political function of the intellectual', *Radical Philosophy*, 17, 12–14, also in C. Gordon (ed.) (1980), *Power/Knowledge: Selected Interviews and Other Writings*, Brighton: Harvester Press.
—— (1979), *The History of Sexuality*, Harmondsworth: Allen Lane.
Hall, S. (1980), 'Recent developments in theories of language and ideology: a critical note' in S. Hall *et al.* (eds) *Culture, Media, Language*, Hutchinson, pp. 157–62.
Kristeva, J. (1974), *La Révolution du langage poétique*, Paris: Seuil.
Lacan, J. (1977a), *Ecrits: A Selection*, Tavistock.
—— (1977b), *The Four Fundamental Concepts of Psychoanalysis*, Hogarth Press.
Macherey, P. (1978), *A Theory of Literary Production*, Routledge & Kegan Paul.

6

The Centre for Contemporary Cultural Studies

MICHAEL GREEN

Though cultural studies was substantially pioneered at the Centre for Contemporary Cultural Studies in Birmingham University, these notes attempt neither a history of significant intellectual developments there, nor a consideration of the distinctive relations between cultural studies and the analysis of literary texts.[1] They are concerned instead with some aspects (productive and also problematic) of marginality in a set of new intellectual endeavours: the relation of cultural studies to the established 'disciplines'; to some received working practices of higher education; and to the purposes and possibilities of intellectual work from such a location. This has involved continual excitements and difficulties hardly mentioned here: difficulties of institutional continuity (particularly of funding), and excitements of comradeship in the complex relations of research and 'teaching'. The main questions concern the breaking of frames and boundaries. In particular, the brief history is of necessity caught in the specific, and rapidly shifting conditions of the politics of intellectual work in Britain between the early 1960s and the early 1980s: from Hoggart to Gramsci, but also from Macmillan to Thatcher.

Cultural studies and the disciplines

When the most basic concepts . . . from which we begin, are seen to be not concepts but problems, not analytic problems either but historical movements that are still unresolved . . . we have, if we can, to recover the substance from which their forms were cast. (Raymond Williams)

Cultural studies began as the outcrop of an English Department. What became known as its founding texts were ambitious, brave, but lonely ventures, whose premises were largely given by their common foundation in 'Left-Leavisism'. In them *Scrutiny*'s concerns were sustained, extended and re-thought, even as the journal itself began to consolidate inwards to a pessimistic retrenchment in higher education. Leavis and colleagues had attempted to unite a close, though untheorised, attention to texts with a wideranging social criticism: the projected idea for an English School (in *Education and the University*, 1943) is still worth reading for its scope. A dissenting stance (alternately self-conscious and paranoid) was taken towards the fashionable and the routinely academic, while new forms of educational organisation, journals and networks were set up in a cultural politics whose lines of development, after the war, became badly blocked. The founding texts in question here were both a diagnosis of those blocks and a set of moves beyond them. Williams's *Culture and Society* (1958) tried to locate and understand Leavis's dissent, while *The Long Revolution* (1961) put together many of *Scrutiny*'s concerns (art, education, politics, communication) in an optimistic view of the future, free of *Scrutiny*'s contempt for the present. Hoggart's *The Uses of Literacy* (1957) sought to describe the containment· and resistance of a class through a reading of its texts: 'listening to the voices' at all levels from idioms and common sense through to magazines and newspapers. If this work refused the élitism of high culture and the great tradition, it was equally opposed to the reductions of marxism understood as a hard determinism of the economic. The aim was not, as it later in part became, to put new questions to a marxist agenda.

These themes took their meaning and force from the political abyss of the left in the 1950s, and from the decade's central (and now ever more powerfully communicated) myths of affluence and embourgeoisement. The much-discussed, highly visible crisis of the interwar economy was superseded by the reconstruction of a capitalist prosperity with a quite fresh kind of 'glossy futurism against the hard, rationed, sharing world of the war' (Williams, 1976/7, p. 87). In the 1950s the forms of domestic consumer production which had been only patchily visible between the wars became more fully developed in the enormous extension of the home market. The mass media, Enzensberger's 'consciousness industries' (and television in particular), constructed a new place for women as at once consumers, symbols and spectators of commodities – ITV born next to *Woman* and *Woman's Own*. At the same time the confrontation of 'the people' with a visibly ruling class was replaced by the longer lines of intermediary managerial groupings necessary to more concentrated production and to the enhanced role and protection of a 'welfare' state. The expanded state education system displaced class differences in the apparent mobility of a 'meritocracy' open to all the talents, with its new rhetoric of intelligence and ability. On top of this, replacing fascism, 'the old gang' and an oppositional popular radicalism, there developed a consensus politics of the centre, the 'Butskellite' convergence. The domestic programme to deliver full employment and low inflation raised doubts whether Labour would ever return to office. In foreign policy, Britain's special relationship with the United States, Europe and the new Commonwealth locked it securely in alliance against the 'god that failed' of the USSR. The discrediting of hope in 'science' was surpassed only by the attempted discrediting of the left and the 1930s together, as an anachronism in which class was an archaic British residuum, a dwindling or removable variable.

The texts in question here were a series of counter-statements to this formation, around four themes. *One*, the demonstration of strong, persistent and complex cultural differences: E. P. Thompson's early industrial working class and its active self-making, Hoggart's resilient near-contemporary northern working-class culture, Williams's working-class achievements of collectivism in the institutions of the labour movement. This emphasis continued in the attention given to the inflections of class and culture inside education (Hoggart, Williams, Jackson and Marsden (1962), later Willis (1977)), and to the highly public and stigmatised symbolic forms of youth sub-cultures, read as the condensed exploration of routes and pressures inside the class or 'parent' culture. *Two*, the account of culture as 'ordinary', as the making and taking of meanings in everyday life. This was put against the strong postwar investment in versions of heritage, tradition and monarchy

(Labour's 'people's' Festival of Britain replaced by the spectacle of the Coronation), themselves linked with the conservatism of Reith's BBC, the Arts and British Councils, and much English publishing in the 1940s and 1950s with its refusal of foreign and difficult work. *Three*, the argument that the new forms of education and communication were profoundly undemocratic: Williams's 'third revolution' or the 'aspiration to extend active processes of learning to all people rather than to limited groups' (1961, p. xi) his strongly (and morally) evaluative critique (as Hoggart's of ITV) of the deformations of contemporary communications and the concern with opportunities for democratic modes of representation, secured in non-capitalist forms of production and distribution. *Four*, the debate around the condition of England and 'decency': the refusal of imperial Englishness, but also of the future as American (and brashly commercial) or Swedish (and mutedly social democratic) – the attempt to prefigure another society (variously through 'community', through Morris and Blake, through the blocked forms of return to the country or region, to another Englishness – or Welshness).

What then started to give such ideas their distinctive 'set' was not an agreed programme of work, even less 'culturalism', but a political condensation around these shared and new themes as they converged with the emergent moments of a 'new' Left. As the 1950s ended, a 'moral' cause became political in both the British CND marches and the American Black Rights campaigns. The issues themselves, and the improvised and original forms of spontaneous tactics employed, were outside the agendas (and imaginations) of the main political parties in both countries. It seemed now, also, that an important agency of change could be found outside the labour movement, in the college-educated, middle-class children of liberal professional parents: 'the ideological dimensions of the revolution are likely to come initially from within the ideologically dominant class', as Juliet Mitchell put it in *Woman's Estate* (1971) – with its symptomatic claim that blacks, students and women were together significant sources of dissent from the management of production and consumption, production and reproduction. The crisis of Stalinism and, to a lesser extent and with many differences of perspective, of the postwar Labour Party was simultaneously the possibility of a new political constituency, with a new political agenda. High on that agenda would be the refusal of academic 'neutrality', exemplified in Williams and Thompson, powerfully by the Wright Mills of *The Power Elite* (1956) and *Listen, Yankee!* (1961) (on Cuba), and later amplified through studies of academic involvement in research support for the 'military-industrial complex'.

There were thus very strong connections between the work on culture and some new forms of politics. Both saw the 'mass' circulation of media images and languages as the treacherous re-presentation of groups and classes to themselves – but also as a site of refusals, of values *not* shared, and as one site of a politics adequate to conflicts in the spheres of reproduction and consumption. In Hoggart's remarkably enduring formulation:

> I have therefore taken one fairly homogeneous group of working-class people, have tried to evoke the atmosphere, the quality of their lives by describing their setting and their attitudes. Against this background may be seen how much the more generally diffused appeals of the mass publications connect with commonly accepted attitudes, how they are altering those attitudes and how they are meeting resistance. (1957, p. 19)

Both, too, saw in strategies of cultural and community politics – the self-making of classes and fractions – the 'speaking' of values inimical to capitalism. Both were concerned not so much with classes or parties but with *cultures* – of resistance. To put it another way, an adequate political understanding, for, both would require a knowledge of the values and motifs and knowledges generated through the forms of everyday life. The strategies of a politics of experience, in a full and ambitious sense, needed to understand and to articulate the 'maps of meaning' of subordinate groups. Those maps lay at once in the media, in the ways the media were received, understood, used and 'handled', and in the informal understandings, the common senses, the lived experience of work, household and street.

To speak of 'both' is to address the tensions between kinds and occasions of knowledges of cultures, and of the sites and forms of such knowledge's production. These tensions form a set of links between cultural studies, the New Left, and the women's movement. The sites of cultural knowledges, or reflexive understandings, have in this period included the shared experience of community or of sexual politics: or shared consciousness of a job (as in the rich range of teachers' journals); or the problem-oriented forms of action-research (as in the Community Development Projects). Only by one route and set of choices did such knowledge become theoretical work, produced within an intellectual field of higher education and at times producing in its turn a mirror-opposite revulsion from 'theory'. Williams's own account of the New Left's formation describes disagreement between the aim for 'twenty or thirty good socialist books' linked to a publishing and discussion programme and the 'big goal' of 'the germs of a new kind of political movement' (adding that he was wrong to 'assume that cultural and educational programmes alone could revitalise the left or alter areas of popular opinion sufficiently to change the traditional institutions of the labour movement' (1979, pp. 363–4)).

From this point on cultural studies could reproduce, inside higher education, the simultaneous concern with forms of knowledge and the forms of their politics, or sometimes (with conviction or regret) allow the one to stand in for, stand as, the other – at some moments with energy, at others ambiguity or antagonism. The tension was stretched further and re-cast by the appearance of forms of structuralism diminishing the importance of experience and meaning; re-cast again by its generation in the women's movement (and later women's studies). It has remained, and it must remain, at the centre of the enterprise. Meanwhile the 'field' was established, not in the political affiliations conjured up by hostile fantasy, but in disciplinary recruitment – in the meeting of three routes out from English, Sociology and History.

The stress lies on routes out, on absences and dissatisfactions and exasperations and dissent within the well-established boundaries of knowledge. The route from English concerned popular cultural forms, along with an interest in texts and textuality outside the 'language and literature' couplet, and/or a challenge to the very construction of 'the literary' and its various exclusions of class and gender. The route from History included in the broadest sense history 'from below', but also oral histories (a re-cast 'listening to the voices') and popular memory (the daily, informally exchanged, construction of a past). The route form Sociology involved ethno-methodologies, interests in meaning-construction, the examination of the structural reproduction of subordination.

There have from the start been rough connections between

these disciplinary 'ways out' and the three different levels which any developed version of cultural studies has, from *The Uses of Literacy* on, attempted to think together: that of *lived experience*, requiring attention to the maps of *meanings* in the daily life of particular cultures and sub-cultures; that of *texts*, requiring a close attention to symbolic forms; that of larger determining *social structures*, requiring a specific historical account of the formation as a whole. Clearly the three can be thought in very different ways (for instance in one view the first two are elided, while in another the specific differences between 'common-sense' understandings and fully worked-up and often substantially ideological representations are stressed). But the strands and the connections between them have recurrently been extremely important – it seems that when any one is lost, or when the question of 'meanings' is no longer central, then what we have is no longer distinctively 'cultural' studies.

In these two senses, then – in the double academic/political insertion and in the mixed encounter of issues – cultural studies has been resolutely 'impure'. In consequence it has neither claimed nor been accorded (any more than has women's studies or indeed marxism) 'disciplinary' status. For that reason it has remained a thorn in the side, grit in the harmony. At all events, it has found only an uneasy lodgement in the academy.

Yet in any case, none of the surrounding 'subjects' could be readily shown to have been either coherent or stable bodies of work. 'English' displayed not only the rift between language and literature, but also that between scholarship and moral/aesthetic evaluation. 'History' subordinated its 'economic' and 'social' concerns to sub-divisions, often separate departments, within the dominant (and unnamed) 'political'. 'Sociology' yoked an English tradition of social policy/research/work to theoretical work where larger tensions between (at their most general) conflict and consensus models went unresolved. From the middle of the 1960s – from the moment of the academic development of cultural studies – the 'crisis' in these subjects was continually discussed and protested. (See, for example, Pateman, 1972, Roszak, 1968).

Two points might be made here. One, that in each subject area the 'crisis' has been contained more readily than then seemed possible. Despite very important new bodies of work in each case, including new kinds of relation to intellectual work itself (feminist writing and criticism, the National Deviancy Conference, the Ruskin historians), the 1970s in many ways witnessed a re-consolidation rather than a re-thinking, or disarray. The university 'apex' of higher education remained almost immune to the changes seen in some CNAA degrees at polytechnics or in mode 3 CSE English. This alone gave the 'break' of cultural studies a high visibility. Two, a materialist explanation of the organisation and continual re-organisation of academic disciplines would need an account related at once to the changing class-composition of post-war education (where the university/polytechnic and grammar/comprehensive contrasts would be salient), and to the social changes of which disciplines are complexly articulated mediations. In both respects the issue is the constant re-composition of the legitimated ('academic') forms of knowledge – in which (whether or not we still speak of 'bourgeois' disciplines) the disciplinary form of knowledge production is itself a sophisticated ideology.

Cultural studies has thus not become a new form of 'discipline'. Attempts to 'unify' the field as the analysis of signifying practices, or as the study of forms of symbolic production, distribution and consumption ('cultural materialism'), are premature or unsatisfactory beneath a very high level of abstraction – though preferable to the view that cultural studies is merely one way of studying communications, or just a 'cover' for a revised and qualified marxism. Equally, the notion of interdisciplinarity no longer seems forceful – not so much because marxism itself has superseded its ambitions (though that is substantially true), but because 'specialist skills' do not just lie ready to collaborate together: the presence of other questions requires the disciplinary knowledges to address their object in quite unfamiliar ways. The relation of cultural studies to the disciplines is rather one of critique: of their historical construction, of their claims, of their omissions, and particularly of the forms of their separation. At the same time, a critical relationship to the disciplines is also a critical stance to their forms of knowledge production – to the prevalent social relations of research, the labour process of higher education.

Group work

It would be possible to look in some detail at academic modes of production and to note their own variety in detail, and of kind.

Basil Bernstein (1975) has commented extensively on the tendency of primary schools, particularly those with a strong middle-class intake, to replace formal by informal pedagogy. In this process the relation of teacher to taught was in some substantial ways made less formal, while group work and group projects were encouraged. At the other end of the education system, graduate research work remains notoriously solitary – a long grind, formed in a super-visor/student, guru/apprentice relation of unequal power, infi-nitely compounded and further distorted when the tenured academic is male, the researcher female. It would be hard to think of a working situation at once so privatised and so necessarily caught up in defensive anxiety. Ironically its outcome ('the thesis') typically bears little relation to later modes of writing and teaching, and may itself be unpublishable until rewritten in an entirely new form. This relation has remained at the centre of humanities research, and almost no challenge to it has been admitted. Cer-tainly a joint thesis is unheard of.

From an early stage the Centre in Birmingham attempted to develop other forms of work, and of necessity – given the already mentioned levels of the work in hand – the primacy of the unex-plored 'contemporary', and the project to democratise academic knowledge forms. Its working groups (usually of six to ten mem-bers) began as forums for the discussion of individual thesis pro-jects in the main areas of cultural studies, of which media studies has been of longest standing, followed by that of work/fieldwork/ ethnographies of work. Weekly sessions would typically alternate between exploration of a central text and individual presentations of work-in-progress, some of which were later put together in the cheap typescript form of working-papers with a view to sharing issues and problems as they were appearing in the projects. These groups were, and are, the working mainstay of the unit. Formally, they lie between a full seminar on problems of theory or studies in cultural history, to which their work may contribute, and the individual thesis project by which their knowledge is advanced. Informally, the friendships and collaborations made have gene-rated new enterprises and altered the direction of others. Typically, such groups have had a three- or four-year lifespan: moving from a preliminary review of an area to a full-scale 'mapping' of the field, then developing a distinctive purchase (through critique) and a particular set of concerns. These have been carried further in both group and individual work, and have usually issued in the Centre's self-published *Working Papers*, later in the series of books published by Hutchinson. In turn this project will often have led to group and individual papers at conferences, and later (often, it must be said, much later) to theses drawing further on particular strands.[2]

This rather formal account is both accurate and highly conceal-ing. Progress in such groups has often been a painful series of pauses, doubts, changes of tack and irruptions. The conditions of graduate work remain almost uniformly insecure – substantially unrecognised and unsupported, uncertainly transitional. To that has been added the relentless procession of new paradigms and bodies of work inside the field, often in a highly combative and polemical mode, crossed by further and often conflicting political imperatives and doubts. It has been difficult for groups so consti-tuted to develop modes of serious intellectual and political dis-agreement, even more of detailed sustained and supportive mutual criticisms of work in progress – or of work not realised. To all these has been added a further set of challenges from feminism, not to be accommodated comfortably (important as this move has been) by the making of gender central to all groups (and no longer ghetto-ised in a separate 'women's studies'). At the same time collective work sits in uneasy relation to individual theses, as do the social relations of the group to the traditional and privatised relation of advisor and advisee which has remained the most unexamined and impregnably traditional area of practice. And if the work of groups has sometimes been so organised as to produce the theoreticism endemic to a review of intellectual 'problematics', so theses have sometimes involved an inversely exclusive attention to empirical detail. Above all, whilst the excitement of group work has been in the opening-up of a connecting, and often proliferating, series of projects, it has also invited and colluded in over-extension to pro-duce a situation in which no piece of work or undertaking can be fully thought out or completed.

The other side of that collusion, another way of understanding it, would be to connect it with the difficulties of assessing priorities. In another form, these are the difficulties of a 'politics of publica-tion'. If one internal aim for group research has been to make it more complexly engaged with particular concrete historical moments, and less a theoretical 'mapping', the other more urgent struggle has been to find forms of writing and forms of making knowledge which do not endlessly reproduce themselves inside the boundaries of higher education. To that extent important distinctions can be made (very roughly) between decades in the intellectual/political relations of cultural studies and of similar ventures.

The constituencies of intellectual work

There were two characteristic modes of 'critical' research in the 1960s. One was the advisory relation to political parties or to semi-autonomous state bodies or enquiries: for instance policy research for the Labour Party, of which the most famous case was the connection, in the campaign to abolish the 'eleven-plus' and later to establish comprehensive schools, between academic sociologists of education, reforming teachers and Labour leaders (see CCCS, *Unpopular Education* . . ., 1981). There have also continually been 'researched' arguments submitted to government review bodies or investigations. The other strategy was that of the 'non-aligned' grouping of independent researchers, loosely linked (as in the New Left case) to political and cultural groups, working generally through educational forms, though by no means always those of the state (Penguin Specials, WEA dayschools). In addition, as suggested, a wide range of cultural 'inquiry' could be found in the working practice of political groupings and of teams dealing with particular situations and problems.

In the 1970s the consolidation of cultural studies as such around some key themes coincided with and helped to shape the opening-up of new syllabi in polytechnics and secondary schools. It relates also to the astonishing proliferation of radical journals and their accompanying left and feminist distribution network. Whether or not reinforced and consolidated by forms of Althusserian marxism (or by a faith in 'science'), this new higher education 'movement' developed an important confidence in its own distinctive intellectual production, support networks, and even in its forms of insertion into political groups and parties – though the near-absence from this picture of a radical/critical/marxist English Studies, and the possible reasons for it, will be of interest to readers of this book. One leading version of intellectual work, in this period, amounted to a fairly unspecified 'making available' of new work: not necessarily in crude forms of translation or handing-down, but in writing of some difficulty making considerable demands of a (usually graduate) reader. Work was often a 'ground-clearing', both conceptually and in opposition to dominant intellectual and political forms. Its typical form was that of critique: the 'interrogation' of dominant practices, and particularly doubts about liberal-humanist and social-democratic orthodoxies and their various disciplinary supports.

Within cultural studies, at least at the Centre, these forms were already being doubted and found insufficient, even before the populist conservative onslaught (at the end of the 1970s) on the left and on its by now quite developed sites of intellectual production. If a key 'model' at the beginning had been Williams, and later (with all kinds of doubts and modifications) Althusser, now Gramsci's work (1971) was both fertile and exemplary. The problem had already become one of 'organic' connections to be made in and through intellectual work, particularly as some men discovered their own distance from the confidence and shared purposes in phases of the women's movement: the connections made between analysis and 'experience', and made also across the division of labour. Inside the Centre, groups attempted to think of their work in relation to the problems of the nearest appropriate constituency, which might not always be that of teachers in higher or secondary education. For example, there could be a connection between media research and the interests of media workers; between research on popular literature and alternative publishers and bookshops, or the Federation of Worker Writers; between studies of the cultural formation of teenage working-class girls and strategies of feminist 'youth work'. More generally, the issue turned from the 'independent critic' of the culture/society 'tradition', through notions of 'science' and rigour, to the classic marxist problem of intermediate class locations and strategies. Where attention had from the beginning been given to cultural forms which were then shown (often without much specificity) to have a class-belonging or class-location, and later (in no simple 'addition'!) a belonging to gender, there had now, in reverse, to be questions about the cultural forms of intermediate groupings in developed capitalism, including those of the 'academic' (or paid) intellectuals whose forms of production arguably confirmed their own knowledge and power, their own 'cultural capital'.

In theoretical terms this involved at once and chiefly Gramsci for his work on the relations of 'common sense' to 'good sense' and on the need for organic connections with popular attitudes and for organic intellectuals of popular classes. It also implied a particular engagement with the various neo-marxist theorisations of 'new middle class' or 'contradictory' or 'professional managerial' class relations – of who or indeed what the 'popular classes' in the 1980s might be. (See, for instance, Carchedi, 1977, Poulantzas, 1978, Olin Wright, 1979 and Walker, 1979.) In practical terms it meant attempts to move through and beyond a politics of publication based in the crucial support networks of higher education (and their defence and redefinition in the early 1980s), to the formation of work with other groups. For the future, it must involve simultaneously the protection of spaces already won (but now rapidly being clawed back); close study of the relations of classes (including political relations) where 'intermediary' groups are ever more prominent (but where classes are no longer thought solely through masculine relations to production); and the development of cultural forms in a 'political' mode (which is not necessarily the same as 'cultural politics').

If cultural studies has become a set of knowledges, or at least an agenda for knowledges, that is not its sufficient goal.

Notes

1 For the first, see Stuart Hall's long essay on 'Cultural studies and the Centre: some problematics and problems' in Hall, Hobson, Lowe and Willis (eds), *Culture, Media, Language* (Hutchinson, 1980). Other versions of this account were published in *Media, Culture and Society*, 2, 1 (January 1980) and in *Annali-Anglistica* (Naples, 1978), no. 3. See also Richard Johnson's important 'Three problematics: elements of a theory of working-class culture' in Clarke, Critcher and Johnson (eds), *Working-Class Culture* (Hutchinson, 1979). For the second, see work in *Culture, Media, Language* and in the Essex conference proceedings, *1936: The Sociology of Literature*, two vols (Colchester: University of Essex Press, 1979) – though the whole issue has scarcely been broached as yet. Much depends on the view taken both of the 'text' and of the 'literary'.

2 The Centre publishes pamphlets, stencilled papers in typescript, a series of books through Hutchinson and individual books through other houses. Pamphlets and stencilled papers can be bought through the Centre, which also distributes lists of all its Centre publications and an annual report on the Centre's activities. (Centre for Contemporary Cultural Studies, University of Birmingham, Birmingham B15 2TT.) There is a network of teachers of cultural studies at all levels, holding

90   Re-Reading English

three dayschools a year in Birmingham, Bristol and London. Contact
M. Dawney, Middlesex Polytechnic, Cat Hill, Barnet, Herts.

References

Bernstein, Basil (1975), 'Class and pedagogies: visible and invisible' in *Class,
Codes and Control* (revised 2nd edn), Routledge & Kegan Paul.
Carchedi, G. (1977), *On the Economic Identification of Social Classes*, Rout-
ledge & Kegan Paul.
Centre for Contemporary Cultural Studies (1981), *Unpopular Education:
Schooling and Social Democracy in England since 1944*, Hutchinson.
Gramsci, Antonio (1971), 'The Philosophy of Praxis' in *The Prison Notebooks*,
Lawrence & Wishart.
Hoggart, Richard (1957), *The Uses of Literacy*, Harmondsworth: Penguin.
Jackson, Brian and Marsden, Denis (1962), *Education and the Working Class*,
Routledge & Kegan Paul.
Mills, C. Wright, (1956), *The Power Elite*, New York: Oxford University
Press; (1961) *Listen, Yankee*, New York: Oxford University Press.
Mitchell, Juliet (1971), *Woman's Estate*, Harmondsworth: Penguin.
Pateman, Trevor (ed.) (1972), *Counter-Course*, Harmondsworth: Penguin.
Poulantzas, Nicos (1978), *Classes in Contemporary Capitalism*, New Left
Books.
Roszak, T. (ed.) (1968), *The Dissenting Academy*, Harmondsworth: Penguin,
1969.
Thompson, E.P. (1963), *The Making of the English Working Class*, Harmond-
sworth: Penguin, 1968.
Walker, Pat (ed.) (1979), *Between Labour and Capital*, Brighton, Sussex:
Harvester.
Williams, Raymond (1958), *Culture and Society 1780–1950*, Harmond-
sworth: Penguin; (1965) *The Long Revolution*, Harmondsworth: Pen-
guin; 'Notes on British Marxism since the War', *New Left Review*, 100
(November 1976–January 1977); (1979) *Politics and Letters*, New Left
Books.
Wright, Erik Olin (1979), *Class, Crisis and the State*, New Left Books.

7

Teaching literature in the Open University[1]

GRAHAM MARTIN

I

Designing and producing academic courses in the Open University is so unlike the corresponding activity in other institutions of higher education that before considering our approach to Literature, a preliminary word about the general context is necessary. Open University academic production is marked by two opposing influences, tight constraint and energetic innovation, both of which directly arise from our conditions of existence. The constraints are partly external and budgetary, partly intrinsic to our teaching methods and to the situation of our students. Currently-available resources limit each discipline or subject-area within the University as a whole to only *two* single-discipline courses at a time, together with limited contribution to interdisciplinary and multi-disciplinary courses.[2] The production of a specific course can only begin after each item (total wordage for printed material, broadcasting, tutorial provision, summer school, etc.) has been budgeted and bid for, not always successfully. Without this detailed procedure, the University would be unable to calculate its overall budget in preparation for the triennial direct negotiation with the Department of Education and Science. The cost of course production is one of the bigger items in our budget.

The practice of teaching-at-a-distance imposes another set of constraints, structural rather than budgetary. A single course (which will also have determining relationships with other courses to enable students to assemble an educationally coherent degree) is a multi-media package (print, radio, TV, modest tutorial support, perhaps summer school), a complex of material written, produced and designed by a large number of people. To work as good teaching, it must aim at intelligible unity (if not achieve it), much as the single author of a book aims at unity, except that we have many authors. The course in existence, its capital costs (print and broadcasting especially) rule out more than minor changes prompted by the comments invited from tutors and students during its first year of use. Major mistakes, that is, must be foreseen and avoided. Planning and producing an Open University course has a certain resemblance to steering an oil super-tanker: you have to think a long way ahead in order to get the right effects in time.

Such constraints have their positive value. To work to a fixed budget, to be obliged from the outset to clarify the aims of a course in order to decide how these aims may best be realised, in what ways the available cash will, educationally-speaking, be most productive, all this concentrates the mind wonderfully; and were current government attitudes towards higher education less obtusely philistine, the discipline could be generally recommended. Yet its effect on the exploratory impulse in course design and content is not always healthy. The long gestatory process (two to four years) severely tests innovative energy. When any major mistake is costly, the cost public, and its consequences for students difficult to remedy, the arguments for playing safe lie all too readily to hand. 'But should we not, within the limited provision for our subject, concentrate on familiar A, rather than original Z?' 'Will these fascinating new approaches work for *our* students, with *our* methods? How will they fit in with earlier courses on more traditional lines?' 'Can we be sure of getting good part-time tutors for a course with such very up-to-date ideas?' These pertinent endlessly-recurring questions present, as it were, a Janus-face: a keen sense of direct responsibility towards adult students, working largely on their own, with little access to adequate libraries; but also, a nervous withdrawal into the safe middle ground of 'the subject'.

Nevertheless, the innovative character of Open University work, if (to one participant in the Faculty of Arts) more limited than the early years seemed to promise, is unmistakable. The Report of the Planning Committee which determined the initial structure of the Open University also remitted to its individual faculties an educational priority: interdisciplinariness. There was a practical reason for this emphatic departure from the pattern of the single-subject honours degree. Many adult students entering higher education could be in no position to decide which single-subject to choose. One task of each faculty's Foundation course is thus to introduce students to the nature of degree study in its particular range of disciplines, which in the Faculty of Arts means Art History, History, Literature, Music, Philosophy. But other reasons were also prominent. We inherited the widespread reservations of the 1960s about the appropriateness of the traditional single-subject honours degree which had already affected the degree structure of such universities as Sussex, Essex, Kent, East Anglia, not to mention Keele whose remarkable Foundation course was an early ambitious pioneer in the field. Long a commonplace in the Sciences, the interdependence of different spheres of knowledge had also become an insistent truth in the minds of (some of) those working in the Arts. In English there was of course the influence of Leavis. From *Education and the University* (1943) the notion of interdisciplinary work in Literature, History and Philosophy was well-known, though perhaps receiving a chillier welcome from historians and philosophers when confronted with Leavis's insistence on the centrality of literary criticism. Raymond Williams's early work with its interweaving of literary analysis and social and economic history offered another model. No reader of, say, 'The Analysis of Culture' chapter in *The Long Revolution* (1961) could remain content either with insulated literary history or with its mirror-image, various selective traditions of Great Works in whose light so much history conveniently recedes into 'background'. Co-operating with such general influences upon many of the new universities, there was also a peculiar institutional factor worth stressing. Our academic unit is not an aggregate of separate single-subject departments, but a faculty sub-divided into distinct disciplines sharing a common responsibility in the creation of interdisciplinary courses. In helping to overcome predictable squabbles over academic territory, this fact was often crucial. Yet against that must be noted the conventional definition imposed by 'Faculty of Arts'. The question, then, arises: have not the concerns of some disciplines in the Faculty of Social Science a significant bearing on study of the 'Arts'? The institutional structure may have helped to overcome certain problems inherent in interdisciplinary work, but it was at the price of importing others, still unsolved. The faculty structure also imposed two further constraints upon inter-disciplinary course-design: the need to cater for all five disciplines within a single course; and a double function for each discipline's contribution, both to the 'horizontal' structure of the interdiscipli-nary course, and the 'vertical' structure to be completed by later courses in each single-disciplinary field. Two kinds of solution to these problems soon emerged: a primary emphasis on theme, or on period. The initial Foundation course (1971–7) illustrates the thematic emphasis. In the first two-thirds of the course, students were introduced to the demands of the different disciplines as a basis both for later courses in each field, and for a concluding interdisciplinary case study entitled 'Industrialisation and Cul-ture', consisting of eight weeks' work:

1–2 The Industrialisation Process, 1830–1914:
     (i)   The Railway: The Evolution of the Machine
     (ii) How the Railway System was Created
     (iii) Glasgow: Transport, Mechanisation and Society
3   The Debate on Industrialisation: Carlyle, Pugin, Arnold, Morris
4   Is Man a Machine?: T. H. Huxley, W. K. Clifford
5–6   Art and Industry: The Great Exhibition, 1851: Ruskin, Mor-ris
7–8   D. H. Lawrence, *The Rainbow*

Course books written for the purpose ('units') discussed aspects of the linking theme in relation to readings separately anthologised in a Course Reader, *Industrialisation and Culture, 1832–1914* (1970), and at the same time, aimed to develop student experience of each discipline: History, Philosophy, Art History, Literature (Music proving, in this case, unassimilable to the theme).

   Students were thus able to read Lawrence's novel in the light of historical study of the formative years of the Industrial Revolution, of the critical debate about its social and moral implications con-ducted by Victorian thinkers, and its reverberations within the sphere of Art and Art criticism. It is not, of course, difficult to spot omissions, or more radically to question the over-stretched chronological span. But as a way of contextualising specific literary texts and establishing the interconnections between literary and other forms of cultural practice, the model may be recommended. Its particular virtue lies in offering the student, not just secondary material from historical and other sources, but some direct study of relevant aspects of other fields: the importance of primary documentation in historical study; the many-sided role of figures like Ruskin and Morris in the development of the 'culture and civilisation' debate, which Lawrence was both to inherit and modify into a powerful twentieth-century myth; the direct access to pictorial art and conceptions of art as a model for work, with its bearing on a figure like Will Brangwen. So constructed, the non-literary subject-matter is neither background nor simply context, but establishes its own presence. Working to this model with the benefit of greater experience in course-planning and of student and tutor response to the earlier version, we designed the current Foundation course (1978–) with a shorter chronological span, increased the number of allotted weeks of study, and shifted the emphasis of the contribution from Philosophy. Entitled 'Arts and Society in an Age of Industrialisation', the case-study was devised as follows:

1 Key concepts: Industrialisation, Romanticism
2 Nature, Work and Art: Constable and Turner
3 The Experience of Industrialisation, 1760–1860
4 Charlotte Brontë, *Jane Eyre*
5 Work, Morality and Human Nature: Marx and Mill
6 From Liszt to Music Hall
7 Twentieth-Century Responses to Industrialisation

A Course Reader, *Nature and Industrialisation*, was again assembled. The 'units' as a whole were planned to approach from different directions conceptions of work, nature and art, the part such ideas played in shaping responses to nineteenth-century industrialisation, and were themselves shaped by such historical changes.

The 'periodisation' formula for interdisciplinary course design may be illustrated by another early course, *The Age of Revolutions, 1780–1830* (1972–8), involving the Industrial, American and French Revolutions; Rousseau, Blake, Wordsworth, and Stendhal; Kant; Beethoven; David and Daumier, with intermittent discussion of Romanticism. As a 'second-level' course (students were recommended, though not required, to have taken the Arts Foundation course), considerably more reading was expected, and students were presumed to have developed an elementary grasp of the methods and procedures of the single disciplines. But the problem of balance between the demands of the latter and the exploration of interdisciplinary connections became considerably more acute. In the literary component, the connections between Blake, Wordsworth, Stendhal, Rousseau and the Industrial and French Revolutions were self-evident but (it should be admitted) of a rather abstract and general kind. That students of Wordsworth should have directly studied the events of the French Revolution underlined once again, and on a bigger scale, the lesson that 'history' is not 'background', not 'context'. On the other hand, the detailed tracing of French events is of smaller import in respect of English Romantic poetry than both the impact of the relevant English history and the struggle against the older eighteenth-century conception of literary practice – in other words of the complex of political, literary and philosophical factors in the development of the writing of Coleridge and Wordsworth between 1790 and 1815.

The 'period' solution to interdisciplinary work can thus sometimes signal a radical shift to merely *multi*disciplinary work, a loose amalgam of the traditionally separate fields of study within a common time-span. It is not only that the concept of 'periodisation' works differently for different disciplines in each specific case (Schubert, not Beethoven, is 'Romantic' in musicological discussion; David is post-Revolutionary and 'Classical' to the art-historian); nor that direct study of Kant's *Critique of Pure Reason* has little bearing on Romantic *poetry*; nor that a historical event of the magnitude of the French Revolution entails excursions into more than one national culture if its reverberations in the 'Arts' are to be fairly represented. A deeper difficulty lies in the fact that the 'period' solution often has the effect of privileging historical study in a manner that students of the Arts need to question. The 'thematic' approach is in this respect sounder since it points to interconnections, interweavings between 'history' and cultural practice, in which a dominant role is claimed for neither. The 'period' solution often involves an implicit 'reflection' historiography, which converts cultural practice into various epiphenomena, a complex of idealist responses to the historical 'real'; or in avoiding this, presents a number of parallel histories – political-social-economic, literary, musical, painting – which despite some limited mutual recognition, are effectively sealed from each other. In one respect, though, such difficulties reflect a situation peculiar to our Faculty with its overriding commitment to the inclusion of five distinct fields of study. Clearly, a course which involved only Literature, History and Philosophy, sharing the chronology of 1780–1830, would have less difficulty in also building round common themes.[3]

Yet it should be said that the choice of interdisciplinary theme requires care. 'Romanticism', for example, can all too easily become a recipe for those predictably arid debates about how nearly or distantly Text A and Writer B approximate an abstract conception of 'Romantic'. With this danger in mind the interdisciplinary course succeeding *The Age of Revolutions, The Enlightenment* (1979–), was built round a group of 'texts' (literary, historical, visual, musical) rather than in terms of competing definitions of the event or condition of 'Enlightenment'. Students are encouraged to work towards a (necessarily incomplete) sense of the complexity of the cultural history through a study of particular texts (Fielding, Hogarth, Gibbon, Hume, Voltaire, Haydn, Frederick the Great, Buffon, Laclos), rather than invited to pummel and stretch the texts to fit some overriding definition of the theme. The period itself, of course, worked in our favour. What we today call 'interdisciplinariness' was then the assumed ideal of anybody with pretensions to education. As far as possible, the course units include contributions from authors in more than one discipline. Thus, those on *Tom Jones* both discuss the novel in its own right, and examine the conception of society which the novel recommends in the light of independent historical evidence, so that while Fielding's work determines the *kind* of history discussed, the latter is not the usual literary critic's 'history', a mere abstraction from the novel itself. The interplay of 'literature' and 'history' is thus achieved, neither 'discipline' being permitted to upstage the other.

II

In the early days of the Open University, it was supposed that we would offer two kinds of degree (both incorporating an interdisciplinary component): a mixed-subject degree combining, say, one

Literature course, two History courses, one Philosophy course; or a degree concentrating on one subject alone. The overall resource constraint mentioned above largely disposed of the second alternative. Academic planning for the University's 'steady state' (from 1984) means for the Literature discipline, that there can be only two specialist courses available at any one time, although, since the average life of a course is six years, students taking five years to complete their degree could probably take three Literature courses.[4] This fact, taken together with the interdisciplinary character of the courses I have described, was (and will remain) influential in the design of our Literature courses. It brings to a head what may be called the pedagogic issue of 'confidence'.

There is a threshold of experience in the study of any subject below which sustained interdisciplinary work is too difficult. A student who has successfully completed both the Arts Foundation course and a second-level interdisciplinary course has still covered a modest amount of reading in the subject *per se*. It can, no doubt, be objected that formulating the problem in this way presupposes both a *kind* of 'reading' and unquestioned assumptions about 'the subject'. Yet some practice in grappling with literary texts is crucial before the complexity of their interrelationships with other subjects can be adequately explored. This is especially the case for Open University students, relatively isolated from direct discussion with fellow students and enjoying a minimum of support from experienced tutors (on average, fifteen hours face-to-face tutorial contact – seminar groups, and/or dayschools – per thirty-two-week course).

Such reasoning led to a decision to concentrate our Literature provision on the two major genres, Novel and Poetry,[5] adopting a 'period' emphasis which provides a sense of chronological continuity. These third-level courses were *The Nineteenth Century Novel and Its Legacy* (1972–8), and *Twentieth-Century Poetry* (1976–83). The design and emphasis of both courses is 'literary' in a familiar mode: text-centred for the Novel, author-centred for Poetry. Certain themes, in the Novel course especially, opened fairly directly into 'history', but there was no direct historical study, only recommended 'background' reading. Individual discussions of novels reflected two principal aims. One was to introduce students to the conception of novels as verbal constructions, possessing an internal economy more or less individual, more or less expressive of their author's sense of the world, or of that aspect of it attended to in the novel. The other concerned the text as a statement about the society it was addressed to and (in some sense) dealt with. Questions of literary history, or of the development of the *genre* conceived as an intrinsic process, were only slightly touched on. Some course units picked up linking themes (e.g. 'Poor Relations', 'Heroes and Heroines', 'Realism'). Perhaps the overall ambience of the course could be described as 'social-historical'. But the concentration on single novels of course created problems in the fuller contextualising of Austen, Dickens, George Eliot, *et al.* In the course on Poetry, whose mediation of social process is more intricate, the access into 'history' was predictably more difficult.[6] There was room to touch on some social and cultural implications arising from, for example, the impact of Modernism on English poetry, the links between Georgianism and Edwardian Liberalism, the relative insularity of the English cultural scene in 1900–20, the impact of historical events on the Auden generation. But the overall priority continued to be giving students reading experience in (some famously difficult examples of) the *genre*.

This brief survey should, finally, mention a fourth-level interdisciplinary course currently in the planning stage, *Art and Society in Britain since the Thirties* (1983–), which involves all the Arts Faculty disciplines, and for which previous experience in third-level single-discipline courses in Literature, History, Philosophy and so on, will be expected. The students' principal task will be writing a substantial essay (*c.* 10,000 words) with attention to more than one field of study on such topics as *Liberal Humanism in E. M. Forster and Angus Wilson, 'The Movement' and the 'End of Empire', The Decline of Nationalism in Music, Art-Books and 'Mechanical Reproduction'*. More than in most Arts Faculty courses, students will have scope for independent work, following guidelines which the course will spell out, but without the close direction characteristic of some less advanced courses. As in more conventional institutions, Open University students have a keen appetite for individual 'projects'. (A third-level course – *The History of Architecture and Design, 1890–1939* – the Arts Faculty pioneer in this respect, has produced some remarkable project work.) The new fourth-level course will offer students a chance to explore interdisciplinary themes of their own choice within a manageable framework. The 'period' concentration (1930s to 1960s) provides some historical cohesion which should not, however, bear in too procrustean a fashion upon the different chronologies that given individual disciplines logically extrapolate; while the topics will encourage concentration on two, at the most three, fields of study, thus avoiding difficulties raised in earlier interdisciplinary courses involving five disciplines.

III

Let me touch finally on some basic questions which Open University work made prominent for us, though giving only modest scope for exploring solutions.* There has been the overriding question: what does 'teaching Literature' mean? In a recent public discussion, one traditional position was put like this: 'The young person knows how to read his own language, and there are the books.' (Bayley, 1981). Such confidence, of course, reposes upon an institutional commitment of time, persons (various ages), and resources which neither the Open University nor its students are in a position to command. The books are indeed *there*. But which books? And why? And what might *reading* these books mean? Contemporary theorists of literature, for whom the latter question is pre-eminent, sometimes use a revealing analogy: 'Poetics is to Literature as Linguistics is to Language', so that Poetics is what teaching Literature *must* mean. But the analogy obscures the fact that Linguistics is able to assume exactly what Poetics can not: wide experience in the language. To insist on Poetics, on theory, before the student is competent in 'the language', that is to say, familiar with a range of literary texts, is to be in the position of teaching, let us say, the linguistics of the French language to those just starting O-level French. The strength of this argument should not be forgotten because of its misuse by those who fail to grasp, or have decided not to recognise, the claim of Poetics to an influential place in degree study in Literature. Indeed, that an invisible 'Poetics' informs the construction of the most conventional syllabus seems scarcely worth mentioning were it not for the cries of indignant outrage that mentioning it so often provokes. For the difficult

* What follows reflects a more personal sense of the issues. It is necessary to stress this, since Open University course production is intensely collaborative. Not all the colleagues with whom I have worked in the planning of these courses would wish to pursue this line of argument.

questions are not *if*, but *when*, in what proportion to the study of texts/authors, to what degree of rigour, should theoretical issues be pursued. To be specific: should an introductory course on the Novel make room for explicit attention to the construction of the 'literary canon' it points to? Should an introductory course on twentieth-century poetry make room for what may be called meta-criticism, a probing of the assumptions about 'reading a poem' which, under the aegis of Richards, Empson, Leavis, Brooks, Warren and many others, have become so widely accepted? (See, e.g., Iser, 1978, De Man, 1979.) By 'make room', I intend something more than an introductory gesture (whether conventional lecture or Open University course unit) alerting students to the existence of such issues.

Certainly, raising the issues in some form is an advance on ignoring them, yet in itself this can never cut sufficient weight. The institutionalised canon of great novelists/poets can only be seriously examined by assembling another canon on different principles. One possibility is the 'vertical' cut into a relatively short chronological period, which includes three distinct categories: writers subsequently canonised for special attention in conventional syllabuses; writers well-regarded in their time, but now unread; and some representation of writing which made no claims to 'literary' qualities. Material for such a course could be unearthed from the pages of Q. D. Leavis's *Fiction and the Reading Public* (1932), a work which powerfully contributed to the 'selective tradition' through which we usually study earlier twentieth-century fiction. Such a procedure would have the additional value of pointing up the moral and cultural assumptions upon which so many conventional syllabi have subsequently been built. It would also foreground the questions of literary production (publishing, advertising, reviewing, marketing) otherwise relegated to the margins of conventional literary study; and (if the chosen period were post-1918) the role of Literature for directly ideological use in the creation of a National Culture as argued in the Newbolt Report on *The Teaching of English in England* (1921).

Such a syllabus would, of course, bring its own considerable problems. One of Mrs Leavis's exhibits is Warwick Deeping's *Sorrell and Son* (1925). Reviewing a reprint of 1957, Kingsley Amis pointed out that the novel is steeped in a variety of social prejudices, not all of them dated:

There is a persistent thread of anti-Americanism; there is continual deprecation of the 'highbrow' and 'clever'; 'sex is nature'
and like eating your dinner, but by a deft synthesis it also
includes 'the mystery of woman'; Freud and all that needn't be
taken seriously, we aren't abnormal – 'the abnormality could be
looked for on the Continent'; people with money and fame, like
film stars, are unhappy and want to be like you and me. To
round it off nicely, savage things are said about the Commission-
ers of Inland Revenue. (Amis, 1972, p. 41)

Many presently uncanonised texts of this century would present a
similar face, while the irrecoverably dated attitudes of older texts
(e.g. the Victorian appetite for theological exchange) pose an even
greater difficulty. We know from conventional syllabi that not
many students leap at the opportunity offered by, say, Chaucer's
translation of Boethius's *De Consolatione Philosophiae*, by Milton's
Paradise Regained, or Blackmore's *The Creation: a Philosophical Poem*,[7]
to acquaint themselves with the central 'ideologies' of the period in
question. Yet a direct consequence of the dismantling of 'Literature', as of the view that Great Literature is characterised by *transcending* mere ideology, must be the confronting in sufficient detail
of the highly visible ideological motifs which characterise so much
'minor' or otherwise neglected writing. It cannot be enough to
encounter such material indirectly, even in a wider than usual
variety of literary texts. Courses constructed on such principles
would evidently stand in need of a new kind of period anthology
offering a range of material, edited to appropriate length, identifying the key ideological formations whose interweaving in selected
texts could then be the principal analytic task. Much of this material would, of course, come from the field of social and intellectual
history, as well as from literary sources.

Only in one area of Open University course production has
there been a more radical quality of interdisciplinary collaboration
than is characteristic of most faculty-centred courses. This is the
independently budgeted 'U-area' responsible for the development
of university courses. These are produced by the direct initiative of
self-selecting groups from all faculties, and must be carefully
designed to attract students from all faculties. Such a course is
Popular Culture (1982–), designed and produced by members of
four faculties – Arts, Education, Social Science and Technology.

Its structure departs widely from the normal compartmentalisation of disciplines (History, Literature, Sociology, etc.), and underlines the crucial interdependence of such disciplines in respect of any course in the field of Cultural Studies. Of interdisciplinary collaboration, the late Roland Barthes has written that

> it cannot be accomplished by simple confrontations between various specialised branches of knowledge. Interdisciplinary work is not a peaceful operation: it begins *effectively* when the solidarity of the old disciplines breaks down . . . to the benefit of a new object and a new language, neither of which is in the domain of those branches of knowledge that one calmly sought to confront. (Barthes, 1979, p. 73)

Barthes reminds us here of one formidable obstacle to any substantial move from Literature to Cultural Studies – present institutional and professional investment in the 'old disciplines'. The Open University 'U-area' is a valuable enabling device whereby it becomes possible to map out the territory of accessible knowledge freshly. In planning the course on *Popular Culture* we moved quickly away from structuring notions like 'popular literature', 'popular music', or 'advertising' and 'television' to a consideration of their place within the history of a conception of 'popular culture' as a site of ideological contestations. With the stimulus of structuralist/semiological analyses we were also able to approach freshly such a question as the formal organisation of texts, thus bypassing standard arguments about their formulaic character.

In another 'U-course', *Inquiry*, which has a strong component of the philosophy of science, there is also a small literature element – the poetry of the Spanish Civil War. This material is approached not in the familiar literary-critical way, but in terms of its value for the enquirer into the nature of that political event. Other 'U-courses' presently in the planning stage, *Women's Studies* and *Third World Studies*, are expected to offer similar opportunities for contributions from the Literature discipline, again in terms of the basic themes and concepts which structure the course. This kind of redefinition of fields of study seems to be one of the really promising developments for the future.

104 Re-Reading English

Notes

1 This is an entirely separate and different essay to one with the same title, by Arnold Kettle and Graham Martin, in D. Craig and M. Heinemann (eds), *Experiments in English Teaching* (Arnold, 1976).

2 The work-load for one course is roughly equivalent to half of the work-load for one academic year of a student in a normal university. The Open University BA degree requires passes in six courses; for honours, in eight courses, individually classified for honours.

3 Some philosophers, though, would dismiss certain relevant philosophical texts as mere 'history of ideas'.

4 Half-courses, however, are permitted. The current Literature plan is for one full course and two half-courses.

5 We were also able to mount a Drama course for 1977–81 only, when Arts Faculty course production was permitted a temporary 'overshoot'.

6 For a criticism of this aspect of the course, see A. Easthope, 'Open University literature courses: a critique', *Teaching at a Distance*, No. 13 (1978).

7 'Warmly praised by Dr Johnson', *The Concise Oxford Dictionary of English Literature* (ed. Dorothy Eagleton) (1970), p. 50.

References

Amis, Kingsley (1972), 'Pater and Old Chap' in *What Became of Jane Austen and Other Questions*, Panther.

Barthes, Roland (1979), 'From Work to Text' in J.V. Harari (ed.), *Textual Strategies: Perspectives in Post-Structuralist Criticism*, New York and London: Cornell University Press and Methuen.

Bayley, John (1981), *The Times Literary Supplement*, 4062 (6 Feb.), 135.

Clayre, Alasdair (ed.) (1977), *Nature and Industrialization*, Oxford University Press.

De Man, Paul (1939), *Allegories of Reading*, New Haven, Conn.: Yale University Press.

Harvie, Christopher, Martin, Graham and Scharf, Aaron (eds) (1970), *Industrialization and Culture, 1832–1914*, Macmillan.

Iser, Wolfgang (1978), *The Act of Reading*, Routledge & Kegan Paul.

8

'English' and the Council for National Academic Awards

JOHN OAKLEY and ELIZABETH OWEN

The Council for National Academic Awards is the largest Senate in the United Kingdom; a third of all degree students in the country graduate under its aegis (CNAA, 1979). Since its Royal Charter was granted in 1964, the CNAA (and in the nine years before this, its predecessor the National Council for Technological Awards) has developed a system of course validation the opposite of the London External degree pattern which previously dominated higher education outside the universities. There, syllabuses were set and examinations marked centrally; the non-university, satellite colleges, or the individual autodidacts, were passive recipients of the requirements of London. The CNAA, on the contrary, engaged in dialogue with its constituents by calling for degree proposals from the polytechnics, colleges and institutes of higher education. Implicit in this was the long-standing British view that learning is not a solitary but a collegiate activity. The CNAA instituted inspections of the environment in which its courses were to be studied and was instrumental in its first fifteen years in directing a portion of the affluence of those times towards the spread of collegiate facilities – libraries, tutorial rooms, common rooms – into public sector institutions.

In 1964, Penguin published *Crisis in the Humanities*, a collection of cries of dissatisfaction and expressions of impotence to effect change in university departments. To propose the change of a detail led to consideration of wider problems, to propose wide changes was 'violent, Jacobinical and un-British' (Plumb, 1964, p. 109). In the requirement of its Statutes (8:5:*b*(ii)), that its Committees should not prescribe syllabuses but only approve those submitted to them, the Council had already to hand an instrument which enabled change to take place while providing the safeguards necessary to make change respectable in Britain. Degree proposals were to be sent in to the Council; the Council set up Subject Boards appropriate to the proposals received; the Boards subjected the submission documents to rigorous and detailed scrutiny, calling for further documentation or information when necessary, and then, when the paper proposals were sufficiently full and coherent, visited the institution to cross-question all the staff involved. Behind these procedures lay the principle that the Subject Board in itself held no view of what a degree proposal should contain; it could only respond to whatever proposals were submitted and would approve them when satisfied of their coherence and of the adequacy of staff support for them.

The initial experience of these procedures in the colleges was one of contradiction. They offered unlimited freedom to design new courses in English to lecturers chafing against the London External orthodoxy, and then subjected their novelty to interrogation from what seemed conservative positions. And to those who considered English to be a well-charted area needing only the mention of the main names on the map, they brought a demand for what seemed radical intellectual re-appraisal of the subject. The requirement that proposals should be written out fully for submission to the Board and then defended against vigorously conducted attack had special consequences. No proposal could go forward without calling out a responsible re-examination of what constituted English and how it should be studied at undergraduate level in the late twentieth century. But the results of this re-examination could vary widely, and in some cases led to the abandonment of the title 'English' altogether. No proposal could rest on the brilliance of an individual leader or the pressure of a small group alone. The visit of the Subject Board to the institution soon revealed whether or not each part of the course, and its general principles, were adequately supported by its teachers. The approval of a degree containing English was not easily won; the subject was no refuge for the intellectually idle. The effect of the somewhat adversarial style of these initial approvals was to create within the polytechnics and colleges teams of teachers who had instituted regular discussion of the principles and practice of English in higher education, who had achieved agreement or an accommodation of differences, and who in the defence of the results of their deliberations had become a committed team. In addition, these proposals were to be resubmitted every five years, when a critical re-appraisal of the course would be required and the opportunity would be offered to make changes – whether major enough to constitute a new degree or involving only minor adjustments – and a further dialogue with the Board would take place. An effective machinery for continuous review had been invented.

It had, of course, the checks and balances required of change in a society devoted to gradualism. The presence of a considerable number of university members on Subject Boards, the use of university external examiners to guarantee results, both assured the public of equivalent standards and allayed university fears of 'dilution'. The Council's principles of non-prescriptive rigour chimed in with the best of the liberal inheritance in the university tradition of tolerant scepticism. It was able to recruit to its (unpaid) service university members who could finally approve courses very different from their own. And as the fifteen years advanced, with some institutions having fundamentally reconsidered English three times, it could set up new boards to consider the new areas of study these reflections generated.

The CNAA now impinges on the area normally referred to in the universities as 'English' through three main boards: the English Board (later with the Drama Board (1972), the American Studies Board (1978) and the Linguistics Board (1978) for related specialisms); the Combined Studies (Humanities) Board, where English figures as one element in joint degrees; and the Communication and Cultural Studies Board where English has merged in a wider study.

The English Board was established in 1967, with seven members from the universities (one in the chair), two from public sector colleges and two independent members.[1] Amongst the universities represented were Aberdeen, Edinburgh, Bristol, Manchester, Sheffield and Oxford. Literature, language and drama were accommodated. But the university members had not been recruited to represent types of university; recruitment had been, and remains so for all Boards, by invitation from the Council.

In its first decade, it approved eight degrees. This small number of approvals was a consequence of the rethinking of the needs of English combined with the Council's tendency to expect that subject areas should be taught by specialists. Where English was felt to involve, say, social history, language study, or the history of ideas, specialists in that area would be expected to participate in the construction as well as the teaching of the degree. This opened the way for a determined effort towards real interdisciplinarity, rather than the juxtaposition of discrete subjects. For their part, the polytechnics preferred to offer courses different from the traditional single-subject degrees of the universities in order to widen the range of choice available to students; English therefore often began life as one element in a loose conglomeration, with which it might later develop selected closer ties.

The Combined Studies (Humanities) Board was set up originally under the title General Arts in 1966 (it was changed in 1968), and grew to be rather larger. By 1971, it consisted of eight members from universities such as Aberdeen, Aston, Essex, Keele (two) and Kent, eight members from the public sector colleges, and four members drawn from other kinds of institution.[2] English has figured in a substantial proportion – but by no means all – of the schemes submitted to this Board, where subjects such as History, Politics, Philosophy, Art History and Psychology are also well represented.

There are many ways in which English might come to the attention of this Board. At its most straightforward the subject may appear much as it does before the English Board (which, in such circumstances, will almost certainly also have an interest); looking, that is, either similar to university English, or appearing somewhat modified as (say) Literary Studies. Here, however, it will normally be neither the sole subject nor a dominant one, but will most likely be of equivalent proportion to one or more other subjects. This may occur in a number of ways and influence the study, through the relations it has entered into, to a greater or lesser degree. Interdisciplinary elements, with their varied consequences for the subjects involved, are not necessarily present. Indeed, the Board has no particular policy for encouraging interdisciplinarity, and the 'Combined' of the title has always (and surely rightly) been interpreted conservatively to refer to proposals where more than one subject is to be studied fully. In fact, with some kinds of modular degree, the structure, while encouraging the development of small-scale interdisciplinary units, may discourage any consistent or extensive experience of joint study. Further, with the familiar proposal of the joint honours type, there may be some kind of relation established between the two or more subjects, or there may not, and, in the latter circumstance, there is no predisposition on the part of the Board to suggest that there should be.

Of course, individual members who have a special interest in kinds of interdisciplinarity may feel it helpful to point out possibilities or potentialities in that direction on the basis of qualities already implicit in the content of the submission or in the unrealised resources of staff research. But such comment is not intended to be substantively critical, unless it points, for example, to a gap between the stated aims of the proposal – in which some gesture towards interdisciplinarity has perhaps appeared – and the syllabus content where it fails to be convincingly picked up. Rather, what is involved here is a more informal aspect of the validation procedure, which, while in no way revealing a commitment to it, may encourage a movement towards interdisciplinarity. The character of the discipline may therefore be affected by aspects of procedure which have just this informal character.

Indeed, these comments on the working of the two Boards may indicate how the redefinition of the subject both 'in itself' and through its relation with other subjects might be encouraged by Council procedure simply as a procedure, rather than as the channel for any policy especially favourable to change. Much, however, will depend on the capacity of staff to appreciate the favourable conditions for such a redefinition established by such processes. The importance of the radicalising effects of institutions and circumstances (where certainly no radicalism was intended) can be readily appreciated by comparing the sorts of thing manifestly possible for the designers of CNAA degrees with the fate (at least so far as the Cambridge Tripos was concerned) of the excellent and still apposite suggestions for joint study advanced close on forty years ago by F. R. Leavis (1943).

It might be useful to distinguish a number of these radicalising institutional elements and explore them further, noting along the way that the vocabulary by which they are registered seems the reverse of radical. These would include the special concomitants of the requirement to write out proposals fully, the often surprising developments stemming from the creation of course teams to do this, and the results of the related CNAA criteria of 'coherence' and 'leadership'. These elements are linked to familiar debates about interdisciplinarity arising from the work of the CNAA and the way in which the Council has, in turn, sought, through the composition of its Boards, to respond to new subject definitions. When one considers the enormous importance of the CNAA in regard to both who and what has been taught over the last fifteen years, it is remarkably little researched, written about or even discussed (with any measure of disinterest), and therefore interpretations of its history and effects are likely to be rather arbitrary and uninformed at this stage. But it would seem possible to attribute special importance to the moment, some eight years ago, when many of these elements were assembled within a formal expression of Council attitudes:

> Based on its extensive experience the Council is convinced that the discipline involved in preparing and documenting a proposal for the approval or reapproval of a course of study is extremely valuable to the College submitting it. When followed thoroughly this discipline contributes to clarifying the aims and objectives of the course and demands the formation of an academic team which identifies itself strongly with the course. The Council believes this latter point forms the basis of a high quality of education. Thus the Council concludes that this discipline is an essential background element to the consideration of courses of study and that no changes in its Procedure should lessen the importance to be attached to it. It is the opinion of the Council that the previous statements in this section are true irrespective of whether the course is one in a single discipline or not. (CNAA, 1972)

Thus the articulation of proposal and course team were seen as both necessary and interdependent, and the interdependent character of the relation has certain consequences in respect of another Council preoccupation not here stated – 'leadership'. It is clear that the *more* intellectually complex the proposal, and the *more* it involved the criticism of existing practices to bring about new disciplinary definitions, the *less* would a conventional notion of 'leadership' be satisfactory. Rather 'leadership' would be deemed to be present as a consequence not so much of qualities in an individual as in the submission itself – especially, the quality of 'coherence'. 'Coherence' shares, with the rest of the implicitly organicist and conservative rhetoric of validation, some repressive overtones, but it has usually been interpreted to mean: (1) that there is a consonance (but not necessarily a comprehensive fit) between the stated aims and the content of the courses; (2) that all staff understand the aims and the part that their contribution makes to the whole; (3) that the enterprise is publicly accessible and that students both know what is expected of them and can develop individually within the experience of the course; (4) that the proposal makes a sense at least comparable to that to be derived from a single-subject honours degree as it is usually understood. It is hardly glib to suggest that this final factor involves no exacting standard, and it is indeed assumed that the notion of 'coherence' should be applied minimally; e.g. staff should not expect students to work out links that they cannot satisfactorily express themselves. To find these qualities present would be in turn to confirm the 'coherence' of the team and to diagnose the existence of 'leadership' although the latter, in the more complex proposals, would necessarily be of a diffused and collective character. The force of 'necessarily' here derives from the anticipation that where the coherence looked for is conceptual, the course teams will naturally expect to see shares in its new wisdom evenly distributed.

We wish to argue that the effect of the CNAA on the evolution of English has been positive, not because of any philosophy that the Boards have about English as such, but rather because the pressure to write is itself the source of a modest critical defamiliarisation in most of us and, where we are working with others, of a greater self-consciousness about our ideas and the way in which they differ from those of other people. The different working relations implicit in the need to write make possible other developments once the challenge to a personal property in such ideas has been made. It is probably still not realised what these CNAA requirements have meant. There is nothing comparable in university practice – except in the Open University, where quite different circumstances have required similar acts of collective expression. In the case of the non-university, public sector colleges, these expectations were presumably introduced as a guarantee of the quality of the staff where publication and other more traditional

testimonies were not always available. They were accepted by the
colleges willingly because of an expectation that they should offer
what the universities do not, and because of a need to convey a
more collective strength where idiosyncratic brilliance was less of
an established virtue. It is usual to find, even in the most predictable joint honours structure approved by the Council, that an
English group has constructed a course on the basis of principles
jointly arrived at, and not simply as an aggregate of competing
interests and attitudes with which staff are variously associated as
individuals. It is certainly not the case that all groups of staff will
have taken this opportunity thoroughly to revise their practices; it
is no part of the CNAA's job to ensure that they do so. But however
satisfied a group of staff may be with established conceptions of
English, the mere obligation to write and discuss creates that possibility. At the very least, this is a different state of affairs from one in
which 'criticism' takes the form of issues about examinations and
personalities, and can only result in the emergence of conceded
alternatives within a reluctant plurality. The Council requirements
seem to create a site for something else.

It might be useful at this point to turn from the rather more
usual degree submissions, where the redefinition of English may
be encouraged through its articulation within joint schemes which
perhaps have some interdisciplinary ambition, to situations which
test what have been held to be the positive aspects of Council's
practice to the fullest. These are the circumstances where a recognisable 'English' is less obviously present. First, however, it is necessary to say that such a proposal will not be regarded as necessarily
creating more problems than other simpler ones; even the most
guarded type of interdisciplinarity has its own difficulties. Let us
look for a moment at an example in which two subjects (say English
and History) are side by side. Usually some trouble has been taken
to ensure that the periodisation is either in rough parallel or not in
embarrassing disjunction. Between the two, there may be some
joint seminars or other projects. These are frequently predictable:
Poetry and Politics in the 1930s or *The Novel and Industrial Society*, to
give some fictitious but characteristic instances. There are a
number of sound courses that do this kind of thing. Most of them
will avoid a simple reflectionism, although there will always be
difficulty in knowing what to put in its place – without a concern
with culture and social structure occupying some central role in the

course. Then the responsibility for making links will fall too heavily on the students, because the literature/society relation, and the ways in which it may be perceived, has not been taught to them as itself a 'subject'. In such cases, the interdisciplinary areas are the site of a negotiation between self-sufficient disciplines whose exclusiveness may in some measure be paradoxically reinforced by attempting precisely that difficult negotiation. The point is not that this is a bad thing – every kind of course has a price, and it is well to consider what it might be – but rather that such an approach, which leaves the student to establish links or compels staff to operate within a very narrow intellectual space, would not always be regarded as 'safer' than a proposal where the more familiar lines of the discipline have been dissolved.

This latter case has, of course, problems of its own but it does at least offer an opportunity for the systematic presentation of its own chief concerns. The situation envisaged here is one in which English enters a field of study – such as Literary Studies (in its more radical versions), Communication or Cultural Studies – in which it is (along with other subjects) restated so as to accentuate where possible its conceptual and other alignments with adjacent disciplines. Here the name 'English' may have gone, but the fact that literature (as it is generally understood) is present, and present in English, involves those who have taught the subject in any of the established ways in an assessment of the new product. This is no bad thing; and it is not necessarily to be distrusted, either, by those who have brought about this redefinition of 'English'. It is neither unreasonable nor sentimental to pose to oneself (and to others) the possibility that something may be being lost in the haste to restate.

But there is a more serious matter. A field of study of the kind mentioned is not a new 'discipline', if by this is meant an acquisition of knowledge organised round agreed categories and procedures and mediated through discipline departments that produce and reproduce such categories and procedures. The field is rather defined by a range of problems (albeit clustered round an object of study – e.g. the culture/society pair) to the solution of which a range of the existing disciplines at some level contributes. These disciplines are, as a consequence, to some greater or lesser extent transformed in turn, and it is valuable if a syllabus in such a field of study can find the forms through which to represent this process of change. In one way, this is only another aspect of the fruitful

CNAA requirement to put a degree course into a written form. Not only are there the immediate comparisons produced by giving formal expression to different subjects within one document, but the very articulation of the categories and procedures of the new 'field' demands that the process by which they were acquired be stated in an accessible manner. New forms of syllabus writing are produced, then, which themselves open up the original disciplines – their history and their 'contradictory discourses' – to scrutiny. So the necessity for CNAA validation of new fields offers advantages for the development of English which have little to do with explicit attitudes or policies.

The Cultural Studies courses (or components of courses) validated by the Communication and Cultural Studies Board are in many ways the clearest examples of how 'English' may partially disappear, but *necessarily* and valuably survives to haunt this new territory with its earlier claims, and of how this ghostly presence must be constantly and seriously engaged with. The term 'cultural studies' itself derives from the Centre for Contemporary Cultural Studies established in the early sixties at Birmingham under Richard Hoggart in order primarily to examine aspects of contemporary British culture which fell outside the area of 'high' culture – still the normal subject matter of Humanities courses. Hoggart's book *The Uses of Literacy* (1957), the debate over which prepared the way for the Centre and, therefore, for the new field of study, has been described as extending the typical concerns and discriminations of the literary critic to the sphere of non-verbal communication, to interpersonal relations, and to the 'reading' of (especially) working-class culture. Cultural Studies will probably always be marked by this filiation from literary criticism, and from *Scrutiny* in particular – not least because it retains, of course, a concern with 'literature' of a recognised kind. Although it is not true any longer that 'English' or literary criticism is particularly privileged within Cultural Studies, it is still true that the impetus to design courses in this area often comes from teachers of literature. The problem for course design is to find a form through which to express the re-enacting of this filiation within the course. *Scrutiny*, for instance, is not a historical curiosity to be crudely mapped in under 'élitism' or some such notion, and the Leavisian formulation for joint study (of the seventeenth century) alluded to earlier, still suggests an initial *method* for engaging questions of literature and society.

This project of Leavis's in *Education and the University* (1943) was concerned with the causes and effects of the survival or otherwise of forms of 'literary discourse'. One consequence of studying liter-ature within Cultural Studies is that students will feel able to discuss this historical dimension of the culture/society relation with almost as much confidence and almost as early as they would be able to discuss, through an assimilation of the methods of literary studies, a poem or a novel. This ability must not, however, be thought possible only as a consequence of spectacular accom-plishments in theory or the prolonged negotiation between discip-lines; and so it is valuable to rehearse, within the course, the resources for a socially-oriented understanding of literature already available to 'English'. These are, anyway, more theoreti-cally subtle than they may seem. To provide some passable account of the seventeenth century, and to be able to involve students constructively in it, does not *require* any particular version of Eng-lish, but it *is* necessary to have a sufficient literature/society para-digm available and the issues problematised. The students can thus work within a *practice* (however ultimately superseded in its implicit theories) which talks about 'literature and society', and they can check this practice as they go along against a 'cultural studies' exposition of the central concerns of the study of culture and social structure.

Similar effects for English may result from its incorporation in Communication courses. Although there are many areas of over-lap (in their contributory disciplines and their central concern with processes of cultural transmission), Communication Studies may be distinguished from Cultural Studies in their greater stress on the socio-linguistic and psychological study of language, and on semiotics, as against the historically informed concern with social structure and cultural forms. An instance of the effects of the Communication appropriation of English is the challenge it must necessarily offer to the notion of 'significant' Literature separated off from other ('minor') literature, from other forms of writing, and from other text-producing processes (film, television). The implicit evaluations of 'literary study', and the central assumption of many teachers of the subject, are thus immediately opened to question. It is a conspicuous example of the debate engendered by the entry of an academic 'discipline' into one of the new 'fields'. But there is no reason why debates of this kind should be finally resolved as a precondition for the design and teaching of courses. The two traditions – one from English as a humane study, the other from social sciences or elsewhere – may both remain available, not in a loose pluralism, but in the 'placing' context of their relations, divergencies and historical development.

Both Cultural Studies and Communication constitute a *field of study* not a 'subject' and, as such, are necessarily critical of what often seems the a-historical closure of the typical discipline. Such a field reveals its own history and compels the subjects entering it to reveal theirs: surveys of the story so far have been a recurrent feature of the development of Cultural Studies in recent years. Yet within such a process a subject such as English has a continuing right of retaliation; as has been remarked, it is possible to underestimate what the discipline offers. So far as the reciprocal effects of CNAA validation are concerned, it seems desirable that this element of conflict should be manifest and, indeed, be part of the field of study in the examples under discussion. This, in turn, resolves itself into a matter of ensuring, through the personnel on the Board, that debates of this sort can be responded to *as debates*: that (say) the claims for literature as a humane study can be made at the time when they are being challenged, in the public context of the discussion of a degree scheme. To this end, those responsible have ensured (again in conformity with some wise attitudes on the part of the Council) that various subject emphases are present on different Boards; that, for example, the English Board is not the repository for some supposedly traditional view and the Communication and Cultural Studies Board for something else.

It may seem that this account of the relation between developments in English and the processes of CNAA validation is tastelessly cheerful, not readily conforming to many readers' own experience of that particular aspect of the human condition. However, it is offered in the belief that the CNAA should now itself begin to be the object of tolerably dispassionate enquiry. The effects of this institution on the organisation and reproduction of knowledge have clearly been considerable. What seems to be important has less to do with the sympathy that individual participants on Boards may have towards new developments in disciplines and more to do with the relation between Council policy (which needs to be evaluated beyond its 'official' rhetoric) and the ways in which that has operated and been interpreted. To see how extraordinary the CNAA was, is to understand why so much has become administratively possible which did not seem possible at the time that Plumb put his book together. The idea of 'coherence' with its implication both for written submissions and course grouping has been, as a consequence of this need for articulation (including the articulation of differences), a basis for developments within English, in its interdisciplinary relations with other subjects, and in its extended evolution within new fields of study. Furthermore, the evolution of the Boards themselves, through their subsequent recruitment, has created a context in which these developments can be appreciated and defended. The designers of degree proposals encounter administrative restraints in a whole number of ways; most particularly, they meet their own college administrators who evaluate their project in terms of competing resources. Assuming the greatest goodwill, it would be difficult for such people to favour innovation. It is therefore the more necessary that a forum can exist where innovative disciplinary trends can be discussed, and where some sort of agreed conventions can be established for knowing what innovation might look like and how it can be expressed within a course proposal. The Council itself is now in the process of developing mechanisms for dealing sympathetically with the problems which arise out of the kind of redefinition of 'the subject' discussed above. As it always has, it will respond to what comes from the colleges.

Notes

1 By 1980, these proportions were markedly different, with ten members from public sector institutions, seven from the universities, and one other.
2 By 1980, these proportions were again markedly different: public sector – 19; universities – 11; and one other. Membership of the Communication and Cultural Studies Board in 1980 was: public sector – 9; universities – 11; and one other.

References

CNAA (1972), Paper C/72/17/a. Report of the Meeting of the Committee for Future Relationships between the Council and the Colleges held on 12 June 1972. Preface 65.

CNAA (1979), CNAA publication, *The Council: Its Place in Higher Education*.

Leavis, F.R. (1943), *Education and the University*, Cambridge: Cambridge University Press.

Plumb, J.H. (ed.) (1964), *Crisis in the Humanities*, Harmondsworth: Penguin.

PART II:

Case studies

9
Re-reading the great tradition
CATHERINE BELSEY

I

There is a sense in which the great tradition of the English novel – the fiction which is unquestionably 'Literature', and which belongs unmistakably on the syllabus – was produced by F. R. Leavis in *The Great Tradition*. Not single-handed, of course. Leavis did not bring any of his 'great English novelists' for the first time before an unsuspecting public. But his critical 'discriminations' established a literary topography which authoritatively distinguished between what was major and minor, mature and infantile in the field of fiction. These judgements, with some small adjustments, have permeated a whole literary culture and a national educational system, and have produced a high degree of consensus concerning the criteria of greatness in literature and the characteristics of novels which are recognised as worth reading. In identifying such novels, Leavis constructed the great tradition itself, made its greatness and its continuity palpable, put it 'plainly', as he himself might have said, 'there'.

Leavis's individual judgements have not, of course, gone unchallenged, but what *The Great Tradition* produced was not simply a canon and a syllabus but a critical discourse, and the assumptions inscribed in this discourse are easily overlooked in the discussion of its specific assertions. In the provocative opening sentence of *The Great Tradition*, for instance, the scandal and the authority (the authority-in-scandal which makes the book so attractive to readers steeped in the novelistic convention of the heroism of lonely leadership) lie not simply in the polemical list of novelists, but in the certainty, nowhere debated in the text, that the object of criticism is to isolate *greatness* and to see it as a property of *authors*: 'The great English novelists are Jane Austen, George Eliot, Henry James, and Joseph Conrad' (Leavis, 1962, p. 9).

Recent discussions of Leavis's work have been sharply critical of some aspects of the Leavisian discourse, paying particular attention to its concepts of culture and community (Anderson, 1968; Eagleton, 1976, pp. 13–16; Lawford, 1976; Mulhern, 1979; Wright, 1979). What I want to do in this essay is approach *The Great Tradition* as itself a text, subject to critical analysis, in conjunction with George Eliot's *Daniel Deronda*, one of the novels it specifies as worthy of inclusion in the great tradition. In doing so I want to suggest that the Leavisian reading is *partial* in both senses of the word – first, in that this way of reading manifests a prior commitment in its reproduction of the values and strategies of the text it undertakes to judge, and second, in that it reduces in the process the plurality of the original novel. Dependent on the texts it isolates for critical attention, *The Great Tradition* limits the possible readings of those texts, confines their meaning within the conventional, the acceptable, the authoritatively 'obvious'. I want then to go on to sketch an alternative approach to *Daniel Deronda*, offering not to *re-evaluate* it in its entirety but to *re-read* those areas to which Leavis himself pays most attention.

II

Daniel Deronda is treated at considerable length in *The Great Tradition* as an instance of the best and the worst in the work of George Eliot. Previous critics have failed to make the judgements of value, understood to be the business of criticism, which enable Leavis to identify the 'fervid and wordy unreality' of the bad half of the book, and to propose that the good half be extricated under the title *Gwendolen Harleth*. This would display George Eliot's art at its most mature, would demonstrate her 'profound insight into the moral nature of man', and would show her 'for us in these days' (1948, the aftermath of the Second World War) as 'a peculiarly fortifying and wholesome author'. The health-giving qualities spring from her commitment to 'life', Leavis's most recurrent if slightly elusive positive value, which manifests itself in the presentation of the characters. These are not only richly and vividly realised 'in the concrete' so that we are made to feel their experience 'from inside'; they are also morally 'placed', judged 'with unfailing rightness'. In *Gwendolen Harleth* George Eliot exhibits for our consideration 'what we recognise from our own most intimate experience to be as much the behaviour of a responsible moral agent, and so as much amenable to moral judgment, as any human behaviour can be' (Leavis, 1962, p. 124). Great novels combine the recognisably real with a complex and humane valuing of this reality. The bad half of *Daniel Deronda*, conversely, is ponderously abstract, remote from life, and not sufficiently 'impersonal'. We feel the direct presence of George Eliot's own weakness, a tendency to exalted enthusiasms and idealisations unworthy of a mature intelligence, and in consequence her analysis lacks discrimination.

The discussion of *Daniel Deronda* is broadly characteristic of *The Great Tradition* as a whole, and especially in its emphasis on *experience*. In this respect Leavisian criticism strikingly reproduces the values which inform the novels singled out for inclusion in the great tradition. Empiricism, the conviction that experience is the source of knowledge, is one of the main determinants of narrative structure in the classic realist novels of the canon. Dorothea Brooke, Gwendolen, Isabel Archer and, in a rather different way, Conrad's Marlow, all learn from experience, moving in the course of the narrative towards an enhanced awareness of themselves and the world. This learning process, which propels the redistribution of the relationships between the characters, constitutes the core of the classic realist story. Ignorance, misunderstanding and misrecognition generate a series of crises (episodes) which finally produce a new and more stable pattern of relationships (closure).

Empiricism also determines the classic realist novel's mode of address, in so far as it undertakes to 'show' in a series of dramatisations the significant experiences of the characters. Dialogue, vivid description and close attention to realistic detail all contribute to the process of *realisation* of experience. And this in turn invites the reader to participate in the experience, to become part of the fictional world, and to learn with (or from) the experience of the characters. This, indeed, is the conventional justification of classic realism as a serious moral undertaking. The novel which not only records the process of learning by experience, but also embodies that process in its own mode of address, is necessarily offering the reader the enhanced awareness which is its theme. According to Leavis, the origin of this awareness is the experience of the author (properly impersonalised). To convey an experience is to have known it. George Eliot's 'richness' is the product of 'a judging vision that relates everything to her profoundest moral experience' (Leavis, 1962, p. 102). Here the Leavisian text takes classic realism on its own terms, accepts its strategies at their face value. In *Adam Bede* the narrator interrupts the narrative to insist on the empirical origin of the 'truth' of the fictional world: 'I aspire to give no more than a faithful account of men and things as they have mirrored themselves in my mind . . . as if I were in the witness box, narrating my experience on oath' (Ch. 17).

The test of the novel's 'truth' is the reader's own knowledge, 'what we recognise from our own most intimate experience', as Leavis puts it. And here it is possible to glimpse a problem: if we know it already, in what sense can we be said to learn it? The answer, of course, is that we come to know it explicitly, come to recognise it *with the help of the novel*. Because to become a source of knowledge experience needs to be interpreted by *a prior subjectivity*. 'Men and things' mirror themselves accurately in the mind able to interpret them. Thus empiricism slides into idealism.

Again Leavisian criticism reproduces the philosophical position of the novels. Dorothea is capable of learning from experience, while Rosamond Vincy is not. Gwendolen's own rudimentary moral consciousness enables her to profit from her mistakes, but she needs the help of Daniel Deronda, whose sensibility is a finer one. It is subjectivity which determines what lessons can be learnt, and which mysteriously transmutes experience into understanding. The reader needs the help of the critic in making sense of the literary experience, and both critic and reader need the help of the author, ultimate source and guarantee of the novel's truth. Thus the experience of George Eliot (in the 1870s) and F. R. Leavis (in the 1940s) converge with mine (in the 1980s) in a single 'recognition', a single 'knowledge' and a single timeless judgement. 'Our' attitude to Gwendolen Harleth 'is, or should be (with George Eliot's help), George Eliot's own, which is that of a great novelist, concerned with human and moral valuation in a way proper to her art' (Leavis, 1962, p. 124).

The phrase 'or should be' in that quotation points to a gap in the seamless concept of shared, timeless novelistic experience, and is a small reminder of the authoritarianism of the Leavisian position. In this instance our attitude should be George Eliot's own, but in others the harmony between author and critic is disturbed, to the point where in *Daniel Deronda* our attitude 'should' diverge so radically from the author's that we reject half her text. In such cases the critic's submission to the author's unfailing rightness is overturned, and it is the critic's human and moral valuation which is offered as authoritative. In order to suggest how this comes about it is necessary to look more closely at the narrative strategies of the classic realist text.

In any utterance, any piece of writing or speech, it is possible to distinguish two aspects: both the action of the speaker in producing the utterance, and the evocation of the world defined in the utterance. In fiction these aspects may be distinguished as the narrative process itself on the one hand, and the presentation of the fictional world on the other. 'These two aspects give life to two realities, each as linguistic as the other: the world of the characters and the world of the narrator-reader couple' (Todorov, 1977, p. 26). The existence of these two realities allows the classic realist text to preserve its characteristic conjunction of empiricism and idealism. The world of the characters is offered as an empirical reality, which the reader not only experiences but learns to interpret correctly, thanks to the guidance of the narrative voice, conventionally identified with the subjectivity of the author. If what the reader learns from the text is to be coherent – that is, if the text is to achieve formal and ideological closure – there must be no sense of discord between these two realities. At the same time, the text is intelligible as classic realism to the extent that it seems to represent 'the evident laws of a natural order' (Barthes, 1972, p. 140). These 'laws', in reality the historically specific mythology of bourgeois society, concern values as well as plausibility. Classic realism requires the narrative voice to evaluate the events it recounts as well as to make sense of them.

This is the real content of the 'unfailing rightness' Leavis finds in the work of the great novelist. To the extent that the two realities in the text operate in conjunction with each other to display the evident laws of a natural order, the text itself is 'mature'. Where this is not so the 'immaturities' must be excised. The nature of immaturity is most extensively discussed in the analysis of *The Mill on the Floss*, though a similar analysis of the inadequacies of *The Portrait of a Lady* illuminates the discussion of *Daniel Deronda* when Leavis characteristically introduces a 'weaker' text to point up the virtues of a 'good' one. In both cases, it seems, the narrative voice fails to 'place' the reality of the characters: Henry James idealises Isabel and does not recognise her 'extremely unintelligent obstinacy'; George Eliot shares Maggie Tulliver's lack of self-knowledge, participates in her sense of Stephen Guest's irresistibleness, and therefore fails to realise that Maggie's motivation is sexual rather than poetic (Leavis, 1962, pp. 127, 54–8).

In these instances the presence of the author intrudes into the reality of the fictional world (a world so real that Leavis 'knows' it as the authors do not). In other words, the narrative voice does not maintain a distance from which to enunciate the evident laws of a natural (moral) order; the subjectivity of the author fails to guarantee a correct interpretation of the experience recounted. The conjunction of empiricism and idealism collapses. But the role of Leavis's critical text is to restore this conjunction. The *critic's* voice now takes over from the author's, and appropriates a corresponding authority. The critical text pronounces the judgements which the narrative voice fails to supply, and thus constructs a shadowy alternative text which does conform to the evident laws of a natural order. It 'places' the experience correctly and so restores the order from which the novel has deviated. Bourgeois mythology is saved.

In *Daniel Deronda*, however, the treatment is more radical. The offending part of the text is simply cut away, to leave a work which does justice to the subjectivity of an author who, in *Gwendolen Harleth*, 'exhibits a traditional moral sensibility, expressing itself . . . with perfect sureness, in judgments that involve confident positive standards, and yet affect us as simply the report of luminous intellegence' (Leavis, 1962, p. 139).

In the Leavisian critical text the two aspects which correspond to the two realities of classic realism are very clearly distinguished. In order that the reader should *experience* the qualities of the novel under discussion there is extensive quotation from it, duly 'placed' by the critical commentary which surrounds the quotation. But whereas in classic realism commentary is conventionally integrated into the narrative, so that George Eliot's generalising moral and philosophical comments are often held to be an 'intrusion', in the

Leavisian text there is a clear gap, indicated by typographical convention (quotations are inset in smaller type), but emphasised by the critical discourse. From the empiricist point of view the quotation should speak for itself, but in reality a quotation of any length is open to a plurality of readings. The object of the commentary is to contain this plurality, not by *analysis* of the passage quoted, which would interfere with the notion that correct reading is a matter of recognition, but by prompting the reader to share the view that the passage is self-evidently ('plainly') an instance of the author's 'sureness of touch'. In *The Great Tradition* at large, the wider the gap between what the reader may safely be left to recognise and the reading offered, the more hectoring the discourse becomes: certain distinctions are 'elementary' (p. 16); specific texts are 'obviously' of a certain kind 'for minds with mature interests' (p. 18, n. 1); 'the adult mind doesn't as a rule find in Dickens a challenge to an unusual and sustained seriousness' (p. 29). The subjectivity of the critic is present in the text, inscribed in the first person pronouns, source of the experience of reading, and authorisation of *this* particular reading. And in many instances, in another strategy Leavis shares with George Eliot, the subjectivity of the reader too is invoked, to ensure a perfect convergence of minds on a single reading: '*we* are made to feel' Gwendolen's situation; '*we* have in reading [George Eliot] the feeling that she is in and of the humanity she presents with so clear and disinterested a vision' (pp. 114, 139, my italics).

To understand the implications of this convergence it is necessary to examine the 'natural order' (or the 'clear and disinterested vision' of 'humanity') which the Leavisian critical discourse serves and reproduces. It is supremely the order of a universe whose sole inhabitant is 'Eternal Man' (Barthes, 1972, p. 140), a subjectivity which precedes all discourse, and whose silent presence both determines and transcends history. This 'human essence', the rightful heritage of individuals, can float free of the destructive forces of a mass society by re-establishing a connection with the 'essential life' inscribed in the great tradition of English literature. Subjectivity thus recovers the humane disposition of discriminating and disinterested intelligence, which is its proper condition, as a means to the recreation of the organic community in the modern world.

The work of this humane subjectivity in its transcendence is to take responsibility for the 'judgment of relative human value' (Leavis, 1962, p. 40). The phrase, in the context of the judgement of relative human value which led to the concentration camps should, in the 1940s, have been spine-chilling. To judge by the success of the Leavisian enterprise in the period since the war, it was not. Here again it is not simply the specific judgements enunciated, but the assumption of hierarchy itself which demands alertness.

In classic realism the hierarchy of discourses, the 'placing' by a privileged narrative voice of the discourses of the fictional characters as more or less astute, more or less unselfish and so on, presents a world in which subjectivity is determining and hierarchies of subjectivity are taken for granted. (See Belsey, 1980, pp. 70–5.) These assumptions are reproduced in *The Great Tradition* not only in its discussion of fictional characters but equally in the theoretical framework inscribed in the opening sentence. The object of the book is to establish the timeless judgements of relative human value which identify those novelists whose special sensibility guarantees in turn their accurate judgement of human value. The reader of the opening paragraphs of *The Great Tradition* is invited to stand on a high mountain, recognising the kingdoms of the novel as they are displayed in patterns of subordination: 'the great English novelists', 'novelists in English worth reading', 'major novelists', 'minor novelists', and finally, 'fiction belonging to Literature', as distinct from mere 'fiction' (Leavis, 1962, pp. 9–10). The task of the book will be to explain and defend the sovereignty of 'the pre-eminent few' (p. 11) in a discourse in which the judgement of relative value is synonymous with understanding. What is judged, it must be emphasised, is not writing but subjectivity itself; novels as access to the identities of novelists.

The basis of this judgement is inevitably intuitive. Present to the disinterested intelligence, humane values are already known and recognised from our own most intimate experience. Just as the great novelist 'knows', the critic 'knows' the novelist's greatness, even when this condition produces an uneasy circularity of argument: 'there must, one reflects, be something more important to say about the moral seriousness of George Eliot's novels; otherwise she would hardly be the great novelist one knows her to be' (p. 41). The reader, therefore, cannot be persuaded by argument. As Leavis himself elsewhere conceded, 'what *Scrutiny's* audience did

not "know already", it could not be told' (Mulhern, 1979, p. 175).
When challenged by René Wellek to defend the philosophical
choices implicit in his position, Leavis refused, on the basis of the
radical distinction between literature and philosophy, adding, 'I
should not find it easy to define the difference satisfactorily, but Dr
Wellek *knows what it is*' (Leavis, 1976, p. 212, my italics).

But the judgement of relative value is not purely a matter of
literary appreciation. It is implicit throughout *The Great Tradition*,
and explicit elsewhere, that there is 'a necessary relationship between the quality of the individual's response to art and his general
fitness for a humane existence' (quoted in Mulhern, 1979, p. 48).
Leavis argued repeatedly in *Scrutiny* and in *Education and the University* for a direct connection between the disinterested play of free
intelligence in the English School and the propagation of humane
values in the community at large. Standing at the centre of a liberal
eduction, literature guarantees to those able to respond adequately to it a mature sensibility and a sureness of perception which lead
beyond the world of fiction: 'the more advanced the work the
more unmistakably is the judgment that is concerned inseparable
from the profoundest sense of relative value which determines, or
should determine, the important choices of actual life.' (Quoted in
Mulhern, 1979, p. 193.) Trained in the kind of discrimination
demonstrated in *The Great Tradition*, the leaders of the community
are to be properly equipped to recognise a hierarchy of subjectivity, mysteriously given to individuals, and judged on the basis of a
knowledge not open to rational argument. By this means, a ruling
élite provides itself with a sensibility which is the source and
guarantee of its right to control and administer experience.

To the extent that the social body concurs with the Leavisian
position, it commits itself to the *scrutiny* of individual subjectivity, to
the surveillance of personal experience, and to the identification of
strengths and weaknesses according to a standard which is purely
intuitive. This process is backed by the power of an educational
apparatus with its system of assessment and examination which
relegates deviancy and permits passage to the next level for finer
intelligences. What is inscribed in the Leavisian model is the making of hierarchies through judgements of relative human value,
not just in literature but in life. The discourse of *The Great Tradition*
helps to guarantee relations of inequality by the endless production of discriminations between subjectivities. Hierarchy is not

seen to be produced by an external ordering of society which is subject to change. On the contrary, it is created through the affirmation of one identity at the expense of another, and maintained by the rejection of any rational criticism of this process itself.

III

What are the implications of a refusal of the Leavisian critical discourse? Does it follow that we reject both the institution of English and the great tradition in their entirety? Not necessarily, I want to argue. A case can be made, of course, for abandoning the whole bag of tricks, but it is finally, I think, a bad case. To desert the institution in the present state of things is simply to hand it over to the Leavisites, whose influence is already dominant. A more constructive strategy is to treat English as a site of struggle, to generate a new critical discourse, to re-read the great tradition not for the sake of valorising it, but in order to release its plurality. I have argued elsewhere that texts are plural, and that their meanings are *produced* by bringing to bear on the raw material of the work itself discourses pertinent to the twentieth century (Belsey, 1980, pp. 125–46 and *passim*). Leavis reads *Daniel Deronda* to find what is 'obvious' in it, the banality of a universe ordered in accordance with poetic justice, 'Hubris with its appropriate Nemesis' (Leavis, 1962, p. 123). Gwendolen errs in marrying Grandcourt, knowing of his relations with Lydia Glasher. What follows is a direct and tragic consequence of 'pride and courage and sensitiveness and intelligence fixed in a destructive deadlock through false valuation and self-ignorance' (ibid., p. 124). I want to argue that this reading is only partial, that instead of looking to *Daniel Deronda* for confirmation of a banal morality, it is more productive to read it, for instance, as challenging the sexual power relations of its society in ways which have an identifiable bearing on our own.

To read *Daniel Deronda* as a feminist text is not necessarily to take it on the terms the narrative voice proposes as its own. But the interest in social relations as relations of domination and subordination is quite explicit and recurrent in the novel. Daniel submits to Mordecai, Mrs Davilow submits to Gwendolen, but above all sexual relations are also power relations, and marriage is presented as a struggle of which the outcome is a foregone conclusion:

One belief which had accompanied her through her unmarried

life as a self-cajoling superstition, encouraged by the subordination of every one about her – the belief in her own power of
dominating – was utterly gone. Already, in seven short weeks,
which seemed half her life, her husband had gained a mastery
which she could no more resist than she could have resisted the
benumbing effect from the touch of a torpedo. (Ch. 35)

I want to read *Daniel Deronda* as the history of an impossible
resistance, a reading which would not have been available to a
reader sharing the mild sexism characteristic of Leavis's period.
(Daniel himself, so lacking in concrete presence that he is to be
largely excised from the novel, is 'decidedly . . . a woman's creation', but we should remember that there is evidence that George
Eliot's was 'an extremely vigorous and distinguished mind, and
one in no respect disabled by being a woman's' (Leavis, 1962, p.
96).) If in offering a feminist reading of *Daniel Deronda* I concentrate on Leavis's 'good half' of the text, this is not to reinforce his
value judgement, but to insist that his partiality is more than simply
a preference for one part of the text. In reality Leavis's dismissal of
the 'bad half' of the text is informative, in that it suggests what
many readers have sensed, that the enigma which the title of the
novel proposes as central ('who is Daniel Deronda?') is repeatedly
displaced by the more insistent question, 'what is Gwendolen Harleth?' In bourgeois mythology subjectivity is a more 'profound'
problem than origins. This is the question with which the novel
opens, and though the question is subsequently motivated in the
text by being located in Deronda's mind, it stands as the whole of
the first paragraph, proclaiming the enigma for the reader:

> Was she beautiful or not beautiful? and what was the secret of
> form or expression which gave the dynamic quality to her
> glance? Was the good or the evil genius dominant in those
> beams? Probably the evil; else why was the effect that of unrest
> rather than of undisturbed charm? Why was the wish to look
> again felt as coercion and not as a longing in which the whole
> being consents? (Ch. 1)

The enigma concerns woman as spectacle, her beauty, the effect
of her beauty and its power, experienced as 'coercion'. The question is never fully answered, but it is none the less at the centre of
the novel. It is posed in the comments on Gwendolen of a series of
minor characters in the opening chapter, and later in the 'fascina-

tion of her womanhood' experienced by Deronda (Ch. 28), as well
as by a succession of rejected lovers. The text presents Gwendolen
as narcissistic – conscious of herself-as-spectacle in the episodes of
the charades, the ball, the archery meeting. We see her repeatedly
gazing at her image in mirrors. But this is not to be understood
simply as a psychological trait, the efflux of Gwendolen's unique
subjectivity, her vanity or egocentrism. Gwendolen-as-spectacle is
posited in the discourses of the other characters: they look, they
explicitly assess her beauty; she is 'the cynosure of all eyes' (Ch. 36).
She is also a spectacle for the reader, who is constantly offered
details of her appearance, fragments of her body (her neck, her
light brown hair, her long, narrow eyes) and the colour and tex-
tures of her clothes.

The text in this presents (whether consciously or not is not in
question) an account of the social production of femininity. Gwendolen identifies with herself-as-spectacle, seeing her image as a
source of power. (Indeed, it is her only available source of power:
her cousin, Anna, who is not 'spectacular', is seen as subordinate to
both men and women.) The mirror scenes are climactic. In the first
of them Gwendolen derives an imaginary transcendence from her
own reflection:

> And even in this beginning of troubles, while for lack of any-
> thing else to do she sat gazing at her image in the growing light,
> her face gathered a complacency gradual as the cheerfulness of
> the morning. Her beautiful lips curled into a more and more
> decided smile, till at last she took off her hat, leaned forward and
> kissed the cold glass which had looked so warm. How could she
> believe in sorrow? If it attacked her, she felt the force to crush it,
> to defy it. (Ch. 2)

But the process of the narrative is the constant undermining of
this imaginary transcendence, in episodes which cause her public
mortification or a nameless and inexplicable fear. The culmination
of these episodes is Gwendolen's hysteria on her wedding night,
'pallid, shrieking as it seemed with terror', unconscious now of her
images in a multiplicity of mirrors, no longer unified, 'like so many
women petrified white' (Ch. 31). The hysteria is in excess of the
immediate motivation: the letter from Lydia Glasher, unpleasant
as it is, after all tells her nothing she does not already know; but it
recalls her reaction to the meeting with Mrs Glasher which, curi-

ously, is defined in terms that have nothing to do with morality: 'Gwendolen . . . felt a sort of terror: it was as if some ghastly vision had come to her in a dream and said, "I am a woman's life".' (Ch. 14).

It is this vision of 'a woman's life' which the text as multiplicity of mirrors displays for the reader. The reality of Gwendolen's power is exposed. Required by her circumstances to transgress the limits the social body has proposed for her, adopt the 'masculine' role of family breadwinner, Gwendolen first thinks of displaying herself on the stage. When this is shown to be impossible (and the 'invisible' role of governess is unthinkable), she puts her image to work for a husband. The element of purchase is made very explicit – the engagement ring is accompanied by a cheque for £500 as an earnest of more to follow – and so is the irony of Gwendolen's belief that she can sell her labour-power and remain free. As her husband, Grandcourt becomes the proprietor and director of the spectacle:

> Why could she not rebel, and defy him? She longed to do it. But she might as well have tried to defy the texture of her nerves and the palpitation of her heart. Her husband had a ghostly army at his back, that could close round her wherever she might turn. She sat in her splendid attire, like a white image of helplessness, and he seemed to gratify himself with looking at her. (Ch. 36)

Wearing Grandcourt's diamonds, Gwendolen becomes the glittering manifestation of his power.

But the story is not wholly one of defeat. The dynamic of the feminine spectacle is sexuality, and marriage is the culmination of the *hysterisation* of women, their confinement to and within their own (neurotic) sexual natures (Foucault, 1979, p. 104). The text confers on Gwendolen a kind of heroism in that she consistently resists her own hysterisation, refuses to identify with her own sexuality. She cannot bear to be touched, experiences a 'physical repulsion' against being made love to, refuses (inexplicably) to 'waltz or polk' (Ch. 11). It puzzles Grandcourt that she resists his offer of marriage for so long. It is a mute (and equivocal) heroism, of course. No discourse, apart from hysteria itself, is available in the 1870s for resistance at the very core of patriarchy, and the narrative voice has in this instance no authoritative 'explanation' to offer of Gwendolen's outbursts of unaccountable and wordless horror. None the less her resistance culminates in the (imaginary?) assassination of the man who extorts obedience. The text is curiously elusive on the degree of her responsibility for his death ('it *seemed almost certain* that her murderous thought had had no outward effect' (Ch. 56, my italics)). But in any case, Gwendolen's disposition to murder Grandcourt invites our ambivalence. It is at all events a refusal of the patriarchy whose oppression is so graphically defined in *Daniel Deronda*.

However effectively interest in the social production of Gwendolen's subjectivity deflects attention from the enigma of Deronda's origins, a feminist reading of the text necessarily attends to Deronda's final encounter with his mother. The normal pattern of classic realism does not strictly endorse the introduction of a character who appears so briefly towards the end of the novel, and the interest of the narrative would permit Daniel's discovery of the 'truth' of his birth in any number of ways. But Deronda's origin and his displacement are the effects of his mother's resistance to patriarchy. Her history, unmotivated by narrative convention, but recounted with such intensity, constitutes a parallel vision of 'a woman's life'.

Gwendolen's story lacks the conventional closure of classic realism: her letter to Deronda gives no indication that she has established a stable position in the social body which produced her. Perhaps none is available. To this extent, and in its speechless refusal of the discourse of femininity, *Daniel Deronda* constitutes a text which both breaks the limits of classic realism and challenges the evident laws of a natural (patriarchal) order.

The feminist reading is, of course, no more exhaustive or final than the Leavisian one, but it lays claim to a good deal less. And in so far as it is a reading which is consciously and explicitly *produced* rather than 'recognised', it is offered as evidence of a form of work that is still available to a literary criticism which refuses the discourse of *The Great Tradition*.

References

Anderson, Perry (1968), 'Components of the national culture', *New Left Review*, 50, 3–57.
Barthes, Roland (1972), *Mythologies* (tr. Annette Lavers), Jonathan Cape.
Belsey, Catherine (1980), *Critical Practice*, Methuen.
Eagleton, Terry (1976), *Criticism and Ideology*, New Left Books.

Eliot, George (1967), *Daniel Deronda* (ed. Barbara Hardy), Harmondsworth: Penguin.

Eliot, George (1980), *Adam Bede* (ed. Stephen Gill), Harmondsworth: Penguin.

Foucault, Michel (1979), *The History of Sexuality*, vol. 1 (tr. Robert Hurley), Harmondsworth: Allen Lane.

Lawford, Paul (1976), 'Conservative empiricism in literary theory: a scrutiny of the work of F.R. Leavis', Part 1, *Red Letters*, 1, 12–15; Part 2, *Red Letters*, 2, 9–11.

Leavis, F.R. (1962), *The Great Tradition*, Harmondsworth: Penguin.

Leavis, F.R. (1976), *The Common Pursuit*, Harmondsworth: Penguin.

Mulhern, Francis (1979), *The Moment of 'Scrutiny'*, New Left Books.

Todorov, Tzvetan (1977), *The Poetics of Prose* (tr. Richard Howard), Oxford: Blackwell.

Wright, Iain (1979), 'F.R. Leavis, the *Scrutiny* movement and the crisis' in Jon Clark, Margot Heinemann, David Margolies and Carole Snee (eds), *Culture and Crisis in Britain in the Thirties*, Lawrence & Wishart.

10

Poetry and the politics of reading

ANTONY EASTHOPE

The basic and apparently universal definition of poetry is language organised into lines. The material of this organisation varies from language to language – syllable and tone in classical Chinese poetry, syllable length in Latin, stress and alliteration in Old English. In each of these the line is marked off as a line by the sound properties of language, not the meaning. In different linguistic forms the principle is the same: poetry consists of lines and lines are constituted through equivalence and parallelism in the signifier. Thus a priority of the signifier is the defining feature of poetry inscribed into its material basis, the line.

This neutral definition of poetry allows us to recognise without prejudice how much of it there is in use in modern British society. There is the oral tradition of nursery rhymes and children's rhymes recorded by the Opies:

> Mrs White had a fright
> In the middle of the night,
> She saw a ghost eating toast
> Half-way up the lamp post. (Opie, 1959, p. 17)

Pop music is a form of popular poetry since the lyrics rhyme and are organised into lines. There are unofficial uses of poetry in football songs:

> Walk on, walk on, with hope in your arse,
> And you'll never walk again,
> No, never walk again . . .

and in demonstration chants:

> The workers/united
> Will never be/defeated.

And there is official written poetry, high cultural poetry, promoted by the state partly through the Arts Council but mainly
through educational institutions. Schools teach this kind of poetry;
it is widely required for public examinations in English; it forms an
important part of the syllabus taught as English Literature in
higher education.

The study of poetry is important, therefore, because poetry is
widely used in modern life – on Radio One, in school playgrounds
and classrooms, in university degrees – though it is not yet fully
understood. The study of poetry in 1981 is particularly exciting
because, following the work of the Russian formalists and subsequent developments in linguistics and semiotics, it is now becoming
possible to construct the analysis of poetry within the human
sciences. A 'science' of poetry is possible; but if (to cite Northrop
Frye) 'there are any readers for whom the word "scientific" con-
veys emotional overtones of unimaginative barbarism, they may
substitute "systematic" or "progressive" instead' (Frye, 1957, pp.
7–8). In order to exemplify the kind of serious work towards
understanding poetry that can be done I shall draw on the linguistic distinction between *enunciation* and *enounced* to analyse a sonnet
from *Astrophel and Stella*; the sonnet is an appropriate example
because it comes from the Renaissance, the founding moment of
the bourgeois tradition. A contrast between the sonnet and
another text, a children's rhyme, may also suggest a way to define
this dominant poetic tradition.

But the attempt to move towards a scientific or systematic knowledge of poetry cannot be an innocent one. It has to be advanced as
a necessary and preferable alternative to the current academic
version of poetry given by literary criticism, and so must begin
from a critique of this. By the term 'literary criticism' throughout
this essay, I mean the traditional forms of bourgeois literary criticism which have centrally in common an ideology of the primacy of

the individual human subject, and which have established a canon of literary works which themselves endorse that ideology. This is a similar point to Catherine Belsey's in the preceding essay where she draws the connections between the 'great tradition' texts and Leavisian criticism of them. Like Belsey, also, I do not believe that criticism need remain the domain of that ideology.

However, at every point such literary criticism blocks the development of a more accurate and complete understanding of poetry. One way it does so has already been suggested. The conventional academic study of poetry accords the status of poetry only to examples of the high cultural tradition, a canon of authors from Chaucer to Larkin. When other kinds of poetry are touched on, the ballad for instance, they are invariably relegated to 'background material' or treated as popular culture rather than as poetry. Written texts with a named author are promoted over collective texts orally transmitted. While this partial and prescriptive attitude characterises all 'genres' of literary criticism (cf. Belsey's essay on fiction above), it operates to a special degree in the criticism of poetry. Poetry – identified with the work of an individual author – is felt to be the essential form of 'the literary' exactly because it can be read, more obviously than drama or the novel, as individual expression. In its account of poetry the contradictions of literary criticism are at their most overt, most easily made visible.

Criticism criticised

Because its methods and assumptions are largely implicit it is not easy to find a definition of poetry in literary criticism. However, as so often, Leavis provides a representative assertion. In defining the poet (presumed to be male), Leavis writes:

> He is a poet because his interest in his experience is not separable from his interest in words; because, that is, of his habit of seeking by the evocative use of words to sharpen his awareness of ways of feeling, so making these communicable. And poetry can communicate the actual quality of experience with a subtlety and precision unapproachable by any other means. (Leavis, 1972, p. 17)

This assumes:

(a)   that poetry originates as the poet's experience;
(b)   that poetry expresses or reflects 'the actual quality of experience';
(c)   that the function of a reader is to re-create or re-live this experience which is communicated to him or her.

Each of these assumptions needs to be challenged.

Literary criticism locates the origin of poetry in the experiences of an individual. In this it works reductively both on the formal properties of poetry and its complex and particular historical significance. Despite protestations to the contrary, literary criticism ignores the formal autonomy of poetic tradition (metre, verse form, modes of representation) to concentrate not on the poetry but the poet. Poetry is conceived to derive from an extra-historical dimension and so the historical cannot be considered except as it is subjectively mediated, as the poet's *experience* of his historical situation. Accordingly, discussion of *Astrophel and Stella* is centred on Sidney, either through biography or critical biography or topics linked biographically; the prevailing attitude is exemplified in J. G. Nichols' subtitle to *The Poetry of Sir Philip Sidney*: 'An Interpretation in the Context of his Life and Times' (1974). Only exceptionally is *Astrophel and Stella* approached in terms of poetic tradition and sonnet sequences, or of sixteenth-century literature and ideology.

The crucial manoeuvre of literary criticism, the one on which its structure and plausibility depends, occurs when it attributes not merely the *historical* but also the *present* origin of poetry to personal experience. It runs together the poet as historical author and the poet as implied speaker in the present ((*a*) and (*b*) above). As can be shown from Sidney criticism, this manoeuvre is to be found in three versions: naive, complex, sophisticated. The naive version (poetry *is* biography) may be represented by Charles Lamb, who, in his essay on 'Sydney's Sonnets', reads the poems as simple expression of the historical author. In practice most modern critics follow this naive model, for invariably and depressingly they tell in their own words the story of Astrophel and Stella as a form of the biographies of Sidney and Penelope Rich. In the complex version poetry is treated as a modification or translation of experience: 'Sidney realises the experience of his love for Lady Rich in the act of giving it poetic form. In him, the activities of lover and poet become one, with the result that personal experience becomes impersonal' (Hamilton, 1977, p. 83). The author's 'personal experience' is transmuted by being given poetic form so that it becomes 'impersonal', while both, somehow, continue to be the activity of 'Sidney'. In the sophisticated version the historical author is recognised as clearly separate from the implied speaker, only for the two to be joined in another way. The implied speaker is other than the historical author, yet the author is responsible for his adopted *persona*, a mask which itself becomes his expression.[1]

Who is this 'Sidney' in whom 'the activities of lover and poet become one'? Is he the man Philip Sidney, who was in love with Penelope Rich around 1581 and wrote poems about it, poems which sometimes relieved his feelings, sometimes made them worse, etc.? Or is he Sidney the voice that can be dramatised in 1981 as speaking in *Astrophel and Stella*? The Sidney of literary criticism is a *third term*, the Poet, a metasubject, partaking imposs-ibly of both historical author and implied speaker in the present, and yet not to be identified unambiguously with either.

It is by means of this equivocation or slide between historical author and implied speaker that literary criticism would account for the effect of poetry. In so doing it provides a method for reading, as in (c) above. Poetry is to be valued because it creates a sense of individual experience, personality, unique voice, what Leavis calls 'the actual quality of experience' and what I shall refer to, in Jacques Derrida's term, as *presence* (cf. Peter Brooker's essay above, Ch. 5). This is what criticism finds in the sonnets of *Astrophel and Stella*: 'when reading them we do think of a real man in a real time and place' (Nichols, 1974, p. 79); 'this sonnet [no. 47] is dominated, as are all the sonnets, by the voice of a man, a living voice fully yet simply human' (Hamilton, 1977, p. 85). On these grounds – 'presence' – the reader is invited into empathy with the Poet, to read 'with the same Spirit that its Author *writ*' (Pope, *Essay on Criticism*, l. 234), in a narcissistic and élitist identification (you too can *be* Sir Philip Sidney).

Poetry is 'presence', and 'presence' is reality and humanity: Sidney died in 1586 yet his 'living voice' is supposedly still speak-ing. It would be no answer for literary criticism to claim that such uses are innocently metaphorical – that we all know all the time that poetry is art and not life – since such criticism depends for its existence on not making this acknowledgement. It can admit that artifice and language are inseparable from experience, are indeed part of experience (the poet has an 'interest in words'), but it cannot admit that poetry consists *only* of artifice. To do so would be to develop the method of analysis beyond literary criticism into a different problematic, another set of questions and answers about poetry.

To summarise the objections to literary criticism and its sustaining notion of 'presence':

(1) Live-or-die existential experience is one thing, the 'experience' of poetry is another. Actuality and representation are different planes of reality: the game of football at Old Trafford on Saturday afternoon is actuality while the television version of it in the evening is representation.

(2) Poetry, like the rest of literature, is fictional; that is, to be read as *if* true, not as true. A historical reference (for example to the husband of Penelope Rich or Sir Philip Sidney's coat of arms) within a poem is no more 'true' than a geographical reference (for example to London as the capital of England). Poetry, then, is not to be read for truth or falsity of reference. By an exemplary coincidence, Sidney's *Apology* recognises correctly that poetry 'nothing affirms, and therefore never lieth'.

(3) As Derrida (1977) makes clear, the poet as historical author is typically dead or absent; what we have as the poem is the message, *writing*, which produces meaning in language perfectly adequately in the absence of its author and remains readable by others in the absence of its original addressee. Philip Sidney as experiencing subject has been absent since 1586; *Astrophel and Stella* is words, not experience. We never have the 'presence' of a poet; what we have is language, fiction, artifice, means of representation, poem.

To refute literary criticism signals a break with it; but a critique must go further than this. To avoid incorporating the same incoherencies into itself, a scientific literary analysis must understand the grounds on which literary criticism rests – it must understand literary criticism as literary criticism can never understand itself. If achieved, this critique becomes evidence for the claim that the alternative approach offers a better paradigm, a *more* accurate and comprehensive knowledge of (in this case) poetry. There is no question of absolute knowledge.

In discriminating 'named' from 'collective' poetry, in discovering the origin of poetry in individual experience, and, centrally, in eliding two separate categories (the historical author and the implied speaker) to produce a notional third term (the Poet), literary criticism manifestly relies upon a preconception from the quotidian world, the idea of the individual as at once 'the *Source*, and *End*, and *Test* of *Art*' (Pope, *Essay on Criticism*, 1.73). It is founded outside the study of poetry proper in the ideological conception of the absolute or transcendent human subject: transcendent, because it is assumed that subjectivity is unconstituted and undetermined, simply a given which is not made. So, for Leavis, the poet exists *prior* to both experience and language, since if he can take an interest in both he obviously transcends them, is not made in and of them. Subjectivity, then, is not recognised as determined socially and historically; nor is it acknowledged as determined in the psychoanalytic process, in the division of subjectivity into conscious and unconscious. Leavis's poet is identified essentially as *individual* (from the Latin *individuus*, 'undivided'), a unified being conscious of his experience as though it were something outside himself, self-consciously able to 'sharpen his awareness of ways of feeling'.

The notion of the transcendent subject is a relatively recent innovation. It is well-known that it did not exist in the ancient world, nor in any developed form in the feudal period. Identification of subjectivity with self-consciousness either in its Cartesian ('I think therefore I am') or Lockian form ('I experience therefore I am') emerges only after the Renaissance in conjunction with the triumph of a new class, the bourgeoisie. At the centre of bourgeois ideology is the idealist conception of the self-conscious individual (typically male) as an unconditioned source of decision and action – owing nothing to anyone, depending on nothing but himself, choosing freely and autonomously to exchange wages for labour power or (more likely) labour power for wages, to own private property, to act within or against the law, to elect political representatives – all as if (in the words of Coriolanus) 'a man were author of himself/And knew no other kin'.

This conception saturates literary criticism, and is a necessary condition for it. It produces the incoherency at its centre, the elision of historical author and implied speaker into 'the Poet'. And it renders this incoherency 'liveable' by inhibiting questions about 'presence'. In rejecting 'literary criticism', in moving beyond it, the first task of a science of poetry is to treat poetry exclusively as artifice, and attempt to explain 'presence' as an effect of language. For this a linguistic distinction will be useful.

Enunciation/enounced

Just as theatre works with actors, stage and script to represent characters in the drama speaking and doing, so poetry can represent 'presence' through poetic means of representation. The terms representation/represented are suitable to drama or film. But poetry is language and speech, so a more appropriate concept is the distinction between *enunciation* and *enounced*. Just as there cannot be a signified without a signifier, so there cannot be an enounced without enunciation. Enunciation is the act within language, the uttering, which produces what is uttered, the enounced. Developing this distinction between 'the speech act (*procès de l'énonciation*)' and 'the narrated event (*procès de l'énoncé*)' in an essay of 1957 Roman Jakobson noted that 'four terms are to be distinguished: a narrated event (E^n), a speech event (E^s), a participant of the narrated event (P^n), and a participant of the speech event (P^s), whether addresser or addressee' (Jakobson, 1971, p. 133). Anglicising rather than translating the French terms we can distinguish the enounced, the enunciation, the subject of the enounced, the subject of enunciation. So if I say, 'She was there yesterday', the 'narrated event', the meaning 'She was there yesterday', is the enounced and 'she' is the subject of the enounced; while the 'speech event', the act of uttering within language, is the enunciation and the person who says 'She was there yesterday' is the subject of the enunciation. As I sit here writing 'She was there yesterday' I am the subject of the enunciation; but you, gentle reader, wherever you are in my absence, when you read this 'She was there yesterday', *you* become the subject of the enunciation.

Whether as speaker/hearer/reader/writer there is always a subject of the enunciation living in what Benveniste calls 'the unceasing present of enunciation' (Benveniste, 1974, p. 84). Language provides a number of signs of enunciation and of the here-and-now of the speaker. In addition to the present tense of the verb, there are personal pronouns (I/you), demonstratives (this/that), relative adverbs (here/there), performatives (I swear that), modifying terms such as 'perhaps', 'certainly'. But we must be very careful over this. It is perfectly possible for these marks of enunciation to figure within the enounced. For example, a character in a novel, very much 'a participant of the narrated event' in Jakobson's phrase, might well speak with all the marks of enunciation, but yet that character would occur entirely within the enounced of the novel.

It is clear enough in the example 'She was there yesterday' that the subject of the enounced (she) and the subject of enunciation (the person uttering these words) are not the same. What is crucial, however, is that they can *never* be the same, even when someone is talking about himself, when I am talking about myself. As Lacan points out, language always intervenes.[2] Enounced depends on enunciation and only takes place 'after' it and because of it. So the person spoken about cannot be the same as the person speaking; the 'I' of enounced is always sliding away from the 'I' of enunciation. When I try to talk about me, 'me' can only figure as a character within my own discourse. It is possible to try to conceal the fact of this process, to contrive a subject of the enounced while concealing the subject of enunciation. This effect depends on several things: the process of enunciation must be effaced as far as possible; the subject of the enounced must be coherent and substantial; the subject of the enounced may have various marks of enunciation. In this way a 'presence' or voice can be represented.

Mrs White/Astrophel and Stella

The significance of these terms can be developed by contrasting two texts, the children's rhyme from the Opie book quoted above (p. 136) and sonnet no. 41 from *Astrophel and Stella*. Freud's distinction between manifest and latent content in the dreamwork applies also to the jokework and so to the rhyme, which is a species of joke – in fact a jest in Freud's taxonomy. What the manifest content of the rhyme seems to conceal and permit is the primal scene, the memory or fantasy of parental intercourse: the Mother did not see a ghost but *was* the ghost (hence Mrs *White*) with its knees parted for the phallic lamp post.

The rhyme is constructed from commonplace colloquial phrases. It works paratactically through juxtaposition and repetition rather than through sustained syntax. Thus, as the second couplet repeats the internal rhyme scheme of the first, there is a syntactic parallel between the subjects of the two clauses and their verbs. This helps to foreground words and sound in language rather than meaning. More importantly, the movement 'white'/ 'fright'/'night' and 'ghost'/'toast'/'post' is not meaningfully motivated in the enounced; but it *is* motivated in the enunciation as phonetic repetition, words used purely as words because they have the same sound. This 'treating words as things' is pleasurable, as Freud suggests (1976, p. 168), and as is confirmed by a nine-year-old the Opies cite as saying, 'I think what's so clever about this is the way it all rhymes' (Opie, 1959, p. 17). The rhyme *insists on itself as enunciation*, an insistence also marked in the heavy emphasis of the four-stress metre (Mŕš Whíte/hád ă frígĥt', etc.). The poem offers itself openly and directly as a pleasurable speaking in the present of enunciation, rather than the representation of 'presence' in the enounced.

In the rhyme, words dominate and determine meanings; in the sonnet they are subordinated to meaning in ways variously contrived. The iambic pentameter, working through counterpoint, lightens the stress relative to the children's rhyme and gives a more natural, prosaic intonation, and this implies a speaking voice rather than a performance:

> Having this day my horse, my hand, my lance
> Guided so well, that I obtain'd the prize,
> Both by the judgement of the English eyes,
> And of some sent from that sweet enemy France;
> 5 Horsemen my skill in horsemanship advance;
> Townfolks my strength; a daintier judge applies
> His praise to sleight, which from good use doth rise;
> Some lucky wits impute it but to chance;
> Others, because of both sides I do take
> 10 My blood from them, who did excel in this,
> Think Nature me a man of arms did make.
> How far they shoot awry! the true cause is,
> Stella lookt on, and from her heavenly face
> Sent forth the beams, which made so fair my race.

In contrast to the children's poem the sense in sonnet 41 rides across the rhyme, notable in four run-on lines, and aims to make the sound an echo to the sense – for example, when in the last two lines the shining of the sun is suggested by a rise in the intonation and the alliteration of 'face', 'forth', 'fair'. It is only on condition that the phonetic materiality of language in the process of enunciation can be backgrounded – either by effacement (sound is incidental) or containment (sound supports meaning) – that the sonnet can proceed fluently to unroll its meaning. Whereas in the children's rhyme words were treated as things, here they are scrupulously handled as meanings, signifier carefully lined up with signified: 'Having this day my horse, my hand, my lance . . .'. A punctilious nailing down of word onto meaning is achieved, above all, through the sustained linear progression of the syntax. From a subordinate clause introduced by a past participle, the syntax develops in a series of parallel main clauses across eleven lines and two further subordinate clauses. This gives the language of the sonnet an effect of transparency such that the reader is led to look through it at what it represents: the events of 'this day' and the responses to them of the implied speaker or subject of the enounced.

Transparency, the 'referential effect', is the condition for classic irony – that which distinguishes between appearance and reality, what the speaker says and what he means. Thus, all those who praised him thought they were praising him impersonally; in fact (Irony 1), self-deception led them to judge him according to their own interests ('lucky wits impute it but to chance'). To all of them his performance appeared due to his own qualities; in fact (Irony 2), it was due to Stella's favour. He appears to be modestly attributing his success to love rather than his own abilities; in fact (Irony 3), the contemporary courtly reader who is meant to overhear the sonnet would have in mind the speaker's skills, which (he reminds us) were praised not only by the English but also by the impartial French. So the sonnet invites us to move from what the speaker says to what he means, to determine his meaning in relation to a reality conceived to lie beyond the words.

By such means the sonnet's narrated events and its speaker are given consistency, solidity and interest. The reader is drawn in, and so led to forget that the events represented take place *in the enounced of which the speaker is the subject* (he is talking about himself). The subject of the enounced is given further dramatic substance, more 'presence', by bearing all the marks of also being the subject of enunciation. Thus each of the six main verbs (including 'shoot', as in Ringler's text) is in the present tense; variations on the first-person pronoun occur ten times; the speaker is situated temporally and spatially through demonstratives ('this day', 'that sweet enemy France'). There is also the vivid and colloquial exclamation, 'How far they shoot awry!'

The subject of enunciation is always the speaker/hearer/writer/ reader producing the poem in the 'unceasing present of enunciation', just as from a script actors and technicians produce a play. It is only through this speech act that events and their participants are narrated, through this enunciation that a subject of the enounced can be represented. The children's rhyme and the sonnet exemplify entirely opposed enunciative strategies. The rhyme foregrounds the work/play of the signifier and insists on itself as enunciation – and so, on the activity of the speaker as subject of enunciation. The sonnet works to efface and contain the phonetic materiality of language and promote consistent representation of the subject of the enounced – 'Sidney' speaking with all the marks of enunciation. But Sidney, in the mask of Astrophel, only addresses Stella or Cupid or a sparrow himself because now, in 1982, I 'produce' this historical text which makes him so speak. Poetic 'presence' is the presence of the poetic, an effect of language.

The sonnet can be understood as a species of realism, aiming to conceal enunciation in favour of the enounced. Through this artifice it contrives to dramatise 'presence', 'a living voice' actually speaking. This presence, the subject of the enounced, is offered to the reader as a point of identification. It is significant that this effect is so marked in a text from the Renaissance: in other words, from the founding moment of the English high cultural tradition (it is also present, of course, in Augustan and Romantic poetry). The English bourgeois tradition is precisely a continuing mode of poetic representation, an enunciative strategy, which would disavow enunciation in favour of the subject of the enounced. It would take much longer to substantiate what must remain only an assertion here, but it does suggest a further explanation for the incoherencies of 'literary criticism'. Because of its exceptional capacity ('unapproachable by any other means') to return a sense of 'presence', the bourgeois poetic tradition lies close to the heartlands of bourgeois ideology and the notion of the transcendent subject. Literary criticism is predicated on bourgeois poetry, and so incorporates the notion of 'presence' into its method – if method is the word for a murmured 'This is so, isn't it?', to which the paradigm response is, 'Yes, but . . .'.

Literary criticism usurps the name of criticism. Far from being critical, it is unconscious, complicit, passive. Approaching poetry as 'presence', it supposes the poem as somehow always already *there*, a product beyond question rather than a production that could have been otherwise. Accordingly, the reader is posed merely as a passive consumer, invited into empathy and identification with the Poet. In this respect literary criticism operates through a structure of alienation: whatever energies readers surrender to their misrecognition of themselves in the Poet, they *deny* themselves as readers. In contrast, literary science will discuss the poem as construction, acknowledging it as labour; and in so doing, it poses the reader as active and productive in reading the poem. (Cf. Catherine Belsey's 'reading' of the novel *Daniel Deronda* in the later sections of the preceding essay). So, as Barthes says, 'the goal of literary work (of literature as work) is to make the reader no longer a consumer, but a producer of the text'. This means that the poem is always in question, rather than assumed as a given. It also means that the *reading* is in question, seeking always to make its preconceptions explicit, constantly probing the ground on which it stands for ideological complicity – a truly materialist 'criticism' therefore. So finally, in transcending literary criticism more is at stake than the principle of science (which would reject literary criticism as incoherent), or the political need to offer a critique of ideology (which would condemn literary criticism as incoherently structured because of ideological penetration). The desire for an alternative practice is grounded in a different conception of reading, in a *politics* of reading.

Notes

1 This loophole was left open by Wimsatt and Beardsley in 'The Intentional Fallacy' (Wimsatt, 1970) when they allow that 'if the poet succeeded in doing it, then the poem itself shows what he is trying to do' (p. 4). Introducing the term 'implied author' in *The Rhetoric of Fiction*, Wayne Booth follows the same path by making implied author an expression of the historical author ('he creates . . . an implied version of "himself" ', p. 70).

2 See Jacques Lacan, 1977, especially pp. 138–41. There is another

account of the subject of enunciation which identifies it as 'the narrator
. . . represented by a book' (see Todorov, 1966, p. 146). The two
accounts remain to be reconciled.

References

Barthes, Roland (1975), *S/Z* (tr. Richard Miller), Jonathan Cape.

Benveniste, Emile (1974), 'L' appareil formel de l'énonciation', *Problèmes de Linguistique Générale*, vol. 2, Paris: Gallimard.

Booth, Wayne C. (1961), *The Rhetoric of Fiction*, Chicago: University of Chicago Press.

Derrida, Jacques (1977), 'Signature Event Context', *Glyph*, vol. 1, 172–97.

Freud, Sigmund (1976), *Jokes and their Relation to the Unconscious*, Harmondsworth: Penguin.

Frye, Northrop (1957), *Anatomy of Criticism*, Princeton: Princeton University Press.

Jakobson, Roman (1971), 'Shifters, Verbal Categories, and the Russian Verb' in *Word and Language*, The Hague: Mouton.

Hamilton, A.C. (1977), *Sir Philip Sidney*, Cambridge: Cambridge University Press.

Lacan, Jacques (1977), *The Four Fundamental Concepts of Psycho-Analysis* (tr. Alan Sheridan), Hogarth Press.

Leavis, F.R. (1972), *New Bearings in English Poetry*, Harmondsworth: Penguin.

Nichols, J.G. (1974), *The Poetry of Sir Philip Sidney*, Liverpool: Liverpool University Press.

Opie, Iona and Peter (1959), *The Lore and Language of Schoolchildren*, Oxford University Press.

Ringler, William A. Jr (ed.) (1962), *The Poems of Sir Phillip Sidney*, Oxford University Press.

Todorov, Tzvetan (1966), 'Les Catégories du Récit Littéraire', *Communications*, 8, 125–47.

Wimsatt, W.K. Jr (1970), *The Verbal Icon: Studies in the Meaning of Poetry*, Methuen.

11
'Not for all time, but for an Age': an approach to Shakespeare studies

DEREK LONGHURST

In this essay I want to examine some of the ways in which Shakespeare has been constituted as 'the National Poet', and therefore how his work has been used, especially since the 1920s, to construct and justify dominant conceptions of a literary education. It will become clear from this how important it is to develop alternative approaches to the study of theatre in general and Shakespeare in particular, and so the later sections of the essay offer in outline three possible ways in which this may be achieved.

A common tendency in both educational study and literary criticism has been to make 'the text' the sole object of 'interpretation', but as we shall see, even a brief discussion of contemporary theatre demonstrates how artificial and limited this is when applied to drama. Theatrical texts are produced by many social determinants, and any materialist approach to Shakespeare must therefore give priority both to the historical and theatrical conditions in which the plays were first produced and to their *reproduction* in later periods through literary criticism or theatrical and television 'versions' of them.

I

Shakespeare is an inevitable and necessary part of school activity because he is . . . our greatest English writer. (1921 Board of

Education Report, *The Teaching of English in England* (Newbolt), p. 312)

Encapsulated here are the crucial notions of Shakespeare as the National Poet and as *the* example of the individual literary genius who transcends his period and produces texts of timeless value which reveal fundamental truths about a 'universal human condition'.[1] The Newbolt Report consistently presents an Arnoldian view of literature as a 'spiritual influence' which may ameliorate, if not cure, the existing 'morbid condition of the body politic' (p. 252). To prevent 'lamentable consequences', educational institutions should promote 'fellowship' through literature, as 'an embodiment of the best thoughts of the best minds, the most direct and lasting communication of experience by man to men' (p. 253). Thus, *via* Arnold, literature is represented as a 'means of grace' to direct 'men' towards 'higher' things than 'the social problem' (p. 255). The Report here tacitly admits that the teaching of English language and literature *is* a political matter 'involving grave national issues' (p. 252), while at the same time asserting that 'literature' has nothing to do with politics, with 'the social problem', that it should be valued instead as a 'source of pride', a great 'bond of national unity' (p. 202).

This sense of the ideological power of culture rests on a definition of 'great literature' as 'timeless', 'eternal', 'universal' (p. 205) – and Shakespeare is used continually to prove it. Although he tells us 'what Englishmen were like' at the beginning of the seventeenth century, he also tells us 'what all men are like in all countries and at all times' (p. 205). Clearly Shakespeare is seen as an *authority* on an unchanging human nature; as such his work is transhistorical, and so replaces history. Thus, Shakespeare is at the centre of our national 'traditional culture', and one of the strategies of the Report is to establish that sense of 'stability' derived from linking a society and its literature with 'the immemorial past' (p. 258). Hence the idealisation of a homogeneous, pre-industrial Elizabethan world in which culture and society were united in an organic totality: 'It was no inglorious time of our history that Englishmen delighted altogether in dance and song and drama, nor were these pleasures the privilege of a few or a class' (p. 319). The message for the present is clear.

Not the least of Shakespeare's functions is to ratify the category of 'Literature' itself, even though he and his contemporaries would not have understood it in the Arnoldian sense the Report assumes. 'Literature' in the seventeenth century meant *all* forms of writing – with drama probably low in any scale of value. In particular, play-texts were more valuable to an acting company when they did *not* exist in book form, and were not therefore subject to piracy by rivals. The notion of the sacrosanct text is alien to the period and yet it is central to the literary criticism of Shakespeare. Just as it is the function of scholarly editors to reconstruct, and of literary critics to 'interpret', these texts, so it becomes the function of education to supply students with the competence necessary to 'read' them. The Newbolt Report, for instance, argues that the purpose of literature is to act as a civilising influence, to teach 'young men and women the use of leisure', to prepare them for 'life', and, through the exercise of reading Shakespeare aloud, to speak 'standard English' correctly.

This Report is, of course, a period document and represents a response to post-Great War educational and political crises. If we turn, however, to the contemporary situation in school education, it becomes clear that much of the Report's conceptual framework has remained intact. No justification is ever offered in 'O'- and 'A'-level syllabuses for the selection of the particular range of texts which students are to study (reference is made to 'major' writers), but the skills to be encouraged are revealing. In the 1980–1 University of London 'O'-level Syllabus A, the examiners warned students that they were looking for 'a detailed knowledge of the text', 'close reference', and the use of 'brief quotation'. Syllabus B demanded the same skills allied to 'evidence of a personal response and a thoughtful approach to the terms of the questions set in the examination. Liveliness of response and sincerity of interest are the paramount considerations.' What is emphasised, then, is the value of subjective response drawn from 'close reading' of 'the texts'. The Joint Matriculation Board (JMB) syllabuses pursue the same objectives, directing candidates towards 'appreciating the spirit of the books, their structure and style' as well as their 'subject matter'. In all cases the approach is based on 'practical criticism', and indeed, at 'A'-level, whole papers are given over to this exercise.

In fact there is a clear continuity of approach and emphasis between 'O'- and 'A'-level syllabuses. Paper I of the JMB 'A'-level, for instance, consists of three questions on two Shakespeare plays and one on a short prescribed work by a 'major' poet. Significantly, the 'context question' for Shakespeare reinforces the techniques associated with 'practical criticism': candidates are asked 'to comment on the nature and significance' of the language used, and on the passage's 'dramatic and literary aspects'. Paper II examines a selection of sixteen texts from Chaucer to the present day and candidates are required to write about four of them, while Paper III is entirely devoted to 'practical criticism' of unseen passages of verse and prose. The study of Shakespeare constitutes almost one third of the examined syllabus – a high priority maintained in the vast majority of 'O'- and 'A'-level English Literature syllabuses. The skills to be assessed by the examination remain consistent: the candidate must demonstrate 'understanding, in some depth' of works studied; 'the response to literature, jointly affective and evaluative (i.e. his personal response and his understanding of the causes of his response)' allied to 'critical powers'; 'breadth' of reading; and clear, organised essays. What is emphasised, yet again, is the primacy of the reader's response, 'the text', and facility with the language.

Finally, let me look briefly at the University of Cambridge 1979 'A'-level Paper II, which is entirely devoted to Shakespeare. The 'context questions' of Section A call for 'appreciation' of: (i) character – judgements of 'behaviour', 'personality', 'state of mind', 'quality and strength of feelings'; (ii) language – 'imagery and tone', 'movement' of speeches and verse; (iii) theatrical effect – 'dramatic function', 'dramatic purposes', assessment of how stage performance might enrich, impoverish or render episodes 'effective'. To a lesser extent, candidates are asked to abstract themes from the passages, or to analyse 'our impression' of the conspiracy in *Julius Caesar* or 'our attitude' to the 'supernatural forces' in *Macbeth*. The essay questions in Section B are predominantly based on thematic criticism: the corrupting effect of 'all power' is offered for discussion as an observation on *Julius Caesar*; 'social rank and money' or 'youth and time' in *Twelfth Night*; the 'positive and negative aspects of order' in *Henry IV, 2*. Alternatively, students are asked to elucidate the 'views' of 'Roman values and civilisation' offered in *Julius Caesar*, or to decide whether they find the ending of *Henry IV, 2* 'unsatisfactory'. The *Macbeth* questions are different – probably because it is a tragedy – in that they ask for an assessment of it as 'a

Christian Play' or for a discussion of the central character – does Macbeth's 'imagination' make him 'heroic'?

This discussion of the study of literature in schools points, first, to a fundamental assumption of the literary value of a 'tradition' of 'major' works in which Shakespeare's plays are given overwhelming priority. But who has made the selection? and on what basis? The answers are by no means self-evident. Second, the terms employed in the examinations ('character', 'personality', 'state of mind', 'language', 'theatrical effect', 'themes') relate uneasily to the conventions of seventeenth-century theatre; 'theatrical effect' is dependent on more factors than can be 'read off' from the text; and thematic criticism tends to impose modern, transhistorical abstractions onto the plays. Third, there is the notion that 'practical criticism', *reading the text*, is *per se* free of interpretative distortion, while its fundamental strategy is, in fact, to remove 'great' works from the period in which they were written and from their relations with other kinds of writing. Simultaneously, the reader is constituted in abstract terms, as an evaluator uncontaminated by extraneous or ideological influences. Clearly, as F. R. Leavis didn't say, this is not so, is it?

II

Much of what I have been describing in contemporary educational practice is also related to the dominant forms of literary criticism and in particular to the widespread influence of the *Scrutiny* movement since the 1930s. The *Scrutiny* project is based on a history which sees our culture steadily degenerating since the ideal world of the Elizabethan period, when language, culture and a rural society were unified within a homogeneous 'organic' community. Although irrevocably destroyed, it is this condition to which we should aspire, and *Scrutiny's* role, by way of literary criticism, was to remind the modern world of lost cultural values. Shakespeare was, throughout, a central concern, and indeed it was the early seventeenth century which provided a focus for L. C. Knights, the founding editor, to establish the all-important concept of a 'tradition' of continuous cultural values which it was the business of literary criticism to preserve in the face of change, of industrialism and mass culture (Knights, 1936). In some measure this was presented as an alternative to crude marxist versions of cultural history and directed particularly against simplistic analysis of the interaction between culture and economic relations.

Numerous studies of Shakespeare's plays were published by *Scrutiny* during the war years, and I shall later discuss, in a brief 'case-study', the contributions by Knights, Leavis and Traversi on *Measure for Measure* published in 1942. In fact, war-time Shakespearian criticism registered a number of influential emphases. It is worth noting, for example, that E. M. W. Tillyard's *The Elizabethan World Picture* (1943) and *Shakespeare's History Plays* (1944) appeared during the period. Although not part of the *Scrutiny* 'team', and indeed probably suspect to them because of his concern with historical, extra-textual material, Tillyard had been one of the founders of the Cambridge Tripos in the early 1920s, out of which Knights and the Leavises had emerged. In his work too we have 'the picture' of an ordered Elizabethan world firmly rooted in medieval notions of hierarchy and the Great Chain of Being, which Shakespeare's history plays 'clearly' exemplify. Thus we have Shakespeare as Tudor apologist, the representative of 'orthodoxy', fearing civil war and rebellion, and caring deeply for 'nature', 'order', monarchy and, most important of all, 'England'. In this account of Shakespeare's values, Tillyard had been preceded by Wilson Knight who had extolled, in his war-time lectures and a monograph, the virtues of patriotism, order, kingship, honour and martial glory, ostensibly through discussion of the history plays. The religious associations of crown and kingship are emphasised, and the plays are seen to represent a psychological growth towards the ideal kingship of Henry V. It is no coincidence that Olivier's 'heroic' film of that play was also made during the war.

Shakespeare's medievalism and his 'belief' in order continue to dominate *Scrutiny's* postwar criticism. Indeed it is possible to detect through it a movement to the right in the journal (see Mulhern 1979 for fuller discussion of this). Two essays by L. A. Cormican traced the cultural roots of Shakespeare's drama to medieval ethics, to the Liturgy and to Platonism, emphasising the influence of religion, philisophy and 'eternal values'. Even Shakespeare's magpie 'practice of widespread borrowing' demonstrated 'the spiritual community' of an age which was to disintegrate under the pressure of puritanism and the revolution. Thus Shakespeare's 'genius' was fostered by the 'objectivity' and the sense of an 'eternal scheme of things' contained in the medieval ethic in which God reigned over an unchanging human nature. He was interested in 'human conduct', the 'human appetites and interests' which 'underlie every important human problem' and his plays were rooted in an ethical system which displayed an 'insouciance about temporal and material things'. Hence Shakespeare demonstrated 'an almost complete indifference to the contemporary forms which political, social and economic problems were then taking'. And yet: 'In diction which is well adapted not only to the Elizabethan audience but also to the ordinary schoolboy today, we find a penetrating portait of what politics is actually like as contrasted with what it appears to be.' Ultimately Shakespeare's tragedies, as 'sane and balanced studies of human nature', provide a model for all time and 'help us to evaluate ourselves and the forces at work within us' (Cormican, 1950, 1951).

Cormican had referred to *King Lear* as one of Shakespeare's 'super-plays'. One of the most revealing examples of 'literary criticism' in the period are Derek Traversi's three lengthy essays offering a blow-by-blow reading of that play. Before the war, Traversi had made his political affiliations clear in an attack on Auden and Spender in a pro-Franco Catholic journal, asserting that 'Marxism always lacked the moral fibre to sustain its natural revolutionary ardour' (Traversi, 1937). Now his literary-critical conception of the Shakespeare play as a 'dramatic poem' was used to register certain not unrelated preoccupations. Lear's initial act of 'passion' disrupts 'reason', 'custom', 'supernaturally sanctioned harmony', leading to an anarchy of egoism and the 'social and cosmic reversal of established values'. Uncontrolled passion, it is repeatedly stressed, causes disorder, the breakdown of 'normal social relationship', and only Kent clings to 'traditional sanctions of moral behaviour' by holding 'a clear conception of natural order, a belief that true authority needs to be exercised . . .'. At the centre of the analysis lies the judgement that '*King Lear* is a great play precisely because it is a play about human "nature" before being a play about the abuses of government or social inequality'. Fortunately, however, Shakespeare saw a need for 'spiritual rebirth', and through Cordelia's 'goodness', 'her state of grace', her firmness about the 'natural foundations of ordered living, she redeems "nature" . . . from the "general curse" of sinfulness'. Thus 'the universal presence of the beast in man' finally meets 'the purgation of unclean impulses from the spirit' (Traversi, 1952–3).

Clearly, then, the literary criticism of *Scrutiny*, like *The Newbolt Report*, is of its time and deeply permeated by ideological, cultural and even theological concepts which, in effect, formulate the critical approach. Ironically, it was always the basis of Leavis's objection to marxism that it was a system of beliefs which got in the way of the critic's responsibility to the text itself. But this latter concept, of the ideal text – which, as we have seen, has been at the centre of Shakespeare criticism, scholarship and teaching for the past fifty years – also carries related implications: about the sanctity of 'the text', about wholeness, unity, coherence and meaning. This has led to the highly competitive critical industry of 'correcting' other critics' misinterpretations, and substituting, by way of a yet more exact reading of the text, its 'seamless' unity and the hidden *real* meaning which it contains. The fundamental character of this apparently innocent criticism is, of course, that it is idealist. In seeking to establish a continuity between the past and the present, and in focusing on 'universal' themes such as justice, chastity, appearance vs. reality, love and marriage, freedom vs. restraint, folly, avarice, time, order vs. chaos, deception, good vs. evil and so on, it abstracts the play from its history and the material conditions of its production. And even marxist *readings* of individual texts are complicit in this.

What I want to propose is a wholly different project for a materialist theatre criticism and theatre studies; one which demonstrates the fundamental inadequacy of analysis based on 'the text'. One way of approaching this is to consider briefly some of the determinations which 'produce' plays in our own contemporary theatre. First, there is funding, and the legal, bureaucratic and political controls exerted through subsidy and the patronage of the Arts Council, which determine the size of companies, the kind of work which can be produced and even where it is performed. Second, the location of the theatre building helps to determine the social composition of the audience – which will 'interpret' the play's meaning in different ways according to class, age, gender, etc. Third, there are factors affecting repertory planning in subsidised theatre, for instance the use of Shakespeare in relation to the annual 'O'- and 'A'-level texts studied in local schools. Fourth, the architecture of a theatre establishes a spatial relationship between actor and audience which, allied to style of acting, produces 'meaning'. Naturalism, for instance, the dominant mode of bourgeois theatre and television, directs an audience towards an empathetic response to individual characters who are largely represented from a psychological perspective. Actors, assisted by 'emotional memories' in their own experience, are trained in creating characters from their own psyches. In addition, the audience is 'left in the dark' witnessing the intense 'circle of communication' between the actors; it is not directly spoken to and is treated as if it were not there. The conventional separation between proscenium stage and auditorium reinforces the way naturalism draws the audience into a self-enclosed theatrical world of illusion in which it sees nothing of the means used to produce that world nor of itself as audience. As Brecht realised, the process of empathy invites individuals to identify exclusively with individual characters; it stimulates no sense of the audience itself as a social group or community. By contrast, acting which expresses its own processes — the means used to produce its effects — must transform the audience's relation both to what is seen and heard *and* to itself, and a 'debate' may thus be set up between actors and audience *about* the characters and the action. Such a theatre directs attention away from individual characters to more general social, political and ideological conflicts.

Performances of plays, then, are not a matter of merely 'realising' or producing the *text*, of giving it 'life', but rather, of constituting a text's meaning precisely by the production processes involved. My point here is that, in the contemporary context, we know that modern texts do not exist statically; *Look Back in Anger*, for example, is a very different play now than it was at its moment of reception in 1956. If this is the case — that a theatre criticism which fetishises the text dislocates it from the social and theatrical conditions in which it is produced (and reproduced in its subsequent moments of consumption) — then surely the appropriation of Shakespeare's texts from the turn of the sixteenth century as the work of the quintessential author-genius of English Literature wilfully misconceives them.

III

It is necessary, then, to develop alternative critical practices which do not give undue priority to 'the author' and 'the text'. We have to recognise, however, that these are amongst the common terms of literary critical discourse and that, given the student's prior experience, we may have to start with them. The real point at issue is what is *done* with them. In the space of this essay I can only roughly sketch three modes of study which aim to controvert received notions of Shakespeare and the more usual approaches to his work, and which may prove practicable in higher (and, to a lesser extent, in secondary) education courses. First, there is the task of replacing Shakespeare firmly within the historical field of his own period. Second, there is the analysis (already indicated in earlier parts of this essay) of the constitutive criticism of Shakespeare, that process which has identified his 'greatness' and produced his 'meanings'. Third, there is the analysis of the mediation of Shakespeare in our own historical period: how he is reproduced and the processes which determine the way we 'receive' and 'understand' his work. The whole BBC Television 'Shakespeare' project could, in this case, be taken as a text-for-study. This third suggestion is, I believe, an important one, starting as it will from the student's own experience of Shakespeare's work.

The first step, then, is to reinstall the plays in their historical context. This involves the examination of writing from the Elizabethan/Jacobean period not usually regarded as 'Literature', and the investigation of relations between different modes of cultural production at that time. Here it is important to break across the common assumption that Shakespeare's work in particular 'defines' the theatre of the period. The theatre must instead be examined as a social, economic and political institution existing within a rapidly changing Jacobean society. This is not to be seen, however, as a necessary but *separate* scholarly activity in the historical reconstruction of the 'background' to the 'great plays', which merely serves to prevent the literary critic from totally 'misreading' their possible meanings. The objective is, conversely, to *foreground* such matters as patronage, the social composition of audiences, economic organisation of the companies, political control through censorship, structure of the repertory, pageantry and ceremony, conventions of dramaturgy, staging and acting – all of which fundamentally influenced the printed play-texts which have survived. Normally these concerns have been separated off as 'theatre history', but together with the study of other kinds of cultural production – underworld pamphlets, sermons and homilies, prose fiction, masques, ballads and poetry, scientific and philosophical writing – they are crucial to a more complete understanding of the drama and its culture.

Of course this culture did not develop in an ideological vacuum, and contemporary concepts of order, authority, kingship, nature, women, marriage and the family, justice and law, usury, religious beliefs, reason, etc. need careful *historical* attention. The tendency has been to isolate such concepts as abstractions but it is vital to locate them in the social, political and economic processes of the period. Again, this should not be viewed as merely background to 'literary interpretation' but as a primary objective, the material context in which the texts were produced.

Of equal importance to a 'historical' understanding of Shakespeare is the examination of his place within the development of English Studies. Such analysis has to be related both to wider educational and cultural relations, as I have indicated in the first part of this essay, and to the strategies of twentieth-century criticism. Students should study criticism and interrogate critical approaches as this serves the important function of introducing them to the notion that 'Literature' has been constituted by the criticism which 'reads' it. It helps to make them aware of the nature of their own 'discipline'.

I would like to take Wilson Knight's essay '*Measure for Measure* and the Gospels' (1930) and the *Scrutiny* debate as an example. Wilson Knight asserts a 'clear relation' between the play and 'the ethical standards of the Gospels', represented largely by the Duke who controls the action, displays 'supernatural authority' and 'like Jesus, is the prophet of a new order of ethics'. Indeed, the 'simplest way' of understanding 'the quality and unity' of the play is 'to read it on the analogy of Jesus' parables', an approach which will explain away any problems or 'strangeness'. The central theme is 'man's moral nature' and, in particular, that 'most universal of all themes', 'sexual ethics', conceived in idealist terms as a clash between 'human consciousness and human instinct'. Wilson Knight's reading 'produces' the play he wishes to read: distant theological associations are adduced and historically static moral assumptions are asserted within his essay to dismiss any challenge to the play's coherence, to establish its 'modernity' and, ultimately, its status as a carefully structured work of 'penetrating ethical and psychological insight'.

In a subsequent issue of *Scrutiny*, L. C. Knight's 'The Ambiguity of *Measure for Measure*' accepts that readers experience a 'sense of strain and mental discomfort' because of 'conflicting attitudes' to characters and unanswered questions about 'social conduct'. His more thematic approach establishes the oppositions between 'natural impulse and individual liberty', 'self-restraint' and 'public law', as the moral problems of the play. Difficulties arise, however, in that 'the paradox of human law' – between 'justice and expediency' – is 'felt' here as confusion. Later in his career Shakespeare was to make 'most political thought look oddly unsubstantial'; he had, 'we know', a 'deep sense of the human worth of tradition and traditional morality', and the more forceful expression of his 'characteristically Elizabethan . . . sense of social *order*' in the tragedies led to 'clarification'. In this essay, then, Shakespeare's play is 'problematised' in relation to notions of social order. Leavis, however, disagreed and, in the same issue of *Scrutiny*, registered his dissent in 'The Greatness of *Measure for Measure*', the very title asserting the play's coherence and moral force. Knights, he argued, had failed to 'read' the text adequately, had adopted a naive conception of character and had been too influenced by the 'bad prepotent tradition' of Shakespeare criticism which had shown its 'incapacity for dealing with poetic drama' and an 'innocence about the nature of convention'. Such error followed from not grounding the argument in the text, and from not accepting what *Measure for Measure* does offer. The play involves a constant challenge to 'our most comprehensive and delicate powers of discrimination' and Leavis's reading demonstrates Shakespeare's 'belief that law, order and formal justice are necessary', while the 'great triumph' is the representation with 'so sure and subtle a touch' of the 'human complexity' involved. Knights's argument that the last two acts manifest hasty plot-resolution is dismissed as not 'significant' for 'interpretive criticism'; on the contrary, the conclusion is characteristically read as 'a consummately right and satisfying fulfilment of the essential design' deriving from 'the poet's sure human insight and his fineness of ethical and poetic sensibility'. In fact, Wilson Knight's essay is the only 'adequate account', and 'the right way' of seeing the play is to regard the Duke 'as a kind of Providence' conducting a 'controlled experiment' in which the 'moral valuations' are clear. Finally, it is important that we have to 'see ourselves in Angelo', otherwise we 'have taken the play and the moral very imperfectly'. The play as a whole 'should come more intimately home to the modern'. This, it is argued, is what is meant by accepting 'what Shakespeare does provide' rather than importing 'your interest and significance'. Through his magisterial evaluation of the text, then, Leavis characteristically 'rescues' it from 'incoherence' and dissonant ambiguity, while asserting the moral values which have remained relevant for a modern world. A final contribution was offered by Traversi in which his preoccupations remain consistent: too much passion/ appetite leads to 'the spread of disease . . . from the individual to the mass of society'. 'A society in the advanced stages of moral dissolution is necessarily ugly', and so *Measure for Measure* justifies 'the necessary ruthlessness of the law' in dealing with the 'instincts which lie at the root of man's normal nature'. Here, as in the other essays, *Measure for Measure* is *recreated by criticism* as a text which contains enduring and universal moral values, which it is then the circular business of criticism to 'find' and elucidate.

It is equally important, however, to examine not only the constitutive criticism of Shakespeare's plays but also their theatrical history – including adaptations, editions, their 'reproduction' through performance in theatre, film and television. The current investment of the BBC in 'the national playwright' (Messina, 1979) is clearly based on many of the assumptions I have been questioning. His work is culturally prestigious: the BBC Television Shakespeare 'has been called the greatest project the BBC has ever undertaken' (ibid.), and it is related to the Corporation's experience of producing 'the great dramatic statements of all ages and countries' as part of discharging 'its many duties as a Public Broadcasting Service'. The objective is to 'make the plays in permanent form, accessible to audiences throughout the world' – especially in the lucrative American market, and indeed, the project is part of a co-production deal with Time-Life Films. For this reason the early productions were permeated by a profound 'Britishness': shots of castles; Sir William Walton (our 'greatest living composer', the composer of music for royal occasions) wrote the 'opening fanfare'; and the history plays were presented as 'a unique record of the chronicled history of that time' (ibid.). The 'greatest classical actors of our time' were to be employed so that students in particular would have 'a wonderful opportunity *to study the plays*' (my emphasis). It should be said that there has been a change of direction since Jonathan Miller took over as executive producer, and indeed he has complained of the limitations placed on experiment by the necessity of creating an English product for an American market. Clearly, then, the BBC 'Shakespeare' needs to be evaluated in terms of the whole determining medium of television rather than of the relation of 'productions' to ideal texts which are being 'brought to life'. Until such issues have a place on the syllabus, there can be no hope of a materialist Elizabethan/Jacobean theatre studies at any level of the education system.

Notes

1 For a fuller discussion of this, see Derek Longhurst, 'Shakespeare in Education: Reproducing a National Culture', in *Red Letters*, 11 (Spring 1981).

References

Cormican, L.A. (1950–1), 'Medieval idiom in Shakespeare: (i) Shakespeare and the liturgy', *Scrutiny*, XVII, 3 (Autumn 1950); (ii) 'Shakespeare and the Medieval ethic', *Scrutiny*, XVII, 4 (March 1951).

Knight, G. Wilson (1930), '*Measure for Measure* and the Gospels' in *The Wheel of Fire*, Oxford; 4th edn, Methuen, 1949.

Knights, L.C. (1936), 'Shakespeare and profit inflations', *Scrutiny*, V, 1 (June). Reprinted as Introduction to *Drama and Society in the Age of Jonson*, Chatto & Windus, 1937.

—— (1942), 'The ambiguity of *Measure for Measure*', *Scrutiny*, X, 3 (January).

Leavis, F.R. (1942), 'The greatness of *Measure for Measure*', *Scrutiny*, X, 3 (January). Reprinted in *The Common Pursuit*, Harmondsworth: Penguin, 1962.

Messina, Cedric (1979), 'Preface' to BBC Edition of *Measure for Measure*, BBC Publications.

Mulhern, Francis (1979), *The Moment of 'Scrutiny'*, New Left Books.

Traversi, D.A. (1937), 'Spain', *Arena*, I, 1 (April).

—— (1942), 'Measure for Measure', *Scrutiny*, XI, 1 (Summer).

—— (1952–3), 'King Lear', *Scrutiny*, XIX, 1 (October 1952); 2 (Winter 1952–3); 3 (Spring 1953).

12

Period studies and the place of criticism

CAROLE SNEE

I

In recent years the left has begun the important and necessary
examination of what constitutes the academic study of English
Literature. Part of this examination has involved the identification
of that discipline as principally concerned with the literature and
culture of a dominant class, and the recognition that the teaching
of English at all levels of education has played an important part in
the reproduction of dominant ideologies.

That recognition led many of us to flee its territory; we did not
want to be contaminated or implicated. We dug our trenches in
cultural studies, in popular culture, in media studies, and we fired
the occasional dart at those still occupying the traditional terrain of
'Eng. Lit.', producing the odd flesh wound but no serious injury.
The development of cultural studies, which can be monitored
through the history of the Birmingham Centre for Contemporary
Cultural Studies, has been of crucial political importance, but it
should not be seen as a refuge from the problems of 'Literature', as
a safe unpolluted haven, nor necessarily as a radical alternative.
Cultural studies is now taught in schools, has its own GCE examinations, is a degree subject, and is rapidly producing its own canon,
hierarchies and 'specialists'. It has arrived on the academic scene,
and is being subjected to the same pressures experienced by the
more traditional disciplines.

Radical interventions are not made simply by changing the object of study (although, yes, it may be more democratic to study *Coronation St.* than *Middlemarch*), but by challenging the conditions of education, by revealing the processes by which and through which it operates in all subject areas. 'Eng. Lit.' will not wither away because the radicals have vacated its territory. On the contrary it will consolidate, become more conservative, more intransigently élitist, and more of a bulwark against change. It needs to be challenged, deconstructed and reconstituted from within. It is not a question of reform *or* revolution, but rather that in the present situation revolution can only be achieved through reforms.

A number of teachers have attempted to break out of the closeted world of 'Eng. Lit.' in our schools and universities, to escape from notions of criticism as the custodian of 'standards', the progenitor of true values, and to look at literary texts as a product of specific societies at specific historical moments. An increasing dissatisfaction with the traditional teaching methods, which dehistoricised literature and saw Great Art as the articulation of eternal values present at all times in all places, led them to look to History for the solution to the discipline's problems, and in consequence 'Period Studies' began to appear on the syllabus in a number of institutions.

The Period Study attempted to escape from the genre-bound approach to literature and the loose periodisation which characterises most university courses. The more radical courses went beyond the notion of history as 'background' or as social context, and attempted to examine literary production as *part of* the historical process. At least that was the theory; the practice has often been very different. At times it has meant simply the identification of a more specific time-span (the Elizabethan Period, the Victorian Period, the Modern Period, etc. – although these are hardly *historical* definitions), and the reading of a few 'non-literary' texts alongside the traditional 'great authors'. Sometimes historians or philosophers are brought in to teach part of the course, leaving Literature for the literature experts – with the result that the concept of Literature is left unquestioned and the sanctity of the individual discipline unchallenged.

At the moment, the Period Study exists on the timetable alongside the traditional genre studies, and is a testimony to the ability of a 'liberal education' to swallow potential challenges to its fundamental premises. Radical critics in the universities and polytechnics argue that we must examine the ensemble of relations which constitute the cultural at any particular moment. Result? A new slot on the timetable called the Period Study. Feminists argue that criticism has desexed women writers and ignored the issue of gender. Result? A slot on the timetable called Feminist Criticism – optional. This incorporation is not simply the result of 'the system', but also of the ways in which we make our political challenges, and our lack of clarity about our political objectives in the sphere of culture and education. We should not be content with a personal timetable which eases our political conscience. In a sense we need to come clean, to say to those colleagues who disagree with our approach: yes, we are talking about politics, we do think that the way you teach and what you teach perpetuates a form of class society with which we fundamentally disagree. We need to become more combative, to fight against incorporation, to resist the temptation to heave a sigh of relief because we have managed to slip something radical into the syllabus. The hegemonic strength of a 'liberal education' resides precisely in its insistence that all points of view can be accommodated, indeed are positively welcomed, so long as they are substantiated by the 'proper' academic research. Unless we challenge at every turn that view of education, we will never break the silken halter which ties us inescapably to its continuation.

Nevertheless, and bearing in mind not only the problem of incorporation but also the need, mentioned earlier, for immediate reforms which challenge from within, I want to argue for a reconstituted Period Study as the basis of a reconstituted discipline, and not merely as an alternative teaching method or approach. The Period Study offers an opportunity to move away from the inevitable élitism of existing approaches to literature. But in order to succeed, it needs to be problem- or topic-centred, and not text-centred, whether the texts be 'literary' or 'non-literary' in nature. If we start from an issue – women's oppression, the family, unemployment, leisure, construction of class, etc. – then any 'texts' studied have an initial common status, they provide an insight into the topic under consideration. Our concern no longer becomes the evaluation of 'good' and 'bad' writing, or explication, but rather the ways in which 'meanings' and understandings of particular issues are constructed. ('The text', of course, does not have to be a book, it can be a newspaper report, a song, a mass demonstration, a campaign, etc., etc.). It is then possible to examine the effects of different forms and structures; how they construct meaning; how our images and understanding of a period are created; which events and texts reinforce the *status quo*, which subvert it; what different discourses were available; what the competing ideologies were at any given time; to whom they 'belonged'; how they manifested themselves, etc. This approach thus tends to dissolve the sharp distinction between the 'literary' and 'non-literary' text, and to look at the production of meanings and their consumption. *All* texts are concerned with significations of reality, the ordering and representation of aspects of experience, and a proper Period Study would allow us to identify the myriad discourses which constitute our 'world-view', their autonomy and interconnections.

However, this can only be done if we break down the barriers which make me a literary critic, you a historian, her a philosopher, all 'knowing' different things. For the Period Study to be truly radical it needs to escape from the notion that there are discrete areas of knowledge which can be parcelled up and labelled, and 'specialists' who are the only ones qualified to decipher their 'own' label and unpack their own parcel. But although the breaking-down of the traditional discipline boundaries is essential in the project I am outlining, this does not automatically mean the rejection of particular skills associated with individual disciplines. Many of the recent radical interventions in English teaching have recognised the importance of the skills of the historian and sociologist for a proper understanding of culture. But there has been a reluctance to identify and reclaim the skills which are part of the training of the literary critic. The critical discourse of 'flat' and 'round' characters, of plot and narrative structure, may appear irrelevant, but it masks and mystifies certain skills which are as potentially valuable to the radical teacher/commentator, as they are necessary to the GCE candidate faced with the question 'Compare and contrast the characters of Iago and Othello'. The student and teacher of literature develops, for example, a consciousness of the importance of structure in the creation of meaning, a sensitivity to language and an ability to pierce the apparent innocence of the words on the page – skills which can be as important in the examination of 'non-literary' material as they have been in 'appreciating' Literature. Many teachers of English have begun to apply the skills of the historian to their own subject, but it is a rare historian indeed who would argue that the skills of the literary critic have any place in the study of 'proper' History.

II

I want now to illustrate the potential use of these critical skills, in the context of what can only here be a notional 'Period Study' of the 1930s, by examining a 'historical document': the Select Committee Report on Government Expenditure of 1931 (the May Committee Report).[1] Within the sort of period study which I have been proposing, a reading of the report would be part of an examination of the 'problem' of unemployment or of government social policy. A full 'reading' of the report would, of course, also require an examination of unemployment in the interwar period, the 1929 Labour government, the development of state benefits and government spending, and so on. However, here, I want to concentrate on only one aspect: the way in which the ideology of its writers is revealed in its language and structure, and to do this will indicate how necessary are those critical skills associated with the close reading of literary texts.

I have read numerous historical and political accounts of the interwar period, and in all of them government reports, enquiries, and Royal Commissions are seen as sources of 'facts', the raw material of history, which the political scientist and the historian then interpret. The recommendations are summarised, their implications and impact discussed, the evidence scrutinised, but the actual language and structure are rarely mentioned. A government select committee is part of a particular political system and has available to it particular discourses. Its terms of reference are constituted not only by the formal order of Parliament, by which it is set up, but also by the informal, unstated, and *already* established political consensus of a modern democratic state which identifies certain issues as problems and proceeds accordingly. The writers of the report have available certain modes of writing, certain forms of language, which are determined partly by their own educational background (which in 1931 would almost certainly be public school and Oxbridge), and partly by the expectations of what a government report, a formal document, should be.

The May Committee Report is now regarded as historically

significant because of its recommendations of selective cuts in the pay of certain government employees (lower ranks of the armed forces and teachers, in particular), cuts in unemployment benefit rates, and the introduction of means-tested transitional benefit – recommendations which split the Labour government and led to the formation of the National government. But it is also an important ideological document which offers an insight into the creation, mediation, and reproduction of dominant ideologies.

In our political culture reports from independent committees established by Parliament are often presented as neutral, unbiased assessments of the problem which they address. They operate according to certain well-defined democratic procedures, taking evidence from all interested parties and then, having weighed the evidence, proceed to make certain recommendations to Parliament, which is of course free to take or reject the advice given. Thus the reports enter into history as a series of recommendations, an influence on government policy, and not as 'texts' in their own right. Yet a close reading of the May Committee Report reveals it as a very committed text, committed to certain dominant notions of the role of government, the function of social services, and the class structure of our society. Also inscribed within it are certain common-sense notions about the nature of the crisis and its possible solution, all of which contribute to the making of the final recommendations, and indeed which make any other set of recommendations impossible.

On 11 February 1931, with the number of unemployed at around two million, the following motion was passed in the House of Commons by 468 votes to 21:

> That this house consider that, having regard to the present burden of Taxation in restricting industry and employment, the Government should at once appoint a small and independent committee to make recommendations to the Chancellor of the Exchequer for affecting forthwith all practicable and legitimate reductions of the national expenditure consistent with the efficiency of the services.

Thus, despite the fact that financial experts were arguing that the principal cause of Britain's economic crisis was the world recession and the resultant collapse of the export market for Britain's major industries, Parliament identified the 'burden of Taxation' as the prime cause, and embarked on the now all too familiar path of proposing cuts in public expenditure as the cure for economic ills. The resultant Committee on National Expenditure was established on 17 March 1931 under the chairmanship of Sir George May, Secretary to the Prudential Assurance Company. It reported four months later.

The introduction to the report sought to give the background to the debate about public expenditure by examining the course of national finance policy in the postwar period, a course which it characterised as an unequal struggle between expansion and retrenchment, concluding that the dice were heavily loaded in favour of expansion. The report comments that:

> The cause is not far to seek. After the heavy sacrifices of the war large sections of the nation looked to the post-war period with the national expectation of a general improvement in the old conditions of life. The disappointment of many hopes in the economic sphere seemed to intensify demands for improvements from political action and all parties have felt the insistent pressure for promises of 'reform' as the price of support, such 'reforms' being in fact mostly of the nature of privileges or benefits for particular classes at the cost of the general taxpayer. The results of this pressure are to be seen not only in the lavish promises contained in the election addresses of the period since the war, but in the undertakings freely given by individual Parliamentary candidates to sections of the electorate. At election times those desiring increased expenditure on particular objects are usually far better organised, far more active and vocal, than those who favour the vague and uninspiring course of strict economy; and as a result candidates not infrequently find themselves returned to Parliament committed, on a one-sided presentation of a case, to a cause which on fuller knowledge they see to be opposed to the national interests. (22)

A close analysis of this passage can help indicate how consensus is established and perpetuated, and reveal the common-sense notions which both inform the report and in turn are reinforced by it.

The introduction and the conclusion to the report are for 'popular' consumption, they provide the 'quotes' for the leader-writers and political columnists and the arguments for the politicians, whilst the substantive part of the report, the detailed statistical evidence, is for the expert. The language of the above passage is clearly *not* that of the expert, and despite the fact that the majority of the members of the committee were from the world of business and finance there is a marked lack of 'scientific' terminology. The introduction uses everyday language and images, and the crisis is represented by the language of everyday experience rather than through an examination of state structures. It could be argued that this makes the report more accessible, more understandable to the 'ordinary' person, yet I would contend that its real effect is to introduce a crucial mystification into the proceedings. The passage above draws upon the language and imagery of war-time Britain with its use of 'nation', 'heavy sacrifices' and 'old conditions of life', and the expansion of state expenditure after the war is seen as an expression of the psychological state of the nation after the trauma of war, understandable but misguided. Thus the demand for increased public expenditure (i.e. old-age pensions, unemployment pay, increased education opportunities for the working class, better social services) is linked to a collective mental state, rather than political and economic realities. This notion is reinforced by the phrase 'disappointment of many hopes'. Disappointment and hope are human emotions and not words which can be applied to state structures, and the grandiloquence of the phrase masks the reality of the situation which it is apparently seeking to describe – no work for returning soldiers, massive increase in unemployment, pay reductions, and until 1926, large-scale industrial unrest.

The passage introduces two familiar categories, 'the general taxpayer' and the 'national interest'. Against these images of unity are pitted 'particular classes' and 'sections of the electorate'. 'General' and 'national' suggest wholeness, all of us, whilst 'particular' and 'sections' are words which divide, split up the whole, and carry the suggestion of minorities. Yet which people and which social groupings are represented by these labels? Who is the 'general taxpayer', and which section of the population would identify itself as part of this category? The 'general taxpayer' is in fact the middle- and upper-class taxpayer, the section of society which regards itself as paying for, and not benefiting from, public expenditure, whilst the 'particular classes' are the working class. Thus the phrases in the passage which evoke the notion of 'all of us together' and unity, in fact refer to a small percentage of the population, whilst those which suggest a minority, and activity which is against the interest of the majority, are in fact referring to the majority of the population.

The passage also implies that governments have been forced to act recklessly; there have been '*demands*' for improvements, and '*insistent pressure*' for reform as the '*price* of support'. This emotive language suggests coercion, and thus that the 'particular classes' are acting in a way foreign to our political culture which is based upon freedom and choice rather than force and threats. The meaning and impact of the passage would have been dramatically altered if it had simply stated that those who advocated increased public spending had been elected to office by the majority of the electorate. There is no attempt to explain what the reforms entailed, and indeed the word reform only appears in inverted commas, suggesting they are not reforms at all in the dictionary sense of 'making better', but rather, as is explicitly stated, 'privileges and benefits for particular classes'. Again the effect of the language is to place the gains made by the working class outside the 'normal' structure of British politics – after all, benefits and privileges are the antithesis of modern democracy. (It is interesting to note how the language of the working-class movement, the attack on privilege, is here used against it.)

The end of the paragraph presents another familiar category, the silent majority. It suggests that expenditure has only increased because those desiring it are 'far better organised, far more active and vocal, than those who favour the vague and uninspiring course of strict economy'. Once again there is the implicit suggestion that those who want reform are a minority who bludgeon and browbeat the majority into accepting increased expenditure. There is a consistent refusal to talk about actual reforms, and the effect of the introduction is to remove from the debate any discussion of the need for increased government expenditure. The strategic sarcasm of the phrase 'vague and uninspiring' reinforces this effect. The authors of the report clearly do not believe strict economy to be vague and uninspiring, rather it means the salvation of the nation. However the phrase serves both as an explanation of why strict economy has not received mass support, and as an ironic and devaluing comment on those who are 'active and vocal'.

The introduction concludes with the observation:

> We fear the country must face the disagreeable fact that its
> public expenditure – and in this we include local as well as
> national expenditure – is too high, and that it must be brought
> down to a lower level. (31)

The tone is the familiar 'more in sorrow than in anger' of the
politician urging the public to *face the facts*, and the effect of the
sentence is to place the 'facts' beyond dispute without actually
presenting the reader with any. Although the introduction has
refused to use the language of the expert, it is in fact relying heavily
on the notion that the 'we' used throughout have access to information which is not available to the general public. There is a similar
suggestion in the first quotation above, when the writers of the
report argue that those elected to Parliament on a platform of
increased expenditure find themselves committed to 'a cause
which on fuller knowledge they see to be opposed to the national
interests'. The clear implication is that once anyone has access to all
the information, the need for reduced spending is apparent; thus
there is no way that the conclusions within the report can be
challenged. The effect of the introduction is to remove the question of the necessity of cuts from the debate, and to suggest that
anyone who proposes increased expenditure is living an illusion
(i.e. refusing to face the *facts*). This established, the report is free to
move on to the detailed consideration of where cuts can be made.

At this point it is important to look at the structure of the report.
Although there is no apparent reason why it should be structured
as it is – for each chapter deals with a discrete area and has no
apparent reliance on the preceding or following chapter – the
structure is absolutely crucial to the report's final recommendations, and it imposes its own logic on the argument. In the introduction the Committee announce that savings of £120,000,000 are
necessary to balance the budget, and they intend to examine five
key areas of government spending in order to determine where
the necessary savings can be made. The first three chapters
examine the Civil Service, the pay and pensions of state employees,
and defence expenditure. They conclude that only just over
£5,000,000 can be saved in these three areas, and thus it becomes
imperative that large-scale economies are made in the last two
areas, Development and Social Services expenditure. If these two
areas had been the first to be examined, and the recommended cut

of £80,000,000 in the Social Services budget had come at the beginning of the report, then the effect of the structure would have been to suggest that the Committee had *already* decided which areas were to bear the brunt of the economies, and the whole notion of the independent and neutral committee would have been undermined. The final chapter on Social Services states:

> Had it been possible to make sufficient reductions in other fields of expenditure we would have gladly been content with comparatively minor adjustments in this field. No such alternative is open. (369)

In order to be able to make this statement it has to appear as if every other possible area for reductions has been explored, and the structure of the report leads inevitably to the conclusion that most of the savings *have* to come from Social Services, because we have seen, haven't we, that there is no alternative. The sentence above is totally self-justifying in its circularity, for if the savings had been made elsewhere then there would be no need to reduce spending on social services! The phrase 'have gladly been content' attempts to remove the sting from the proposals which are about to be made and suggests that the Committee have no principled opposition to Social Services expenditure: it simply happens to be the only area left where cuts can be made. Thus the apparently random structure imposes its own logic. Readers have certain 'structural' expectations of most written texts, anticipating progression to a conclusion, to a solution to the problems which have been raised. The May Committee Report fulfills these expectations, and is indeed structured by them.

In the final two chapters there is a significant change in the language and structure of the argument. The chapter on Development looks at those areas of government expenditure which were designed to promote economic development. The report states:

> There has been in our view an unfortunate tendency since the war to confuse economic development, or to put it plainly profitable development, with what we might term 'amenity development', especially in the field of Trade Depression Services. (275)

And that:

We cannot endorse a policy of great expenditure on capital works, irrespective of their economic value, as a means of providing work. It is too expensive. On the usual calculations of 4,000 man years of labour, direct and indirect, for £1 million expenditure, it costs £250 to keep a man in work for one year. The saving on maintenance is usually put at £60 a year. Thus proceeding on this basis, unless the man's work is worth at least £190 to the nation when it is done, the nation loses economically by carrying it out. (358)

The economic expertise and technical language previously restricted to the statistical analysis within the text, and notably absent from the explanatory sections, is now brought into full play. If one compares the above passages with the previous quotations one can see a marked change in style. The language is more formal and technical (Trade Depression Services, capital works, amenity development), and the lay person is excluded from its mode of argument: if one does not know that 4,000 man years etc. is the 'usual' calculation, then one cannot possibly challenge the conclusions. The use of the words 'usual' and 'usually' further distances the reader; clearly these calculations are not 'usual' to the vast majority of the population, but if they are apparently 'usual' to the authors of the report, then they must know what they are talking about, mustn't they? It is also worth noting the strategic importance of 'unfortunate' and 'to put it plainly', and the way in which 'economic' becomes synonymous with 'profitable'.

In the introduction to the report the 'burden of Taxation' is given as the major cause of the financial crisis, but in the final chapter the argument becomes more focused. The Committee observes that the cost of Social Services has increased seven-fold since 1911 (they omit to mention that until 1911 there was hardly *any* such expenditure), and conclude:

Under the difficult conditions of the post-war period, the increase of burden has been a grave handicap, and we cannot shut our eyes to the fact that the enormous increase in the Exchequer charge of these services has been the prime cause of the present crisis in the national finances. (368)

This paragraph marks a significant shift of emphasis, for it is no longer government expenditure *in toto*, nor the burden of taxation,

which is the cause of the crisis, but specifically the expenditure on
Social Services. The tone is measured and weighty, and we are back
to the apparently 'everyday' language of the introduction – no one
could fail to understand what is being said. Yet what kind of
everyday language is this? People in the street don't usually talk
sonorously of 'difficult conditions', 'increase of burden' and 'grave
handicap'. Nevertheless, it is a language with which we are all
familiar: it is the language of crisis, of the speech to the nation, of
the political leader columns in the press, and it is a language which
refuses contradiction. 'We cannot shut our eyes to the fact': there *is*
a crisis, this is fact not opinion, and to disagree is to ignore 'reality'.
Thus having identified the *real* cause of the crisis, the way is open
for the solution – or, in literary terms, for the *dénouement*: major
cuts in public services, and in particular savings on unemployment
pay. The authors recommend a saving of £66,500,000 by cutting
the benefit rates by 20 per cent, increasing contributions, and
introducing a means-tested benefit for those who have exhausted
their insurance rights – the increasing majority of those on the
unemployed register.

The report proposes cuts totalling £96,500,000, and in the conclusion the Committee recommend that the government should
adopt the whole package, for

> if economies are only attempted where little opposition is antici-
> pated, if certain classes are called upon in the national interest to
> suffer serious reductions of emoluments while large unprofit-
> able expenditure goes unchecked in other fields, resentment
> and opposition will be aroused, and the eventual result in savings
> will be negligible; the object of our appointment will remain
> unfulfilled. (566)

Worthy sentiment, but what does it actually mean? 'Where little
opposition is anticipated' presumably means amongst the middle
class, yet the only proposed cut which affects a section of the
middle class is the recommended cut in teachers' salaries.
£88,000,000 of the proposed cuts were to come directly from the
'particular classes' and 'sectional interests' of the introduction, i.e.
the working class. The conclusion, like the introduction, evokes the
unifying image of the national interest, and stresses the need for
all-round sacrifices, yet the report's recommendations only
require a sacrifice from one section of the population.

The type of reading I have attempted here, situated in the larger context of a Period Study, can begin to reveal how 'meanings' and ideology are both reproduced and consolidated. I am not suggesting that the May Committee Report is evidence of a ruling-class conspiracy against the working class, nor that the structures and meanings identified above are a deliberate and conscious part of the construction of the report. The May Committee did not 'create' the argument that public expenditure was the cause of the financial and political crisis of 1931. But the report is an important document in strengthening that explanation; it gives it further legitimacy and authority, and makes it even more difficult for other explanations to have credence. It reinforces the attack on government expenditure by providing 'evidence' of the correctness of the dominant explanations, and is thus part of a process of consolidation and legitimisation.

The Times' leader on 14 August 1931 observed that:

> The committee have proved beyond doubt the fact that the nation is living beyond its means, and they have challenged contradiction of the fact that terrible dangers can be averted only by cutting down public expenditure.

The Daily Mirror the next day took up the report's call for sacrifices all round:

> As to equality of sacrifice we have, in this column, urged again and again that it should apply in appropriate measures to the *whole of the voting community* and not to one – the direct taxpaying section – which has hitherto been sacrificed to the others: to the dole-takers, the recipients of social benefits and the myriads who do not worry about public expenditure because they do not have to contribute towards it.

The role of the press in the production of meanings, and its mediation and transmission of documents like the May Report, would of course be another part of the Period Study. All we may notice here, however, is that the manipulations of style and structure analysed above are already acquiring, by way of the Press, the status of objective and factual authority. Indeed, it is my argument that these 'literary' elements serve to invest the report with its 'authority' and are a crucial aspect of what it tells us.

178   Re-Reading English

Note

1   *Committee on National Expenditure* (1931) Cmd. 3920. All references
    hereafter are to the numbered paragraphs of this report, and appear in
    brackets in the text.

13
Socialist-feminist criticism: a case study, women's suffrage and literature, 1906–14

WENDY MULFORD

In this essay I want to look at two manifestations of the treatment of suffrage in literature in the period of militant suffrage activity, Elizabeth Robins's novel *The Convert* (1907) and the work and organisation of the *Women Writers' Suffrage League*, in order to raise questions to do with our objectives in teaching English literature in higher education. At the outset, I wish to make certain points about the position from which I am writing, and in conclusion to argue for the validity of this approach.

Feminist criticism

Feminism includes a number of quite widely varying political positions, but probably the major divide occurs in the question of the relationship of class-oppression to gender-oppression in the social subordination of women. The position from which I proceed is within the socialist-feminist region of this debate, in which both class and gender are seen as crucially determining that subordination. The problem is to analyse and make visible the articulation of class and gender oppression. Within this field, feminist criticism has a particular task to perform, in the scrupulous and attentive study of all aspects of literary production. The connections between literary and historical studies will become more powerfully established as we seek to understand the formations of our lame society in which, as one feminist critic, Ellen Morgan, has put it,

'Women grow up in order to grow down' (Morgan, 1972). It is to free human potential from the crippling restrictions of habit and assumption that we study; and feminist critical work comprises, amongst many other topics, the enormous range of the representations of men and women in literature; women readers and writers; the treatment of women's books by critics; women and the conditions of the writing profession; women and language; and women and the literary tradition.

However, it seems that feminist criticism is now become grown up: it has 'come out' into society, made its curtsy, and been accepted. There is a danger that, as Lillian Robinson warned ten years ago, it is about to become 'bourgeois criticism in drag . . . to contract what can only be a mesalliance with bourgeois modes of thought and the critical categories they inform' (Robinson, 1978, p. 21).

I would like to digress briefly to take an example of such modes of thought. In 'The Difference of View', an essay I have found most stimulating, Mary Jacobus (1978) argues for the 'otherness' of women's writing as making possible, potentially, nothing less than a rewriting of fictions and the interrogating of writing itself. I am excited by such a possibility. I can even think of a few women writers to whose work I could relate Jacobus's ideas – Helene Cixous, Monique Wittig, Lyn Hejinian, Alice Notley, for example (there are others). But Mary Jacobus admits in her essay that these concerns extend to very few people (how few, I have myself indicated in an article in *Red Letters*, 'Notes on Writing: a Marxist-Feminist viewpoint' (Mulford, 1979)):

> Woman and artist, the feminine and the avant-garde are elided in the privileged zone of contemporary intellectual and aesthetic concern: writing. . . . *Difference* is redefined, not as male *versus* female – not as biologically constituted – but as a multiplicity, joyousness and heterogeneity which is that of textuality itself. Writing, the production of meaning, becomes the site both of challenge and Otherness; rather than (as in more traditional approaches) simply yielding the themes and representations of female oppression. (Jacobus, 1978, p. 12)

The problem is that this kind of critical approach is limited, by the terms of its own discourse, to a limited audience, and that it consequently addresses only a limited aspect of 'writing', and indeed of sexual difference. All writing is not 'writing' in the restricted, élite sense in which Mary Jacobus uses it; is it even an important, let alone crucial, kind of writing for us to be grappling with now, in the 1980s? The absence of any reference to class difference lends such considerations a curious air of unreality: if it is true that women generally have been silenced by their sex, it is nevertheless equally true that many middle-class women have been most eloquent, while most working-class women, until quite recently, have not; and that working-class men, unless 'liberated' by their occupation, or participation in the labour movement, have been just as silent. It is equally imperative for working-class men, as for all women, to engage with the traditional modes of writing to articulate their oppression, and their desire, if we are to change the lives of both women and men.

With this perspective, I would argue that socialist-feminist critics, of both sexes, should address all forms of writing and literary production from the dual perspective of gender and class. We are consciously partisan for, to paraphrase Lenin, nobody if (s)he understands the relationship of the classes can avoid joining one class or another, or can shield her/himself from some kind of partisanship, whether in politics, literature or art. Nor can anyone escape their gender designation, nor the implications of gender, if they understand the relationship of the sexes. So here also, as critics and writers, we are partisan, for: 'Partisanship is the conscious struggle of the theoretician or the artist, using the means of science or art, for the ideals and interests of the class, and is indivisible from the class struggle' (Kunitsyn, 1971, p. 128). Our dual perspective as socialists and feminists is to make feminists address the problem of class-oppression and socialists address sex-oppression, even though 'the habits and priorities of the Labour movement and socialism express inherently a whole web of political givens – the great unsaids – which have women's subordination at their centre' (*Red Rag*, 1980, p. 2). As critics, if we seriously wish to put our students in touch with the 'subversive power of writing, its power to destabilise the ground on which we stand' (Jacobus, 1978, pp. 18–19), we cannot stay in our present unhappy marriages of feminism and either traditional or latest-Parisian-model literary criticism. We have, I would argue, to make a new political and linguistic move.

It is for this reason that in looking briefly at the relationship between fiction and the Suffrage Movement in this chapter I want to highlight the value of attending to other aspects of literary production than the text itself. My first 'case study' is indeed a text – Elizabeth Robins's highly successful novel *The Convert*, written 'at white heat'[1] to propagandise for the suffrage movement – and my reasons for choosing it are that it is a useful focus for considering questions of art-value and social and political relevance, and most particularly, of how we look at the relationship between the two. My second 'case study' is a literary organisation, the Women Writers' Suffrage League, founded in 1908 to advance the cause of suffrage by 'the methods proper to writers – the use of the pen' (WWSL Prospectus, in Robins, 1913, p. 106). The conclusion of my argument is that those of us who define ourselves as feminist and socialist teachers of English in higher education need to shift the ground of our study, and the goals we set our students, away from aesthetic and moral questions of the value of the text, to a broader analysis of literary production in its period, and to see this as one of the manifestations, and shaping forces, of the social and political reality of the time.

The Convert

The Convert was adapted from Elizabeth Robins's successful stage play, *Votes for Women*, which she wrote in 1906. Fearing that no stage management would be willing to undertake such a subversive piece of propaganda, Robins turned it into a novel, by which means she hoped to reach a wide audience. In fact the play was staged at the Court Theatre in April 1907 before the novel was published, and both play and novel brought critical praise and commercial success.[2] At a crucial point at the outset of the militant Women's Social and Political Campaign against the new Liberal government, therefore, Robins used her literary and dramatic skills to make a clear intervention on behalf of the suffrage cause, and an emotional plea to the women and men of her class to support it. Two years later, she became the first president of the Women Writers' Suffrage League (WWSL), the first organisation of women writers formed to work for a political objective.

The Suffrage Movement shares with Vida Levering, the society beauty with a mysterious past, the role of protagonist in *The Convert*. It is rare enough to find a bourgeois novel that deals directly with social movements rather than using them to contextualise the drama of interpersonal relations, but Robins's novel not only counterpoints the development of the 'heroine' with her growing awareness of the developing forces of the Movement, but it also affirms, structurally, the triumph of the cause in despite, or in disregard, of personal happiness. In a melodramatic plot-resolution Robins has Vida Levering force her former lover, who ten years earlier abandoned her when she was pregnant rather than lose his patrimony, pledge his support in the coming General Election, as an influential Tory politician and likely Cabinet minister. The means to achieve this *dénouement* lie in Stonor's fiancée who, influenced by the Suffrage Movement and by Vida, is determined that he shall 'make amends' to Vida. The conventions of romantic melodrama would have required that one of the women die of a broken heart at the very least, or Stonor be stabbed to death and *both* women die of broken hearts. But at this point Robins discards the conventions and has her heroine bargain quite cold-bloodedly with Stonor for Jean Dunbarton and his happiness as the price of his political support. Vida's personal pain is not glossed over or made to look trivial, but it is seen in perspective as one aspect of the wider forces at work which can be harnessed for change:

> One woman's mishap – what is that? A thing as trivial to the great world as it's sordid in most eyes. But the time has come when a woman may look about her and say, What general significance has my secret pain? Does it 'join on' to anything? And I find it *does*. I'm no longer simply a woman who has stumbled on the way. . . . I'm one who has got up bruised and bleeding, wiped the dust from her hands and the tears from her face – and said to herself not merely: Here's one luckless woman! but – here is a stone of stumbling to many. Let's see if it can't be moved out of other women's way. And she calls people to come and help. No mortal man, let alone a woman, *by herself*, can move that rock of offence. But . . . if many help . . . the thing can be done. (Robins, (1907) 1980, p. 304)

The polemical, oratorical quality of the writing is characteristic not only of this work but of much of the impassioned prose writings of the militant suffrage supporters. Both the pitch and the biblical resonances of the language ('stumbled on the way', 'bruised and bleeding', 'rock of offence') have an appropriate place in the fiction of public action such as *The Convert*, although it is less easy to accept that a woman or a man *would* speak in these accents to a former lover. Clearly Robins violates the conventions of the social-realist novel here, and indeed in many other parts of the book. But the interest and the value of *The Convert* as an object of study do not depend upon her skill in exploiting those particular conventions. The novel is exemplary for us precisely in posing the question as to how a writer may render passionate political commitment fictionally, and achieve a wide audience; in what way can (s)he represent the drama of that commitment centrally in the novel, and what compromises, tensions and artistic strains may be caused by the attempt? All these questions are, I would argue, crucial for our clearer understanding of the relationship of politics and art, and for confronting the challenge that political commitment makes to our evaluation of literature.

One way of approaching at least a part of these related questions might be to ask in what way does *The Convert* appear to be a less satisfactory novel, to be fictionally cruder, because of its reliance upon romance conventions and melodrama to mediate that part of the plot that deals with personal relationships. But having asked that question, it has immediately to be said that we are in effect looking at only one half of the novel. For all that part which deals with the suffrage meetings, the encounters, the speeches, the heckling, the preparations and departures, the organisation, the opposition, the hopes and ambitions of countless different women from different classes, occupations, life-styles and family backgrounds, Robins used a documentary approach.[3] Consequently the wider public world of struggle into which Vida Levering is gradually introduced is created for the reader substantively by way of careful and detailed accounts, or of descriptions of the meetings from Vida's point of view. And the 'other' world, beyond society's dinner-tables and elegant weekend house-parties, comes increasingly into view – as Robins has her heroine report on her experience of finding out for herself what the treatment of women in the hostels for homeless women was really like:

> I put on an old gown and a tawdry hat . . . you'll never know how many things are hidden from a woman in good clothes. The bold free look of a man at a woman he believes to be destitute – you

must *feel* that look on you before you can understand a good half
of history. (ibid., p. 224)

Perhaps the novel too must put off its 'good clothes', its traditional
and ideologically determined modes, in order to reach out to this
hidden half of history.

There is much that is worth discussing in *The Convert* of relevance to contemporary socialist and feminist struggles, particularly in its articulation of political and personal struggles. But I
want to conclude by noting how Robins has focused the sexual
dimension of power relations as one that differently manifests
itself according to class position. In the upper classes, women are
apparently protected to some extent by the respect and patronage
of men – provided they do not step outside their 'proper sphere'.
But beneath this veneer lies a different reality – soon unmasked if
women should presume to reject that sphere, take themselves
seriously and make demands upon society:

> Lots of women used to be taken in by that talk about feminine
> influence and about men's immense respect for them. But any
> number of women have come to see that underneath that old
> mask of chivalry was a broad grin. (p. 205)

When Vida ventures out in disguise into the world of London's
streets, squares and parks, she soon discovers how that mask
belongs only to her own class-reality: at first, there is the 'curious
direct . . . cooly watchful, slightly contemptuous stare. . . . Vida
was conscious of wishing she had come in her usual clothes' (p. 74);
later, the apprehension that having slipped out of her protective
class-identity she is fair game for all the sexual humiliations, the
'degrading discomforts, the cruelties' (p. 201), inflicted on powerless women. As she reflects towards the end of the novel: 'The
thing's largely a matter of economics' (p. 289); and the women who
suffer the worst are those who are most powerless and exploited:
'the nail and chain makers of Cradley Heath, the sweated girls of
the slums . . . the army of ill-used women, whose very existence I
mustn't mention' (p. 288). The worlds of *The Convert* are inter-
linked, economically, sexually and politically. The same set of
power relationships encircle the middle-class women as exploit the
labour, and reject the basic human needs, of the working-class
women. Vida's education is completed when she realises that it is

the same system of male dominance by the ruling class that has created both her personal suffering at the hands of her lover, who rejected her right to have a child in favour of his right to his patrimony, the gilded cage of her social equals, and the miseries of Cradley Heath, the girls in the sweated workshops and the army of prostitutes. In the final melodramatic scene of the novel, Robins makes her protagonist sacrifice any personal claim to happiness in order to secure a political advantage for 'The Cause'. But by this stage 'The Cause' *is* the protagonist too. Personal happiness as an ultimate goal, and the sense of past suffering, are superseded by the conviciton that 'There is work to do' (p. 303).

The Women Writers' Suffrage League

> On balance, the suffrage movement was not a happy stimulus to women writers. If they participated in its militant phase, they did get some sense of effective solidarity, but not as writers . . . no real manifesto of female literature was produced; the Women Writers' Suffrage League remained a political and, in many ways, a social organisation. (Showalter, 1978, p. 239)

Elaine Showalter's negative estimate of the WWSL follows directly from her concern with standards of excellence in the writers she discusses. I don't wish to dispute that much of the work produced by the League, or by members of the League individually, was either fairly tendentious or light-hearted burlesque, nor that fund-raising and various forms of upper-class social activities (soirées, dinners, etc.) formed a large part of the activities of the League. Like its sister organisations such as the Artists' Franchise League and the Actresses' Franchise League it was shaped by the class-composition of its members (although the latter arguably incorporated a greater variety of social strata).[4] But the political significance of this organisation both in the evolution of women's emancipation and, more broadly, in the developing politicisation of women through their awareness of their oppression as women, is missing from Showalter's account.

For the first time, as far as I am aware, a group of women writers – poets, journalists, novelists, playwrights – banded together *as professional writers*, to help to win a common political objective, the 'Parliamentary Franchise for women on the same terms as it is, or may be, granted to men' (Robins, 1913, p. 106). The qualifications for membership were clear: 'the publication or production of a book, article, story, poem or play *for which the author has received payment*' (ibid., my emphasis); and the methods were described as: 'the methods proper to writers – the use of the pen'. The aim was 'to influence public opinion': the founding members, Cicely Hamilton and Bessie Hatton, believing that 'a body of writers working for a common object cannot fail to influence public opinion' (ibid.). The League had a constitution, annual subscriptions of 2s 6d, and a fully-constituted committee with officials elected at the Annual General Meeting. It sent delegates to women's and suffrage conferences, and supported the large suffrage demonstrations in Hyde Park in 1910 and 1911, marching behind its own scriveners' banner one hundred strong. It published both fictional and polemical work, some by men (who are also mentioned in the reports of social events), although mainly by women; but the greater part of its work lay in promoting the suffrage cause through contributions to the press, in the form of letters and articles. Between its foundation in 1908, and its gradual demise in the period of ebbing militancy prior to the outbreak of the First World War, the WWSL was very active in many different ways.

Some idea of the range of work the League produced can be gained from an account by Elizabeth Robins in May 1911: her list of the League's activities includes highly successful plays such as *How the Vote Was Won* by Cicely Hamilton and Christopher St. John, a farce on the theme of men's capitulation to a total general strike by all women (a heartening theme . . .); a cartoon postcard of 'Justice'; polemical pamphlets on 'The Suffrage Question' and 'Feminism' by Madeleine Riley and May Sinclair; a poem 'Woman's Plea'; and pamphlets by Laurence Housman and Elizabeth Robins ('Time Table – May 1911', Robins, 1913, pp. 225–6). Members of the League seem to have been more productive in poetry, essays and pamphlets, masques, farces and burlesques, than in fiction, although Ethel Sharp produced an acclaimed collection of sketches and short stories, *Rebel Women* (1909), which went into two editions, and fiction was published in some of the suffragette papers, notably the Women's Social and Political Union's *Votes for Women*. Full-length fiction on the suffrage theme was written during the militant phase of the suffrage struggles (two frequently cited examples are G. Colmore's *Suffragette Sally* (1911) and Charlotte Despard and Mabel Collins's *Outlawed* (1908)); but those writers who had an immediate political and educational end in view, such as the League's members, tended to choose rather different forms. An audience could be reached more swiftly and readily through 1d, 3d, 6d or even 1s pamphlets available through the local suffrage shop,[5] than through a full-length 6s novel; and even a seat at the theatre to see *Votes for Women* or *How the Vote Was Won* could cost as little as 3s 6d.

Other members of the WWSL included women such as Alice Meynell, Olive Schreiner, Sarah Grand, Violet Hunt and Edith Lees, whose work was not necessarily directly linked to the League but who almost certainly took part in the kinds of newspaper debates to which Robins refers in 'Time Table'.[6] Aside from its roles as publisher, fund-raiser for the suffrage cause and prop-agandist, the League seems most importantly to have acted, in a non-sectarian way, as a consciousness-raising body. It enabled women to come together and collaborate on work in pursuit of their common aim, and to use their professional skills as writers to fight society's relegation of their sex. It allowed them to question the place of literature in the formation and maintenance of that inferior position granted to women – as Elizabeth Robins pointed out more than once in her speeches to the League: 'How much, we ask, how much of woman's past and even her present futility is due to writers constantly dinning it into her ears that for purposes of all activity, save one sort, she is a poor creature . . .' (4 May 1909, Robins, 1913, p. 111). That the contradiction between private artistic determinations and these wider goals of making a literary intervention in order to educate people about the iniquity of women's lack of enfranchisement caused some conflict, some resis-tance and heartache, is apparent from the tone of some of the women later looking back on the period.[7] A commitment to the suffrage cause with any degree of seriousness, whoever made it, in whatever way, was a costly commitment.

Since most of the productions of the WWSL were anonymous, much remains to be pieced together of its history from the files of the suffrage papers and the national press before a full assessment of its contribution to the political struggles of the period can be made. This work has indeed begun, and it is in this direction that I would argue our work in English in higher education should also proceed: towards a mapping of the writers of a period in terms of the social and political force which they constituted. We should be looking more fully and systematically than our present contextual and period studies allow at the positioning of writers amongst the forces for change at any given time, and we should be making it our clear choice to study those periods, organisations and writers whose work is exemplary for us in terms of our social and political struggles today. As long as we allow the major concern of our studies to be with the appreciation and evaluation of the individual text, and the individual great writer's work, however much we juggle with the canon and contextualise our texts, devise new methods of analysis, ask new questions, the end result of our labour will not greatly differ from that of New Critics, Leavisians, post-structuralists or any other group of academic critics. We will be training 'sensibility' in an updated guise.

If the relationship between women's suffrage and literature in the period 1906–14 holds a value for us today as an object of study, it is because we have as teachers and critics a particular and declared interest in the nature of the interrelationship between literary production and the social matrix. So long as our students are made clearly aware of the position from which we speak, and are not bamboozled by any claims to exclusive and authoritative 'truth' by their teachers, we need have no fear of the inevitable charges of 'bias' and 'coercion' that will be made by those speaking from a different interest. To take as an example for study a period when the relationships between literary work and the society of which it forms part are necessarily and evidently acute, both in terms of the social and political crises of the time and the self-conscious response of certain sections of writers to those crises, is to make a deliberate choice of terrain.

For socialist-feminist critics my two 'case-studies' might develop in rather different ways. The study of *The Convert* could lead, for example, to the recovery and exploration of little-known, contemporary popular fictions dealing with the theme of suffrage, such as *Outlawed, Suffragette Sally,* May Sinclair's *The Tree of Heaven* (1917) or Cicely Hamilton's *William an Englishman* (1919). We could usefully be looking at the differing representations of political struggle in works produced at the height of the militant period and in the years afterwards: between 'high art' fictions such as Virginia Woolf's *Night and Day* (1919) and the more popular fictions, or between fiction produced by men, such as H. G. Wells's *Ann Veronica* (1909), and that produced by women. We could be examining the different literary and artistic forms in which women addressed their public, how they used the conventions of romance, melodrama, masque, burlesque and pageant. We could be asking why they turned to drama and song or sketch more often than to prose fiction; and what part fictive writing of whatever kind played in their weekly and monthly papers. We could be looking at the responses of their opponents in the anti-suffrage league, discussing the ideological reinforcement of woman's role in the home in the works of its leading members such as Mrs Humphrey Ward, and analysing the tensions and contradictions in her fiction resulting from the contemporary debate over that role. And in trying to piece together the history of the WWSL, we could be led to the crucial question of the nature of the relationship between public practice – the organised activity of working together, publishing, selling, publicising, attending meetings and speaking for a particular politics – and the writer's individual perception and shaping of her work and role.[8]

Notes

1 Letter to Mrs Millicent Fawcett, 1 November 1906, Fawcett Library Collection, City of London Polytechnic. Robins wrote in the same letter that *The Convert* was the first work she'd been really satisfied with – she had already published several successful novels in the 1890s.

2 'The hullabaloo in the press gave publicity to the cause and it took columns of newsprint to debate the issues.' Jane Marcus, Introduction to *The Convert* (1980, pp. viii–ix). Robins divided the money gained from both the play and the novel between the Women's Social and Political Union (WSPU), led by the Pankhursts, and Mrs Fawcett's constitutional National Union of Women's Suffrage Societies (NUWSS). Politically, she was closest to the WSPU, and both Christabel and Mrs Pankhurst criticised successive drafts of the play and the novel (Marcus, 1980, p. viii). Some of the money from both the works was also used to buy a farm in Sussex, which became a retreat for, amongst other women, suffragettes after their ordeals in prison.

3 Robins took considerable care with the documentation by accompanying the Pankhursts on the Huddersfield by-election campaign in 1906. She kept detailed notes of the progress of the big open-air meetings, the speeches made, the heckling, and the events. She also talked to working-class suffragettes, and made use of some of their views and accounts, as Hannah Mitchell noted in her autobiography, *The Hard Way Up*.

4 Julie Holledge's *Innocent Flowers* (Virago, 1981) will be helpful here. The actresses' profession seems traditionally to have had a more mixed social composition than that of the women writers, which, as far as we are able to ascertain, was almost without exception middle-class.

5 Suffrage shops were set up in the high streets of some districts of London and of provincial towns where support for suffrage activities was high. Staffed by volunteer shopkeepers, they displayed a varied range of literature from bodies such as the WSPU (which had its own literature department, later to become The Women's Press), the NUWSS (which also ran its own shop in central London), the Artists' Suffrage League, the WWSL and publications by sympathetic independent publishers. An example of the latter is A. C. Fyfield whose strongly progressive list of cheap books and pamphlets included the second edition of Evelyn Sharp's popular collection of suffrage stories, *Rebel Women* (1912). The stories originally appeared in papers such as *The Manchester Guardian*, and the book contains an enthusiastic preface by Elizabeth Robins: one of the stories is a wryly amusing sketch of the contradictions and absurdities of well-meaning and earnest middle-class women making their intervention into the commercial life of a working-class neighbourhood where they set up one of the suffrage shops.

6 'An opening for propaganda was presented to writers when, in response to the new demand for information about the fight for Enfranchisement, a great London daily (*The Standard*) for the first time devoted columns of its space, daily, to full accounts of meetings, deputations, debates, and to articles for and against the Suffrage. A vast amount of the most effective work done by the Writers [from the WWSL] has been anonymous.' (Robins, 1913, p. 225)

7 I am thinking here of accounts in the autobiographies of writers such as Flora Annie Steele, *Garden of Fidelity*, and Cicely Hamilton, *Life Errant*; others, such as the indomitable Evelyn Sharp, were more stouthearted – her autobiography, *Unfinished Adventure*, betrays no regrets.

8 With a more detailed knowledge of the whole range of women writers' activity in the opening decades of the twentieth century we should be in a position to look again at Elaine Showalter's contention that 'women writers found themselves confronted through the suffrage movement by a number of challenges and threats: by the spectre of violence, by the ruthlessness of female authoritarianism, by the elimination of class boundaries, by a politics of action rather than influence, by collectivism, and by the loss of the secure privacy in which they had been cultivating their "special moral qualities" ' (Showalter, 1978, p. 239). Her argument that they then retreated from social involvement into a 'leisurely examination of sensibility' does less than justice to the two writers she discusses as examples of this retreat – Woolf and Richardson. On the contrary, I would argue that there is a continuity, not a discontinuity, between the political involvement of the earlier period, and the tough, feminist awareness of male-female power relations in, for example, Richardson's *Pilgrimage*.

References

Jacobus, M. (1979), 'The difference of view' in M. Jacobus (ed.), *Women Writing and Writing About Women*, Croom Helm.

Kunitsyn, G. (1971), 'Lenin on partisanship and freedom of creativity' in C.V. James (transl.), *Socialist Realism in Literature and Art*, Moscow: Progress Publishers.

Morgan, E. (1972), 'Form and focus in the neo-feminist novel' in S.K. Cornillon (ed.), *Images of Women in Fiction: Feminist Perspectives*, Bowling Green, Ohio: University Popular Press.

Mulford, W. (1979), 'Notes on writing: a marxist feminist viewpoint', *Red Letters*, 9.

Red Rag (1980), No. 9.

Robins, E. (1907), *The Convert*. Reprinted with an introduction by Jane Marcus, The Women's Press, 1980.

—— (1913), *Way Stations*, Hodder and Stoughton.

Robinson, L. (1978), 'Dwelling in decencies: radical criticism and the feminist perspective', reprinted in C. Brown and K. Olson (eds), *Feminist Criticism: Essays in Theory, Poetry and Prose*, Nantucket, New Jersey: Scarecrow Press.

Showalter, E. (1978), *A Literature of Their Own*, Virago.

14
Reading the lines: television and new fiction
PETER HUMM

Re-reading has been a particularly English form of critical practice. Disregarding any literal hint given by the term *novel*, critics on the left as well as on the nostalgic right have circled untiringly around a long-exposed body of work. This preference for picking the bones of a past tradition rather than finding new ways to read new work is not restricted to critics of literature. Television criticism has stayed largely within the literary tradition of singling out the responsibly-authored work of a select canon of writers and producers.[1] The emphasis is on authorship and notions of creativity and not on the process and institutions of broadcasting; this in turn serves conveniently to distinguish the remote skills of the reviewer from the ordinary experience of viewing. Yet television and new fiction are alike in undermining any fixed practice of reviewing and re-reading: their changing and elusive structure requires a reading that is equally open-ended.

The critical movement which has approached this need most closely has been structuralism. While marxist critics have refined their readings of the realist tradition, analysis of the anti-mimetic practice of modernist and post-modernist fiction has been significantly influenced by structuralist theory. Similarly, most recent work on cinema and television is informed by the related theoretical perspective of semiotics. In the meantime, booksellers and publishers continue to stack, alongside the best-selling Top Ten paperbacks and the ranks of Horror and Romance, the latest 'TV and Film Titles', covers trailing their recent or imminent screen celebrity. And while the 'novelisation' of a high-rating television series may be formally closer to naive nineteenth-century realism than to the self-conscious stylistics of new fiction, it too, like most popular fiction, is ignored by most marxist critics.

Structuralists 3, marxists 0. The marxist comeback is concentrated on structuralism's main defensive weakness: while it has championed the critical reading of this neglected range of contemporary writing – from the *nouveau roman* to the mythologies of popular magazines – it has tended to ignore the specific formal and historical shaping of each text in favour of a generalising concern with the structures of language. In this, theory is complicit with the practice of many writers of new fiction. Sometimes, as with the American writer, Ronald Sukenick, theory *is* practice:

> the more we talk 'about' a work, the less we participate in it, the less we are engaged by the experience of it. . . . When consciousness of its own form is incorporated in the dynamic structure of the text – its composition, as the painters say – theory can once again became part of the story rather than about it. (1975, p. 430).

That passage comes from an essay, but the next comes from the title story in Sukenick's collection *The Death of the Novel and Other Stories* (1969):

> The contemporary writer . . . is forced to start from scratch: reality doesn't exist, time doesn't exist, personality doesn't exist. . . . In view of these annihilations it should be no surprise that literature also does not exist – how could it? There is only reading and writing. (p. 41)

The gap between theory and practice is denied because in that gap grow the tangles of reference and reflection that the writers and critics of new fiction are trying to escape. It is this suspicion of the story-telling abilities of criticism that leads critics to call their books *Against Interpretation* (Sontag, 1966) or *Paracriticisms* (Hassan, 1975) or to begin an essay on 'The Fictional Criticism of the Future':

> Criticism has taken the very idea of 'aboutness' away from us. . . . It is because reality cannot be recorded that realism is dead. All writing, all composition is construction. We do not imitate the world, we construct versions of it. There is no mimesis, only poiesis. No recording, only constructing. (Scholes, 1975, p. 233)

Yet it is still necessary to insist on the material circumstance of the most self-consciously hermetic text while, at the same time, persuading marxist criticism to let go of the faded, endlessly resewn security blanket of realism. A criticism is needed which can reconcile or establish a useful tension between the formalist analysis of structuralism and the 'aboutness' of marxism.

This essay, then, is an attempt to establish a correspondence between the structuring codes of television and some of the routes travelled recently by writers in retreat from realism. That movement has led in so many and often criss-crossing directions that I have stayed with the laconic hospitality of 'new fiction' rather than choose between the more quarrelsome manifesto claims of 'postmodernism', 'metafiction', 'surfiction' or, loudest of recent contenders, 'superfiction'. Such terms exclaim the exaggerated fictitiousness of writing which refuses to trust any reality beyond its own making, and yet new fiction, in its rejection of the conventions of realism, can move closer and closer to that outside world, can become reportage, the non-fiction novel. Again, it is television with its panoramic ambition to be a window on the world boxed within its own familiar solipsism, that provides a metaphor for the restless ranging of new fiction from fact to fable. However, a metaphor is no more than that. Macherey and others have warned of the idealist aesthetic consequences of resting content with noting the similarities between different forms of fictional writing or cultural production.[2] So I have tried to set this comparison back in the differing material contexts of television and fiction production and to suggest ways in which the highly visible materialism of television can help us to recognise that more easily concealed or ignored but still crucial aspect of fiction.

Norman Mailer is tracked through *Armies of the Night* (1968), his confessional account of a 1967 protest march against the Pentagon, by a British television crew making a documentary on him for the BBC.[3] The documentary tradition, with television as its new patron, at first seems the obvious parallel to the work produced in the sixties by those writers who reacted against the compromises of realism by claiming the paradoxical freedom of reportage. Just as the documentary photographers and film-makers of the 1930s had provided a model for those writers anxious to serve as camera-eye-witnesses to what Christopher Isherwood called the 'fantastic realities' of the times (1972, p. 34), so there was felt an equivalent need during the violence and disruption which spilled from America in the Vietnam years to hold down an incredible reality by taking on the authority of fact. But where Isherwood and Dos Passos took on the formal guarantee of accuracy given by the stare of the newsreel or still camera, Mailer comes out from behind the camera to consider the ways in which the formal structures of television have influenced the reading as well as the writing of his book. Mailer makes the mediating processes of television a parable for his own nervous switching between History as a Novel and The Novel as History: a nervousness increased by his uncertainties about his audience's response. He is marching with, hoping to be read by, a generation which

> had had their minds jabbed and poked and twitched and probed and finally galvanized into surrealistic modes of response by commercials cutting into dramatic narratives, and parents flipping from network to network – they were forced willy-nilly to build their idea of a space-time continuum (and therefore their nervous system) on the jumps and cracks and leaps and breaks which every phenomenon from the media seemed to contain within it. (Mailer, 1968, pp. 86–7)

Mailer, acting as novelist, historian and television performer, suggests one route towards bringing together a formalist and a politicised criticism. His emphasis on the Vietnam generation's surrealistic response to what is happening around them is simply a more convincing explanation of the restless discontinuities of American culture than the crudely reflectionist assumption by writers such as Philip Roth that the fact of American experience is so incredible that fiction must stretch in every way to accommodate it. The American writer becomes for Roth a site-wearied tourist, sending home his 'You won't believe this' postcards: he 'has his hands full in trying to understand, and then describe and then make *credible* much of the American reality. . . . The actuality is continually outdoing our talents' (1977, p. 34).

It is important, however, not to step back from Roth's determined confrontation with 'the American reality' to an abstracted concern with the formal talents of the writer or television director. The crucial correspondence is not between the 'drama documentary' now often promoted as the quintessential television genre and the 'non-fiction novel', but between the ways in which we read both the galvanising, switching leaps and breaks of television and the equally unstable forms produced by writers such as Norman Mailer, Kurt Vonnegut, Donald Barthelme, Robert Coover, who refuse to settle on any one title or style or genre for their work. The marked American presence in any map of new fiction has been sustained both by the strong tradition of anti-realism in American literature and by the new electronic challenge to any fixed boundaries separating fact from fiction.

Kurt Vonnegut's distrust of genre is shown on the title page of *Slaughterhouse Five* (1970). Like Norman Mailer or the author of any of the collections of short stories which new fiction has revived as a significant form, Vonnegut gives his book more than one title. Below the three titles, he gives a leisured, eighteenth-century prospectus: his book is to be a confessional memoir, an eye-witness report of war and finally, but not conclusively, 'a novel somewhat in the telegraphic schizophrenic manner of tales of the Planet Tralfamadore where the flying saucers come from'. Later, Vonnegut extends his theory of Tralfamadorian literature. Books on the Planet are laid out

> in brief clumps of symbols separated by stars . . . each clump of symbols is a brief urgent message – describing a situation, a scene. We Tralfamadorians read them all at once, not one after the other. There isn't any particular relationship between all the messages, except that the author has chosen them carefully, so that, when seen all at once, they produce an image that is beautiful and surprising and deep. There is no beginning, no middle, no end, no suspense, no moral, no causes, no effects. What we love in our books are the depths of many marvellous moments seen all at one time. (p. 76)

Kurt Vonnegut not only describes the appearance and method of his and others' new fiction but, like many of those others, he makes that literary definition part of the total structure of the fiction itself. Donald Barthelme gives one of his characters in *Snow White* (1967) a similar opportunity for a critical comment on the kind of book he is appearing in:

> We like books that have a lot of *dreck* in them, matter which presents itself as not wholly relevant (or indeed at all relevant) but which, carefully attended to, can supply a kind of 'sense' of

what is going on. This 'sense' is not to be obtained by reading
between the lines (for there is nothing there, in those white
spaces) but by reading the lines themselves or looking at them
and so arriving at a feeling not of satisfaction exactly, that is too
much to expect, but of having read them, of having 'completed'
them. (p. 106)

The self-consciousness of new fiction becomes one of the subjects of those lines of text. 'Subject' in fact seems too distant and
immaterial a term – a gesture towards that secreted meaning which
is only to be revealed at the moment of epiphany. There is no gap
between those lines and a hidden text which invites or at least
allows readers to trace their own deconstructive reading. New
fiction resists the interpretation which comes from reading between the lines and yet there are plenty of white spaces: there is
something there on the paper besides words. New fiction simply
looks different from the stories and novels written by those who
continue to traffic in 'climaxes and thrills and characterisation and
wonderful dialogue and suspense and confrontation' (Vonnegut,
1970, p. 4). A piece of fiction by Vonnegut, Barthelme, Robert
Coover or Richard Brautigan is typically divided into page-length
chapters or paragraphs of a dozen lines or less. Paragraphs are
numbered or arrowed (———►) divided by plain white space or by a
patterned line of type. In *Breakfast of Champions* Vonnegut fills
those spaces with felt-tipped scrawls and graffiti; Donald Barthelme adds to the stories in *City Life* his own collages of borrowed
nineteenth-century engravings, and in *Guilty Pleasures* these are
further mixed with photographs, the *dreck* of advertising. The
effect of all this typographic dazzle is both disruptive and additive:
the text is broken and reformed into a mosaic which looks never to
be completed. Equally, the sense of an ending, the tendency for
any narrative to head towards some rest, if not resolution, is deli-
berately hobbled. Vonnegut and Brautigan explain in earlier chapters exactly how *Slaughterhouse Five* and *Trout Fishing in America* are
going to end. The circularity which is implicit in the modernism of
Virginia Woolf or William Faulkner is printed into the typographic
devices by which post-modernist writers avoid what John Fowles
(or whoever it is who represents him in chapter fifty-five of *The
French Lieutenant's Woman*) calls 'the tyranny of the last chapter, the
final, the "real" version' (1971, p. 349). The final hand-printed
word of *Breakfast of Champions* is ETC.

One difficulty in writing about new fiction is its resistance to paraphrase – the continual slipping away from any one authorised version of the story. The final two paragraphs of Robert Coover's story 'The Babysitter' read:

> She wakes, startled, to find Mr Tucker hovering over her. 'I must have dozed off!' she exclaims. 'Did you hear the news about the babysitter?' Mrs Tucker asks. 'Part of it', she says, rising. 'Too bad wasn't it?'. Mr Tucker is watching the report of the ball scores and golf tournaments. 'I'll drive you home in just a minute dear', he says. 'Why, how nice!' Mrs Tucker exclaims from the kitchen. 'The dishes are all done!'

o   o   o

> 'What can I say, Dolly?' the host says with a sigh, twisting the buttered strands of her ripped girdle between his fingers. 'Your children are murdered, your husband gone, a corpse in your bath tub, and your house is wrecked. I'm sorry. But what can I say?' On the TV, the news is over, and they're selling aspirin. 'Hell, *I* don't know', she says. 'Let's see what's on the late late movie.' (1973, pp. 192–3)

Coover supplies several more possible narratives than are completed here: he does not supply any guidance as to which reading he intends as the real story of that evening. Some stories, some evenings, are dull; some are exciting, but switching between the news, the ads and the late late movie we learn that none is necessarily more credible than any other.

There are 108 paragraphs in 'The Babysitter' and the television is on in forty-three of them. Television is not a pale flickering in the background: it actively invades the story, as when the children are relentlessly tickling their babysitter:

> he grabs a stocking foot and scratches the sole ruthlessly and she raises up her legs trying to pitch him off, she's wild, boy, but he hangs on and she's laughing, and on the screen there's a rattle of hooves and he and Bitsy are rolling around and around on the floor in a crazy rodeo of long buckling legs. (ibid., p. 170)

The babysitter switching between the Western on one channel and the murder mystery on another is in the position of the reader trying to construct a meaning from a structure that is continually dissolving, interrupting itself, setting up new patterns. Television, particularly in a country with many more than three channels and with unannounced commercial breaks every few minutes, repeats the essential formalist premise that its structure – broken, discontinuous, episodic – is central to its meaning. Like the babysitter we 'watch television' rather than watching distinct and separate programmes on television. The serious joke in Monty Python's 'and now for something completely different' is that however bizarre or inconsequential that something, it is still television. The mock credits and repeat endings that have become a convention of television comedy work, like the prefaces and open ends of new fiction, to undermine any sense of a distinct and completed experience which is available for interpretation. The broadcasters' term for the white spaces between programmes emphasises the confusion of boundaries: 'continuity', with its armchair reminders of the time and what to watch out for later tonight and in next week's TV Times, becomes the invisible thread which holds television together. Continuity takes up almost as much time as the news or drama: the BBC in 1974–5 had 4.6 per cent of its output in this category compared with 5.0 per cent for news and 5.7 per cent for drama (Fiske and Hartley, 1978, p. 167). Continuity is a gap which serves simultaneously both to separate and to fuse the distinct units that go to make up the 'flow' of a day's or an evening's television.

It is Raymond Williams who has distinguished the need to analyse television not in terms of discrete programmes, but in a way that represents more closely the actual experience of watching television. 'In all developed broadcasting systems the characteristic organisation and therefore the characteristic experience, is one of sequence or flow. This phenomenon, of planned flow, is then perhaps the defining characteristic of broadcasting, simultaneously as a technology and as a cultural form' (Williams, 1974, p. 86). This concept, defining both the production and consumption of television, is an equally useful way to describe the way in which Vonnegut or Coover write and we read new fiction. Television with its trailers, its repeats and replays, its instant switches in mood and between genre, is a continuous challenge to the beginning, middle and end of realism. In Reading Television (1978) John Fiske and John Hartley set out in opposing columns 'the modes by which television is organised on the one hand and the modes characteristic of dominant literate culture on the other':

Oral Modes	Literate Modes
dramatic	narrative
episodic	sequential
mosaic	linear
dynamic	static
active	artifact
concrete	abstract
ephemeral	permanent
social	individual
metaphorical	metonymic
rhetorical	logical
dialectic	univocal/'consistent' (pp. 124–5)

Without having to argue for every single selection on that team list, it is clear how much more easily new fiction fits the pattern of the oral rather than the literate mode. Not only is the formal structure of a book like *Slaughterhouse Five* episodic rather than sequential, mosaic rather than linear, dynamic rather than static, and so on down the line, but we are made to read the book in a way that is closer to the switchback experience of watching television than to the smooth ride of realism. Those roller-coasting paragraphs provide a dizzying simultaneity of views; at the same time they reassert the authority of the one who has designed the ride – we cannot guess what the next paragraph or chapter is going to say – there's no time to set up our own narrative or personal reading.

Television does suggest a new variety of formal techniques which writers can add to the devices, such as dissolves or montage, an earlier generation of novelists learned from the cinema. But any comparative reading of television and new fiction must extend beyond the formalist considerations that generally have restricted the comparison between film and novel, to the wider ideological implications of authorship and authority. The flow of television, the 'telegraphic schizophrenic manner' of new fiction, both depend on a structural continuity established by presenter or author: that presentation in turn draws repeated attention to the fragile boundary between fiction and fact, representation and reality. Any one programme, any one paragraph or chapter, may maintain a formal coherence that works like the 'can't put it down' seductions of realism. But inevitably that illusion is ended by the urgency of the next message from our sponsor. Vonnegut insists on telling us so much about his 'famous book about Dresden' –

explaining his publishing contract, whom he has dedicated the book to and why, what he has learned from it, what we are to learn from reading it – that we can create our own reading only by registering the tension between the worlds Vonnegut describes and the reality of massacre and mass bombing in 1969, the year *Slaughterhouse Five* was published and Lieutenant Calley was charged with murdering civilians in My Lai. Television seeks a similar authority and risks or invites an equivalent side-stepping by its audience. The breaks which television presents as natural may capture an audience for an advertiser or an agent of the Ideological State Apparatuses. They also provide repeated opportunity to leave the room or to switch channels. While Vonnegut may intend or expect his readers to move from fiction to fact, television hurries nervily between proclaiming and disguising the distinction. The warnings posted before any 'drama documentary', the edgy smiles assuring us before any break that there's still plenty of action to come, suggest that the television programmer cannot be as confident as Raymond Williams that 'experience' flows directly from 'organisation'. It is this uncertainty that calls for a criticism which can move confidently from fiction to fact, can recognise the formal strategies of an author or programme-maker and the material context which defines and limits his or her authority.

Television adds a further twist to the tension created in film criticism between a theoretical emphasis on the author/director and the counter-insistence on studying the enclosing (studio) system of production. *Slaughterhouse Five* exists as a film as well as a novel: directed by George Roy Hill with a screenplay by Stephen Geller, it was released in 1972. Any comparison of these two 'texts' can easily wander into the dead-end aestheticism of questioning Hill and Geller's 'faithfulness' to Vonnegut, their ability to 'translate' novel into film. Yet, show this or any version of *Slaughterhouse Five* on television and the structure of the medium, governing both production and consumption, will replicate without any fuss the full range of devices used by Kurt Vonnegut. Trailers will promote and simultaneously flatten any suspense or climax; commercials will cut in their display of the 'simulated earthling habitat . . . from the Sears and Roebuck warehouse' (p. 97); the news will force the recording of an event against its interpretation; and each viewer, in following or resisting the baited trail laid by the programme controller, creates his or her own television version of *Slaughterhouse*

Five. While the cinema produces another text to put alongside that written by Kurt Vonnegut, television dissolves that concept so thoroughly that it calls into proper doubt any notion of text at all. Television, like new fiction, is forever moving our attention sideways to the next image in its kaleidoscope collage. Television, like new fiction, tries to deny or subvert the attempt, learned from an earlier literate tradition, to look through the text to discover and fix what it is really about. The text, in television and in new fiction, becomes all and nothing.

This, then, is the way in which the comparison between television and new fiction can lead from the simple formalism of the 'medium is the message' to a politically-complicated consideration of television and fiction as forms of cultural production, to be scheduled and marketed. That first formalist reading establishes the essential break with 'the fallacies which have bound literary criticism to ideology: the fallacy of the secret, the fallacy of depth, the fallacy of rules, the fallacy of harmony' (Macherey, 1978, p. 101). As Macherey insists, a 'true reading . . . is not a question of perceiving a latent structure of which the manifest work is an index, but of establishing that absence around which a real complexity is knit' (ibid., pp. 100–1). A formalist analysis is needed to trace the text to its final disappearance, but something more is required to support the reader who rightly decides to follow the words from the page. Continuity is the 'absence' around which the complex experience of television is structured, and a true reading of fiction would be one that established an equivalent of that essential concept. Just as it is necessary to read television beyond the boundary of a single programme, so it is equally necessary to read any fiction beyond the boundary of its authored text.

Jerome Klintowitz calls his illustrated guide to 'Super Fiction' *The Life of Fiction*, and he shows a groupie's enthusiasm for crashing the reserve that has traditionally distanced writer from critic. 'Vonnegut & Co are living writers. The substance of their writing is widely available not only in their fiction, but also in their commentary, reviews, interviews, letters, phone calls and personal adventures' (1977, p. 2). Abandoning the 'metaphysic of the text' cannot be compensated for entirely by a critical life spent waiting for an adventurous phone call from Kurt Vonnegut; but there is an important sense in which the career of a writer like Vonnegut can only be understood by a criticism which extends to the creation of his public/published personality through the agency of press and television promotion and the patronage of university workshops and presses. Vonnegut's own readiness to include within the first chapters of *Slaughterhouse Five* or *Breakfast of Champions* information previously reserved for the book-jacket or a trade blurb calls for a criticism that is equally adept in establishing the material circumstance of fiction.

The critical response to Vonnegut's career has often nagged at the implications of his promotion from the lower divisions of slick magazines and pulp paperbacks to the review pages of the *New York Times* and Writing in Residence. Vonnegut himself in his ventriloquist exchanges with Kilgore Trout has mocked his vulnerability to being typed a writer of black humour, science fiction or merely popular fiction. Moving between television and new fiction shows the increasing implausibility of such classifications and the variety of hybrids that are already supplanting them. The delight of Donald Barthelme in the *dreck* of popular culture, the readiness of new fiction to celebrate the 'trash' of the American folk-story with its cowboy, detective or space-travelling hero, is met by the arbitrary power of television to elevate a forgotten fiction into a BBC classic serial or a presentation of Masterpiece Theater.

Two other natural children of television and fiction, the 'novelisation' and *The Book Programme*, show in contrasting ways the tension between the oral mode of television and the literate mode of the dominant culture. The novelisation exists to convert the frustratingly episodic appearance of television's popular heroes and families into a steady supply of narrative. It stands against the restless discontinuities of television and new fiction, and provides a reassuring reminder of the dependable commercial value of good old-fashioned realism. If the TV tie-in or spin-off is the tribute paid by an oral culture to the earlier, still resilient, literate tradition, then the talking heads of *The Book Programme* or the chat show promotions of *Read All About It* suggest in their formula jargon the steady conversion by television of print into talk. This clearly has a formal equivalent in the conversational lay-out, the open confidences, of much new fiction; but again it is important to go beyond a formalist comparison to consider the surrounding questions of cultural politics.

The American writer Adrienne Rich has spoken recently of a

'crisis in naming' which has hampered the drive of women's writing
to find new ways of describing their experience. Publishers are
made uneasy by texts which move constantly between poetry and
autobiography, personal history and a collective political demand.
While Adrienne Rich's own recent work provides exemplary proof
of the rewards gained from a refusal to be held down by naming,[4]
this is a problem and an opportunity that reaches beyond the
specific practices of feminist writing. Television and new fiction
have found new ways of escaping the traditional limitations of
genre, and yet it is not enough to recognise and analyse the new
names and forms they have created. Reading the lines of television
and new fiction reveals not only the formal complexity of their
structure but also the need to set that against the equally compli-
cated institutional and cultural structures which have channelled
their meaning.

Notes

1 This question is discussed in several of the contributions to *Screen Education*'s issue on Television Drama (1980) No. 35.
2 Tony Bennett discusses this problem in the Conclusion to his *Formalism and Marxism* (Methuen, 1979).
3 *Will The Real Norman Mailer Stand Up*, directed by Dick Fontaine (1969). The film was not shown on BBC until 1975.
4 Adrienne Rich made this comment in a talk at the ICA in October 1980. Her own answer to this crisis is best exemplified by *Of Woman Born* (Virago, 1977).

References

Barthelme, Donald (1967), *Snow White*, New York: Atheneum.
—— (1970), *City Life*, New York: Farrar, Strauss & Giroux.
—— (1974), *Guilty Pleasures*, New York: Farrar, Strauss & Giroux.
Brautigan, Richard (1967), *Trout Fishing in America*, San Francisco: Four Seasons Foundation.
Coover, Robert (1973), 'The Babysitter' in *Pricksongs and Descants*, Picador.
Fiske, John and Hartley, John (1978), *Reading Television*, Methuen.
Fowles, John (1971), *The French Lieutenant's Woman*, Panther.
Hassan. Ihab (1975), *Paracriticisms*, Urbana, Illinois: University of Illinois Press.
Isherwood, Christopher (1972), Foreword (1947) to Edward Upward's 'The Railway Accident'. Reprinted in Edward Upward, *The Railway Accident and Other Stories*, Penguin, 1972.
Klinkowitz, Jerome (1977), *The Life of Fiction*, Urbana, Illinois: University of Illinois Press.

Macherey, Pierre (1978), *A Theory of Literary Production*, Routledge & Kegan Paul.

Mailer, Norman (1968), *Armies of the Night*, Weidenfeld & Nicolson.

Roth, Philip (1977), 'Writing American fiction' in Malcolm Bradbury (ed.), *The Novel Today*, Fontana.

Scholes, Robert (1975), 'The fictional criticism of the future', *Tri Quarterly*, 34.

Sontag, Susan (1966), *Against Interpretation*, New York: Farrar, Strauss & Giroux.

Sukenick, Ronald (1969), *The Death of the Novel and Other Stories*, New York: Dial Press.

—— (1975), 'Twelve digressions toward a study of composition', *New Literary History*, VI.

Vonnegut, Kurt (1970), *Slaughterhouse Five*, Jonathan Cape.

—— (1973), *Breakfast of Champions*, Jonathan Cape.

Williams, Raymond (1974), *Television: Technology and Cultural Form*, Fontana.

15
Historicist criticism

DAVID CRAIG
and MICHAEL EGAN

I

We call our approach historicist in order to mark it off from other ways of reading imaginative literature, yet recognise that by impli-cation we are also laying claim to the entire practice of modern literary criticism. Historicism, in our view, potentially reconciles and advances the principal theoretical and practical difficulties now being encountered by students of literature.

The term *historicist* is not perhaps the best we could have chosen, especially since we do not include within it the special meanings assigned by Karl Popper. But we retain it because it emphasises our sense of the centrality of the study of history to the study of literature (and vice versa). Part of the contemporary crisis in liter-ary criticism – this book is, if nothing else, evidence of that – derives on the one hand from the collapse of the late Victorian compart-mentalisation of knowledge, and on the other from the increasingly-apparent bankruptcy of the two intellectual traditions which have dominated critical practice in recent decades: New Criticism and what we could loosely call Althusserianism. New Criticism is now felt by a large number of critics to be both wanting in theory and, at the same time, to be carrying hidden in its baggage political and social assumptions of an unacceptable kind. Althusserianism, on the other hand, using this term in the sense propounded by E. P. Thompson in *The Poverty of Theory* (1978), has proved in its applications to literature and aesthetics to have been wilfully obscure and limited, stiflingly élitist and jargon-ridden, and extraordinarily incapable of generating fresh (or even stale) insights. What is evident is that an intellectual vacuum in the practice of criticism is now felt to exist. Historicism, it seems to us, offers to fill it.

We shall show that historicist criticism is properly eclectic. Its historical method is both materialist and dialectical in the full marxist sense; we hold that the superiority of Marx's approach to historical knowledge is evident and demonstrable. At the same time we have willingly learned from New Criticism, and wish to retain its practice of close reading and of supporting one's judgements with illustration and quotation. Banal as this point may seem to some it must be made, because there is a strong current of opinion among radical critics, semioticians and structuralists alike that the mere scrutiny of texts in Leavis's manner is inherently reactionary and limiting. We understand some of the philosophical difficulties involved, but think they can be overcome.[1]

The nub of historicist criticism, however, is the conviction that some works of art are demonstrably superior to others. Again, this point may seem painfully obvious to some readers, yet so deeply has the confusion of relativism bitten in recent critical practice – and the difficulty is compounded by the legitimate argument that the élitism of the 'Great Tradition' has defined out of the discussion whole areas of popular culture and radical art – that it is now seriously put about that any attempt to distinguish comparative levels of quality is quite illegitimate. We see the problem well enough but also note the soggy mess which evading it, rather than confronting it, has led to. Historicist criticism negotiates the difficulty of aesthetic criteria, and the continuing debate in marxism of the uses of literature as social evidence, in the following propositions: the more historically accurate a piece of imaginative writing is, the better it is likely to be. And the better it is aesthetically, the more historically accurate it is likely to be.

We shall show that these are not circular propositions; they are fully dialectical, rich in the interplay between historical knowledge and artistically-creative witness. Nor are they axioms, since we offer them only as statements which are probably true. Working out the considerable theoretical difficulties flowing from them constitutes a principal item on the historicist agenda, just as the repeated, concrete illustration and testing of them becomes a major activity. And the one is not abandoned for the other, they move in necessary tandem. Theory and practice, as Lenin understood, are inseparable.

II

During the First World War the British press was full of patriotic verse whose purpose, especially after the military disasters of 1916, was to revive the sagging morale of the troops and their families. The following, by Gerald Cumberland, is an example:

The Winging Souls

When good men's bodies die, their souls go winging
To God: go winging and singing
Through space. And God, smiling but august,
From heav'n, of angels sends a little throng
To meet the happy souls so newly freed from dust –
To greet the happy souls singing their song.

In bed I lay one night wakefully thinking
Of France: lay thinking, and shrinking
From Death. I saw smitten, and wet with Death,
A thousand men of Britain – brothers, sons.
Twisted and torn were they, their latest breath
A cry crushed by the thunder of the guns.

Foulness below . . . But up above?
O, up above was Love . . . .
I saw a thousand souls
Winging to God.
He met them on Heav'n's stair
And took them in His care.

Heav'n's corridors and ways
Are open to them all their days.
And as I fell on sleep I heard their winging
And as I woke this morn I heard their singing.

Our point is this: that only an historicist reading of this poem renders the right judgement as to its quality, and a judgement of its quality in effect becomes an act of historicist criticism. For instance: can the poem be read as religious satire? If so, then the awkward archaisms of speech (august, throng, latest, Heav'n, etc.) will resonate somewhat differently. But the act of contextualisation, both social and literary, provides the answer No. We have already noted that the poem was written by an Englishman at a time when there was a widespread need to bolster the depressed feelings of those whose 'brothers, sons' were dying by the tens of thousands in the mud of northern France, when the prospect of victory was an insufficient compensation for megadeath, and when the British press, almost daily, contained poems such as this one, all making essentially the same point: that while perhaps death in the trenches was no longer a cleansing and purging experience (as poets such as Rupert Brooke had claimed when the war broke out), at least the Almighty was on our side and our dead children could look forward to the consolations of the afterlife. Whether or not we consciously deploy historical information when reading it, the knowledge that this is not a satire presents itself both from within the poem and from the public accessibility of images and facts woven now inextricably into our consciousness. There can be no 'innocent' reading of this or any other literary work.

But despite Cumberland's wish to console the bereaved and encourage their continued support for the war effort, his language and imagery, inseparable as they are from the poem's overall compensatory stance, are limp, clumsy and conventional. The image of the winged souls flying happily upwards with a song on their lips is mawkish because Cumberland's outworn, Sunday-school imagery is in every sense the conceptual equivalent of his imitative, linguistic bombast ('And as I fell on sleep . . . and as I woke this morn . . .'), clearly an effort to infuse a grandeur into ideas that are felt to be exhausted. So the poem evokes not genuine sacrifice, martyrdom and struggle against Evil (it is only the British soldiers, after all, who are 'good men') but merely the literary-heroic, a stagey gesture. Cumberland, indeed, appears to be offering a palpable fiction that he had a vision of angels issuing from the Hand of God to greet dead Englishmen. And why are they dead? And what is the source of their goodness? They have been slain in a war against Germans. The Hun may be presumed to go to the other place. Cumberland's suggestion, then, that God is an Englishman entirely subverts the broad humanitarianism at the heart of Christianity. This jingoism is in fact the source of the tatty theatricality of the language and the imagery.

To write at second hand is to acknowledge that one has not in fact experienced the thing at first hand, and this question of direct personal experience is an important and even crucial dimension for the historicist critic. It seems as a general rule that the immediacy of direct experience is inseparable from literary vitality. What we have in mind here is Brecht's notion that the dramatist should speak with the energy and urgency of someone describing an automobile accident he has just seen or been part of, or Trotsky's more intellectualised observation that an analyst of events must also be a participator: that is, the two things are dialectically linked. Cumberland's flaccidity, then, is the direct consequence of his not having seen what he claims to have seen, even in the second stanza which 'approaches' the war itself.

Compare Cumberland's images and language with those in another war poem, written, again, by a little-known poet but one who was actually there, Robert Nichols:

The Assault[2]

The beating of the guns grows louder.
'Not long, boys, now.'
My heart burns whiter, fearfuller, prouder.
Hurricanes grow
As guns redouble their fire.
Through the shaken periscope peeping,
I glimpse their wire:
Black earth, fountains of earth rising, leaping,
Spouting like shocks of meeting waves,
Death's fountains are playing,
Shells like shrieking birds rush over;
Crash and din rises higher
A stream of lead raves
Over us from the left . . . (We safe under cover!)
Crash! Reverberation! Crash!
Acrid smoke billowing. Flash upon flash.
Black smoke drifting. The German line
Vanishes in confusion, smoke. Cries and cry
Of our men, 'Gah, yer swine!
Ye're for it,' die
In a hurricane of shell.

One cry:
'We're comin' soon! Look out!'
There is opened hell
Over there; fragments fly,
Rifles and bits of men whirled at the sky:
Dust, smoke, thunder! A sudden bout
Of machine guns chattering . . .
And redoubled battering,
As if in fury at their daring!
. . .
Time. Time!

I hear the whistle shriek
Between teeth set;
I fling an arm up,
Scramble up the grime
Over the parapet!
I'm up. Go on.
Something meets us.
Head down into the storm that greets us.
A wail.
Lights. Blurr.
Gone.
On, on. Lead. Lead. Hail.
Spatter. Whirr! Whirr!
'Toward that patch of brown
Direction left.' Bullets astream.
Devouring thought crying in a dream.
Men crumpled, going down . . .
Go on. Go.
Deafness. Numbness. The loudening tornado.
Bullets. Mud. Stumbling and skating.
My voice's strangled shout:
'Steady pace, boys!'

The still light: gladness.
'Look, sir. Look out!'
Ha! Ha! Bunched figures waiting.
Revolver levelled quick.
Flick! Flick!
Red as blood.

Germans. Germans.
Good! O good!
Cool madness.

This is precisely not an antiwar poem, of which it could be said that we consider it superior because we prefer its sentiments. The speaker is an officer with all his class's paternalism towards 'his' men, and the poem runs the gamut of emotions, from fear of death through religious feelings (he prays twice in the course of waiting for the signal) and the nationalist hatred of Germans to the concluding bloody rage and murder.

Yet it is also clear (isn't it?) that Nichols has produced a superior poem to 'The Winging Souls'; and the reason is that he is writing about something learned at first hand. This does two things for him. First, he is able to include in his poem images of striking sensuousness, not only those of his own seething emotions but of the trenches themselves: the 'shaken periscope'; the fury and noise of the guns; the 'rifles and bits of men whirled at the sky'; actual words and phrases – 'Gah, yer swine: Ye're for it!'; the comradeship of shared danger; the frightened suspense of waiting to go over the top. And it becomes one of the few examples in literature dealing with what must have been a daily experience for millions of men caught up in the war. Nichols, like Cumberland, uses the analogy between thunder and gunfire, but succeeds in infusing it with fresh power because he has established it in a context of storm, the hurricane of trench warfare. So the thunder is not asked to carry the entire evocative load but grows organically from the 'spouting shocks' of earth, the 'fountains' and 'waves' of death which draw the unexpected, but wholly authoritative and descriptive, parallel between the exploding earth and a monstrous sea. In 'Dulce et Decorum Est' Wilfred Owen was driven to a similar analogy describing a gas attack, so that war itself is seen as an inversion of the natural order, air and earth transformed into hostile ocean.

The second effect of Nichols's direct involvement is to force him to find a poetic form appropriate to the experience. Where the thin internal rhymes of 'The Winging Souls' ('thinking and shrinking', 'smitten . . . Britain', 'up above? O, up above was Love',) are jangling and irritating, a distraction rather than an enhancement, in 'The Assault' the shape of the poem itself fragments, allowing

images, emotions and half-formed thoughts or recollections to
flicker by in a concrete enactment of the process. This is done even
though the rhyming is exact. There is a creative tension between
the disintegrating lines and irregular stanzas and the steady tick of
the rhymed line-endings, a structural parallel to the tension between Nichols's churning terror and the act of self-conscious will
that eventually forces him up and over the parapet into the storm
of bullets.

'The Assault', then, creates a potent, sensuous image of extreme
danger and potential injury breaking in on the dazed and gruelled
weariness of infantry at the front line. We are plunged into the
situation, but while it is given in all its chaos it remains uncannily
precise. We are there, we feel, on the Somme or at Ypres perhaps,
harrowingly near the shellbursts. And this arises, as we have seen,
from the masterly detail, almost all of which is not invented but
experienced.

Yet we ourselves have not been in a battle. Our sense that much
of the poem's imagery is not only unexpected but accurate (good
evidence) cannot, therefore, arise from a comparison between the
writer's phrasing and our own experience. It must derive from a
general experience of language, which leads us to recognise that a
striking image – 'Shells like shrieking birds rush over' – is able to
give us a new mental sensation, which we value as such, while
staying materially true to the original object. It is at this point that
'excellent writing' and 'good evidence' intersect.

How much more are we saying than that a poem like 'The
Assault' or 'Dulce et Decorum Est' is a remarkably intense evocation of what one man perceived at one stage in his life?[3] The poets
obviously intend more than this. 'Dulce et Decorum Est' evokes a
particular episode which is then broadened and broadened until it
turns into a fairly generalised indictment of those people (recruit-
ing sergeants, War Ministers, jingo journalists, headmasters, belli-
cose parsons) who had helped to put about the official propaganda
message that it is sweet and fitting to die for your country. It is not,
claims the poem; it is in fact filthy and terrifying. In 'The Assault', a
less conscious poem, the frightened, homesick officer becomes an
insane killer. Thus 'The Assault' is finally a poem against the war,
not because Nichols set out to preach, but because the accumula-
tion of bloody detail – the poet's integrity as a witness, in fact – leads
to this inescapable conclusion.

Of the two views – Cumberland's and Nichols's – which is the truer? Is 'The Assault' better history by virtue of its being better written than the jingo journalism or the many poems which took the official line? Ultimately, our grounds for trusting the poet as a witness lie entirely in our sense of the relation between language working well on the page and the experience it purports to represent.

But can we say more? Can we claim that Nichols's poem offers good evidence, not only of one area in the north of France late in the war, but also of how great numbers of people were coming to think and feel as the conflict wore on? The lines of our argument, in the space here, can only run roughly as follows. We are talking of millions, to whom no one homogeneous frame of mind can be attributed. Nevertheless, there are tendencies in social behaviour: morale collapses or remains high; votes swing; millions did, in fact, on the Eastern Front, 'vote with their feet' and stream back to the Russian countryside and the Russian cities. We know they had been among carnage and chaos not unlike that described by Nichols – the shellbursts, the drowning, the destroyed tissue. The common-sense *prima facie* case would be that what Nichols suffered (both the immediate terror, the resulting revulsion and – in Owen's case – still later the disillusion with the official propaganda) was felt also by significantly large numbers of soldiers throughout Europe.[4]

We have now made the move from the poem to the continental, even global history to which it bears witness. To recapitulate the process: we encounter the poem; we are stopped by it – held by it; and we feel it to be aesthetically pleasing. (Already, of course, our own *parti pris* is creeping in. We know our own tendency, as socialists, to go along with, and even particularly admire, work that criticises or exposes the brutality of imperialist war. But we believe that none the less we are also focusing clearly on the features in 'Dulce et Decorum Est' or 'The Assault' which exact our aesthetic admiration, and we are encouraged in our judgement when we remember that we often dislike and disapprove of socialist works which are poorly written – tub-thumping, written to order, etc.) Having then taken the force and noted the exactitude of the more descriptive parts of the poem, we are encouraged to agree with the argument (especially, in Owen's case, the polemical ending) for which the rest of the poem has offered the grounds. The flung accusation of 'the old Lie' is nothing like a petulant gesture, some private grudge cloaked in a concern for the general good. We would expect to find it shared by many, and even to be acted on in that war, at that stage. To confirm these expectations we must go to history (Sassoon's rejection of his Military Cross, the mutinies which Pétain drowned in blood, the massive desertions of soldiers and sailors who went home to create the Soviets), and having done so we find evidence of widespread political disenchantment with the war. The behaviour of armies and voters, of whole regiments and cities, is in the historical record to that effect. One agonised minute in the life of one man is in the poem. Yet the historical evidence and the poetic testimony are only at different points on the same scale: namely, the record of what our species has undergone.

Remarkable literature, then, is good evidence because of the salient quality for which we appreciate it whether or not we have a conscious wish to read it historically. In essence, it is its vividness in giving us the feel of particular ways of life. At the more lifelike (realistic) end of the spectrum, it is expert in mimicry. At the more stylised (symbolic, visionary) end, it is notable for its foregrounding of certain elements in reality, giving rise to a texture or ensemble which may strike us first by its powerful and original use of the means in its own medium (metaphor, rhythm, flexible use of time, etc.) and then by creating a vision or imaginative overview which is a model of experience that stirs us deeply and challenges us to realign our sense of how things are.

Thus our sense of how things are – our view of reality – is inalienably fundamental to literature. However independent of fact or mundane observable conditions a work may seem to be (Blake's *Prophetic Books, Flash Gordon*), it cannot in practice avoid for long our almost instinctive – certainly our habitual – reference to 'likeness': is this how things are? or (if the work is historical) is this how things were? or (if the work is futuristic) could things as they now are conceivably develop into that? It follows that literature is, at however many removes, evidence of present reality; that of a person who is in the world and who is moved by his or her experience of it to select this or that element and compose it with others into a representation of life, giving a dark image to what is opposed, a glowing one to what is admired, a double-edged or satirical one to what is cared about but feared for, and so on. We may therefore ask of writers: where were they? what were they looking at? from what angle? were they observing or taking part? how clearly did they see it? and through what prisms? And if good writing flows from precise awareness, as we have argued, the excellent writer will be a reliable witness and his work is likely to be good evidence.

III

It is evident from what we have said, and also not said, that the interaction between history and literature is one of complex dialectical interplay, and full of theoretical difficulties.[5] But what we want to do now is consider the other side of the equation, the ways in which the historical matrix shapes literature and art in their more general manifestations. For we are not saying only that history – by which we mean reality in process of evolving – gives writers their subject matter, which they then interpret according to their temperaments, upbringing, class, etc. They interpret it also according to their culture or – in specifically literary terms – by means of the forms which they invent or adapt, innovating upon what comes to them via the media in use in their society. What follows, then, is a necessarily curtailed illustration of the way in which an historically-informed critical practice deals with the issue of artistic evolution.

The instance we choose is that of the novel, the most accessible and well-known example of the historical phylogeny of an art form in modern times. It had few significant precedents before the late seventeenth and eighteenth centuries; soon after that it became the major vehicle for imaginative writing in English. Why this development at that time?

It is our view that a major cultural form or medium – epic, the novel, cinema, television, or whatever – is as it is, and is superseded when it is, because of the social arrangements prevailing in the culture as a whole. The roots and the prototypes of the novel lie in the motley range of forms which society needed for its business, just as, for example, the form of the sentence (two nouns linked by a copula or a verb) originated in the labour process (the person, the object of his/her work, and its instruments); metre, verse, and refrain originated in work-songs; and drama originated in rituals.[6] The forerunners of the novel of Defoe and Fielding were various bread-and-butter media which evolved as a result of the struggle between the aristocracy and the gentry which some call the Civil War and others the English Revolution. These media included newsletters and newspapers, printed parliamentary speeches, lives of famous soldiers, sinners and convicts, and Civil Service documents.

In the 1620s newspapers were still newsletters – weekly or monthly magazines, for subscribers only, and full of exotic oddities and rumours, such as an item 'reporting' that a woman in Switzerland had given birth to a calf. By 1650, such was the demand for news of recent crucial events, newspapers were on sale widely and consisted of more or less factual home news with lively descriptive writing and human-interest stories about the armies. They also mattered enough to be censored by government and, at times, a monopoly to publish them was vested in safe sympathisers such as Roger L'Estrange. The same demand generated the printed speech. In 1640 three or four copies of a speech in Parliament might be made by the scriveners, sometimes commercial, sometimes in the pay of unusually wealthy or vain MPs. By 1645 a crucial speech or piece of business, such as the Grand Remonstrance addressed by the Commons to Charles I, might be printed in as many as 20,000 copies and sold generally – a brand new form of political appeal to the people.[7] A little later lives of prominent people began to appear abundantly. The country, as it took stock of what had happened during the war, wanted to know in detail what sort of men had been active. The form that resulted, as in various memoirs, in Clarendon's and Burnet's histories, or in Halifax's 'character' of Charles II, belongs to historiography, biography, and the essay, but approximates the novel when it specifies the details of a person's behaviour.

Another popular form of activity had been preaching, often with a political message, by working-men to the democratically-organised sects which had sprung up.[8] This medium, along with and inseparable from the heightening of personal consciousness which issued in potent new sects such as the Quakers, gave rise also to candid self-revelation such as Bunyan's autobiography, *Grace Abounding*. At the other end of this same gamut lies the 'true confession' type of life, perhaps of a famous forger or prostitute, which was run off to be sold among the crowds who gathered to see the subjects of them hanged at Tyburn or the Edinburgh Grassmarket. Defoe had a large collection of them in his library. Finally, the Civil Service, which grew up as the new state machine won more and more powers from the monarchy, and which employed many notable writers (e.g. Milton, Marvell, Pepys, Defoe), developed a staple prose, forerunner of the Augustan, which was formal, judicious, given to generalisation – in every way a change from the highly spontaneous and 'oral' prose of the Elizabethan proto-novels such as Nashe's *Unfortunate Traveller*. It has been suggested that the new prose arose because civil servants had to take care not to commit themselves, in their reports and memoranda and minutes, in case their masters changed policies.[9]

What these ingredients fused to create was a prose which aimed to imitate, and to moralise about, the actual present life and speech of recognisable people from its own society, even when the characters were invented. Such is the realistic method of novels as different as *Moll Flanders*, *Tom Jones* and *Pamela*. They are unprecedented: they cater for a consuming appetite for impressions and discussion of our own way of life, and both the root of this appetite (a sense that society is what we make for ourselves, in the teeth, perhaps, of what royalty or divinity may ordain) and the linguistic medium needed to satisfy it may be traced directly to the media which were engendered by the class struggles of the seventeenth century.

Of course the novel is a 'bourgeois form', inseparable from the rise of the middle classes, as Ian Watt has argued,[10] and of course artistic ingredients went into the mix, for example, epic and the picaresque. But to explain and account for the novel only by referring to the ascendance of the bourgeoisie – as if that were all that needed to be said – or to talk only about existing forms – which were both exotic and dated – is insufficient. By and of themselves they cannot explain the extraordinary power and complexity of the form, with its incomparable ability of detailing the lives of real people in real societies. We have to be both historians and critics to get the argument right. We need the procedures of historicist criticism.

IV

If our theory is correct, that the best literary works are good evidence, then the history which they build up will be true in outline, reasonably full, and strikingly accurate in its recounting of particular episodes – a civil war, perhaps, a drift of population from country to town, or a slump in the morale of a class. In practice, of course, we alternate between history and literature, deepening and making more inward our sense of, for example, the industrial revolution by reading Dickens's version of its relentless ideology in *Hard Times*, then correcting or supplementing his view of local trade union politics (as travestied in the character of Slackbridge) by consulting eye-witness accounts (including Dickens's own) of contemporary meetings.[11] What is also true in practice is that we are usually reading a literature from a culture (most often our own, or a close neighbour such as France or the USA) which we have already frequented in other ways: travel, television, printed reportage, what friends have told us, and the like. From these and other sources we build up the historical and cultural *view* that runs abreast of and dovetails with the *vision* we then derive from the literature. Nevertheless, as an illustration of literature as good evidence, let us consider the social history embedded in the series of novels from Fielding through Jane Austen to Dickens and George Eliot.

A reader ignorant of Britain's past would learn that in the eighteenth century the country was dominated by rural landowners living brutally but vigorously (*Tom Jones*) but that gradually their way of life was refined to the point where they came, as a class, to be felt as an incubus (*Northanger Abbey*, *Persuasion*). During the nineteenth century the centre of social gravity increasingly shifted to the towns and cities, places notable for their squalor and extremes of poverty, but also where a large and resentful working population, living by its labour in the textile and metal industries, was becoming politically self-conscious and challenging to the established order (*Mary Barton*, *Dombey and Son*). But the proletarian uprising feared by the middle and upper classes never materialised (*Sybil*, *North and South*, *Hard Times*). The propertied went on to develop an affluent and self-regarding life-style set at a distance both geographically and morally from their workers and tenants (*Adam Bede*, *Middlemarch*, *Daniel Deronda*, *The Portrait of a Lady*). People coming new to our literature and history would not be misled if they inferred the shape of British social development and its political and moral implications from this particular sequence of novels. On the contrary, and this is our point, they would be remarkably well informed.

Historicist criticism, then, opens out into a series of projects, since it is not intrinsically hostile to any of the major schools or activities in modern critical practice. A historicist history of literature is still to be written. The relevance of structuralist and semiotic theory is still to be assessed. The insights of the Freudians, perhaps via the work of materialist psychologists such as Wilhelm Reich, must obviously be incorporated. What is more, and perhaps initially, we have to show that there *is* a tradition within marxist literary theory – to be found for instance in the work of Brecht, in Trotsky's *Literature and Revolution*, in Caudwell's *Illusion and Reality*, and in some of Raymond Williams's later work (especially *The Country and the City*) – which starts from particular texts and social situations, and is saturated with a sense of history as a major intellectual discipline. It is this criticism, and our own, that we call historicist, and it is in this tradition that we feel the growing points in literary comment and analysis are to be found.

Notes

1 As a partial answer we point to our own practice, particularly in *Extreme Situations* (Macmillan, 1979).
2 We cannot, unfortunately, reproduce the whole poem here. It was originally published in *Ardours and Endurances* (Chatto, 1917).
3 Clearly, not just on a single occasion. 'Dulce et Decorum Est', for example, was based mainly on an action of 12.1.17, but the gas attack belongs to other actions (for instance, one nearly a week later; see J. Stallworthy, *Wilfred Owen* (Oxford University Press, 1974), pp. 156–7.) We are precisely *not* saying that good poems are simple reportage.
4 The mutinies of the French soldiers at Craonne and elsewhere are well-known from *Oh What a Lovely War!* and Leon Wolff's *In Flanders Field*.
5 We cannot pursue them here, but have recently done so elsewhere. See David Craig and Michael Egan, 'What is Historicist Criticism?' in S. Knight and M. Wilding (eds), *Radical Reader II* (Sydney: Wild and Woolly, 1981).
6 See George Thomson, *The First Philosophers* (1955; Lawrence & Wishart, 1973), pp. 39–41 and *The Prehistoric Aegean* (1954; Lawrence & Wishart, 1978), pp. 445–51; also J.M. Manly, 'Literary forms and the new theory of the origin of species', *Modern Philology*, IV, 4 (1907), 5, 7–8. These cases have been brought together, and their theoretical bearings discussed, in David Craig, 'Marxism and popular culture' in C.W.E. Bigsby (ed.), *Approaches to Popular Culture* (Edward Arnold, 1976), pp. 140–3.
7 Joseph Frank, *The Beginnings of the English Newspaper, 1620–1660*

(Cambridge, Massachusetts: Harvard University Press, 1961), pp. 7–31, 302; Christopher Hill, *The English Revolution 1640* (Lawrence & Wishart, 1955), p. 41.

8 See D.W. Petegorsky, *Left-Wing Democracy in the English Civil War* (Gollancz, 1940).

9 David Ogg, *England in the Reign of Charles II* (Oxford University Press, 1963), pp. 703–5.

10 In *The Rise of the Novel* (Chatto & Windus, 1957), Watt argues, in a sophisticated version of 'the ethos of the age' approach, that the genre originated in the economic individualism which began to thrive in the mercantile age following the down-grading of the feudal monarchy.

11 See Dickens's 'On Strike', *Household Words*, 203 (11.2.1854); 'The Diary of John Ward of Clitheroe, Weaver, 1860–64', *Transactions of the Historical Society of Lancashire and Cheshire* (1964), 115, 140, 150, 156; James B. Jeffreys (ed.), *Labour's Formative Years, 1849–79* (Lawrence & Wishart, 1948), p. 61.

16
Text and history

TONY BENNETT

> You cannot just 'write the truth'; you have to write it *for*
> and *to* somebody, somebody who can do something
> with it.   Brecht

I

In his *Aspects of the Novel* (1927), E. M. Forster imaginarily insulates
the English novel against the inruptions of history by visualising
the English novelists as 'seated together in a room, a circular room,
a sort of British Museum reading-room – all writing their novels
simultaneously' (p. 16). Although empires may fall, he later asserts,
'those people writing in the circular room . . . have entered a
common state which it is convenient to call inspiration, and, having
regard to that state, we may say that History develops, Art stands
still' (pp. 27–8). Needless to say, Forster's ideal reader is also safely
ensconced in the British Museum with the critic scurrying between
writer and reader, clasping them, through the text, in a perfect and
completed cycle of communication, all the while shushing those
new entrants who threaten to disturb this timeless, circular
exchange with the muddied boots of history.

The view that the literary work is formed, communicated and
received, passed on from writer to reader within a system of
exchange that is untroubled by the intrusions of history has, of
course, always constituted an integral component of the bourgeois
critical enterprise, and one made possible only by the curious and
contradictory status it has accorded the concept of 'the text'. Curious and contradictory because although an inordinate emphasis
has characteristically been placed on the text as the point at which

reading must start and – whatever else may be encountered on the way – to which it must return, the text is simultaneously conceived as a mere vessel, a carrier of the meanings which, secreted within, beneath or behind its surface workings, constitute the critic's or reader's ultimate objective. In spite of its honorific status, then, the text is valued only as a shell placed around the meanings it contains, preserving these intact and inviolate, passing them on from writer to reader uncontaminated by the history that intervenes. And the goal of criticism, as of much teaching, has been to dispense with this shell, to distil from the text the meanings it contains, to unwrap them from the dense textual structures in which they are enveloped and, in so doing, to place the reader in direct, unmediated contact with them.

This view of the text, characteristic of the dominant forms of interpretative criticism, has been seriously challenged in recent years, mainly by structuralist and semiological schools of criticism. According to these, the text has no within, beneath or behind where hidden meanings might be secreted. Attention is instead focused exclusively on the processes and structures of the text and on the ways in which these produce meanings, positions of intelligibility for the reader or the specific effects of realism, defamiliarisation or whatever. The very antithesis of interpretative criticism, structuralist criticism does not seek to read through the material properties of the text to reveal 'the work' they contain; rather, it examines the way in which the text, as a set of material notations, 'works'.

In this essay, I want to challenge both of these conceptions of the text and the constructions of the critical enterprise which they support. In their susceptibility to the seductive facticity of the text, to its apparent self-containedness, solidity and discreteness, both views misleadingly fetishise it in abstracting it from the concrete and historically varying relationships in which it is inscribed during the successive moments of its history as a culturally active, received text. A condition of any text's continuing to exert long-term cultural effects within any society must be that it is constantly brought into connection or articulated with new texts, socially and politically mobilised in different ways within different class practices, differentially inscribed within the practices of educational, cultural and linguistic institutions and so on. I shall argue that it is only in the light of such historically concrete, variable and incessantly changing determinations – determinations which so press in upon the text as fundamentally to modify its very mode of being – that it is possible to assess, at any given moment, the effects that might be attributed to any given text or set of texts.

However, in developing these criticisms, I want also to point them in another direction. For marxist criticism, in both its interpretative and its structuralist guises, has successively subscribed to either the one or the other of these views of the text. The *credo* of marxist criticism, of course, has always been that the study of literature should be based on protocols and procedures that are impeccably historical and materialist. Works of literature, that is to say, should be viewed as material phenomena inserted within historical relations and processes, the purpose of analysis being to explore the connections between the two. Yet this is seldom the case in practice, where marxist criticism has often proved to be seriously flawed by its implicit retention of idealist concepts and procedures. An arguably more serious limitation, however, consists in the fact that marxist criticism has sought to historicise literary phenomena only one-sidedly. For the greater part, attention has focused on returning literary texts to the conditions of their production and on the insistence that the practice of writing can be understood only when placed in the context of the varying historical and material determinations which condition its pursuit. Although this stress on the determinations of literary production is a *necessary* part of any thoroughgoing marxist criticism (see Lovell, 1980), the historical and material determinations which, as it were, flow into the literary text through the diverse and changing structures which condition the modes of its consumption are of no less importance. Yet considerations of this sort have been almost totally neglected within marxist criticism. Although the writer has been inserted in the flow of history, the text, except for the privileged moment of its production, has not. And the reader, to all intents and purposes, has been left in the reading-room of the British Museum: ideal, abstract and disembodied.

This failure to consider the determinations which structure and condition the practice of reading and which, in so doing, constantly re-work the text, as well as the related tendency to think of the reader as ideal and singular, the product of purely textual processes, rather than of *readers*, concrete and plural, have seriously distorted the ways in which questions concerning the relationship between literature and politics have been posed within marxist critical debates. Far too often, the political effects that might be attributed to different practices of writing have been calculated on the basis of their formal properties alone, without any reference to the different ideological formations within which different groups of readers are inserted or to the determinations which regulate the consumption of specific texts in specific periods. It has been in this way that we have been invited, successively, to choose for or against realism (of the Lukácsian variety), for or against modernism, for or against the avant-garde, for or against the classic realist text. Literary-political debate has typically taken the form of a choice between abstract and polarised options posed, seemingly, without any regard to the possibility that different literary-political strategies might be appropriate in different historical contexts or in relation to different groups of readers.

II

There can, of course, be no doubting the *materiality* of the text, its physical existence as a set of written, material notations. Indeed, properly understood, it is this very materiality of the text which disables the view that the text can be fetishised as either the container of a meaning, single and irreducible, or the source of an effect. Jacques Derrida has demonstrated this perhaps more forcibly than anyone. In an analysis of the view of the written text which underlies interpretative criticism – the text as a vehicle for the transportation of thoughts and meanings from writer to reader – Derrida contends that the very materiality of the written work *necessarily* entails that the life of the text exceed such a closed cycle of communication. In order for writing to function as writing, he contends, it must continue to be structurally readable – 'iterable' – beyond the confines of any particular set of author-reader relations.

> To write is to produce a mark that will constitute a sort of machine which is productive in turn, and which my future disappearance will not, in principle, hinder in its functioning, offering things and itself to be read and re-written. . . . For a writing to be writing it must continue to 'act' and to be readable even when what is called the author of the writing no longer

answers for what he has written, for what he seems to have signed. (Derrida, 1977, pp. 180–1)

This 'iterability', Derrida goes on to argue, liberates the text from any possible enclosing context, be it the context of the originating moment of inscription favoured by interpretative criticism or the context of the semiotic code favoured by structuralism. The very structure of the written text is such that it carries with it a force that breaks with its context; and, indeed, with each of the contexts in which it may be successively inscribed during the course of its history. It cannot be limited by or to the context of the originating moment of its production, anchored in the intentionality of its author, because 'the sign possesses the characteristic of being readable even if the moment of its production is irrevocably lost and even if I do not know what its alleged author-scriptor consciously intended to say at the moment he wrote it' (ibid., p. 182). Nor can the text be tied down by the authority of the semiotic code, as a fixed system of rules, which allegedly inhabits it:

> As far as the internal semiotic context is concerned, the force of the rupture is no less important: by virtue of its essential iterability, a written syntagma can always be detached from the chain in which it is inserted or given without causing it to lose all possibility of functioning, if not all possibility of 'communicating', precisely. One can perhaps come to recognize other possibilities in it by inscribing it or *grafting* it onto other chains. (ibid.)

A radical and thoroughgoing critique of both interpretative and structuralist criticism, Derrida's remarks speak against any and all attempts to pin the text down, to limit it to a single context. Instead, they open up to investigation what might be called 'the living life of the text'; the history of its iterability, of the diverse meanings which it supports and of the plural effects to which it gives rise in the light of the variant contexts within which it is inscribed as it is incessantly re-read and re-written. The important questions, from the standpoint of a materialist theory of the articulations between literary phenomena and social processes, concern the nature of the determinations which bear in upon the 'living life of the text', the changing matrices which condition the concrete and variable forms in which it is available to be re-read and re-written.

Most immediately, there is the question of the text's relations with and to other texts. This, as I have argued elsewhere (see Bennett, 1979), was a question that centrally preoccupied the Russian formalists. For the formalists, the question as to whether a given text counted, on their definition, as 'literary' – that is, whether it fulfilled the function of 'defamiliarisation', of making the world strange and an object of renewed attentiveness – could not be resolved abstractly with reference solely to its formal properties independently of the changing relations of intertextuality in which it might be installed during the different moments of its history. They viewed the position of any single text in relation to other texts, and hence the meanings which it might support, the signifying functions it might serve or the effects to which it might give rise as being liable to constant shifts and displacements as new forms of writing transform and re-organise the entire system of relationships between texts. Thus they convincingly established that the notion of 'the text itself' as the source of some pure or essential meaning could not be anything other than a metaphysical concept. To this there needs to be added the role of criticism which, in constantly re-classifying texts, discursively re-orders the relations between them. No text, as Colin MacCabe has argued, 'can escape the discourse of literary criticism in which it is referred to, named and identified' (MacCabe, 1978, pp. 2–3).

From a materialist perspective, however, such immediately literary and critical determinations need to be thought in relation to the broader ideological processes through which the sphere of fictional writing is connected with adjacent areas of social and political practice. It is here that, in recent years, the work of Antonio Gramsci has been so important. Ernesto Laclau and Chantal Mouffe have argued that Gramsci's writings on the subject of hegemony constitute both a resounding critique of and a valid alternative to reductionist conceptions of ideology according to which specific ideologies are viewed as the expressions in thought of specific class situations and of the interests flowing from such situations (see Laclau, 1977 and Mouffe, 1979). According to Gramsci, they argue, particular ideological discourses – those of populism or nationalism, for example – do not have an essential class-belongingness. They cannot, that is to say, be attributed, for all time, in some essential way, to particular classes as their 'world-views': ideologies do not stay in one place but may, so to speak, swap sides in the class struggle. Indeed, as Mouffe suggests, the objective of ideological struggle is precisely this: to break down ideological ensembles into their constituent elements and to re-articulate the connections between them, pulling them together in a different way and on a different side in the class struggle, rather than opposing one ideology to another in an eternal struggle of truth versus illusion (see Mouffe, 1980, p. 192).

The same processes are at work in relation to 'the living life' of the literary text, albeit not so directly or in ways that connect so immediately or perceptibly with the flux of class struggle. The mediation through which such connections are forged is the arena of criticism. It is through the operations of criticism that the relations between different practices of writing are constantly broken down into basic elements and built up again into new, discursively constructed orders of intelligibility, and, in the process, grafted onto specific ideological interventions within the social formation at large. The position which a text occupies within the relations of ideological class struggle at its originating moment of production is, from this point of view, no necessary indication of the positions which it may subsequently come to occupy in different historical and political contexts. Indeed, to speak of the 'occupancy of a position' is, in any period of the 'living life of the text', misleading. The text does not occupy a position but is always and forever installed in a field of struggle, mobilised, placed, positioned, articulated with other texts in different ways within different critical practices which, sometimes obliquely, sometimes directly, themselves play into and register effects within neighbouring areas of ideological struggle. From the point of view both of a theory of the connections between literary phenomena and social processes and of the conduct of a politically conscious criticism in the present, an understanding of the historical determinations which thus flow into the text through the diverse forms in which it is discursively mobilised in changing relations of ideological class struggle is vital. The aim of such a criticism should not be that of revealing the truth of the text, laying bare its structures, unpicking its devices, analysing its effects or whatever; at least not as ends in themselves. Rather, it should be that of the *strategic* mobilisation of texts in specific contexts of class struggle; not a question of what texts mean but of what they might be *made to mean* politically. To cite Colin MacCabe again:

In analysing literature one is engaged in a battle of readings, not chosen voluntaristically but determined institutionally. The validity of interpretation is determined in the present in the political struggle over literature. (1978, p. 26)

The rider 'institutionally' is important. Althusser has taught us that signifying practices are always inserted within and have no concrete existence apart from the material practices of specific ideological apparatuses or institutions (see Althusser, 1971). In the case of written texts, the ways in which these are discursively mobilised by the practice of criticism thus need to be inserted within or set alongside the practices of cultural and educational institutions, particularly the latter as, especially since the nineteenth century, these have constituted a privileged site for the circulation of those texts which have been regarded as of special value; that is, as 'literary' in a specialised and restricted sense. The work, in France, of Renée Balibar and Dominique Laporte has been of especial importance here (see Balibar, 1974, 1978 and Balibar and Laporte, 1974; see also Davies, 1978 and Bennett, 1979 for summaries). In studying the uses to which literary texts were put within the educational institutions of post-revolutionary France, Balibar and Laporte have shown how these functioned so as to construct and maintain class-based inequalities in relation to the newly constructed unified French language. Within primary schools, the children of all classes received their education in the national language in the form of an administered grammar – a set of codified rules to be learned by rote and applied mechanically. The élite schools preserved for the sons and daughters of the bourgeoisie, however, sought to inculcate a superior facility with the language by means of the privileged place that was accorded so-called literary texts within the study of comparative grammar. The aim was to promote an awareness of those properties of language that exceeded the requirements of mere communicative competence. By thus, in effect, producing two languages within one – the ordinary linguistic competence shared by all classes, and a special, literary awareness of the properties of language restricted to the bourgeoisie – the objective functioning of literary texts, Balibar and Laporte suggest, was such as to produce and maintain for the bourgeoisie a position of dominance in language.

   In addition, the work of Balibar and Laporte registers a decisive methodological advance in the respect that it analyses the effects of specific forms of writing (those nominated as 'literary') not only with regard to their formal properties, but also, more importantly, to the ways in which, in the context of late-nineteenth-century France, such texts were 'produced for consumption' in specific ways by virtue of their inscription within a pedagogic practice of a particular kind. Nor is this of importance solely from a methodological point of view. One of the more arrestingly peculiar features of marxist criticism is the extent to which, so far, its 'recommended reading' has amounted to different selections from bourgeois reading – realism or modernism, for example – in spite of the fact that, objectively speaking, these have formed a part of a privileged exchange from which the great mass of ordinary people have been, not accidentally, but *systematically* excluded. It is clear that marxist critical debates cannot continue to take the form of a series of disagreements about precisely which versions of bourgeois literary culture should be handed down to the working-class reader with the approval seal of 'radical effect' stamped on them – at least not without regard to the ways in which the relations between such texts and different categories of readers are concretely structured.

Which brings us to the critical question of the reader and the moment of consumption. Stuart Hall has argued that the text itself is not the place where 'effects' are located: texts achieve effects only through the decoded meanings that are taken from them and only in the context of the ways in which those meanings are invested in social practices of varying sorts (Hall, 1980, pp. 128–30). Characteristically, the issues to which these considerations point have been virtually wholly neglected within British literary scholarship. Two recent studies on the subject of reading, welcome though they are, make no attempt to pin down the extra-textual determinants which bear on the process of reading (see Slatoff, 1970 and Iser, 1978). For Iser, the 'act of reading' has to do with the ways in which the reader's experiencing of a text is made possible, with how the reader – not the empirically real reader but the reader within the work – activates the text's processes. 'Effects and responses', he writes, 'are properties neither of the text nor of the reader; the text represents a potential effect that is realized in the reading process' (Iser, 1978, p. ix) – an important advance but none the less significantly marred by its stress on the singular: on '*a* potential effect that is *realized* in *the* reading process' rather than on different *effects* that are *produced* in different relations of reading. Similarly, whilst disputing that we can 'talk meaningfully about an ideal or correct sensory response' to the text (Slatoff, 1970, p. 33), Slatoff keeps alive the notion of the unsullied integrity of the text as 'that which is responded to' (albeit differently), and, try as he might, is unable to speak about different 'responses' to the text without attempting to distinguish the appropriate from the inappropriate, the valid from the invalid, grouping responses in a hierarchic relationship that is ultimately warranted by the authority of the text and/or its author.

Fortunately, the question of reading – or, more accurately, of viewing – has been raised in a more theoretically informed and empirically concrete way in film and television criticism. The context within which these considerations have been raised has been largely that of an ongoing polemic against the protocols of structuralist criticism, especially as represented by *Screen* in the 1970s. In particular, exception has been taken to the structuralist view of the text as, so to speak, unilaterally fixing a position for the reader, imprisoning him or her in its structure so as to produce a singular and guaranteed effect. The polemic has, however, been circumspectly conducted in the respect that, anxious not to throw the baby out with the bath water, the critics of the more extreme forms of structuralism have nevertheless granted much of the structuralists' case. The text may, it is admitted, stitch the viewer or reader into position in certain ways; it may offer the subject specific positions of intelligibility; it may operate to prefer certain readings above others. What it cannot do, it is argued, is *guarantee* them. Nor has this tempered rejection of structuralism given rise to the opposing *reductio ad absurdum*: namely that, since the text cannot guarantee its readings, the range of readings is potentially infinite and randomly distributed with as many readings as there are readers. Rather, attention has focused on the determinations which structure and pattern readings into identifiable clusters, on the factors which make for a limited repertoire of readings.

Of the various considerations that have been raised within this perspective, I will single out two for special mention here. The first concerns the use to which Michel Pêcheux's concept of the *interdiscourse* has been put, particularly by David Morley (see Morley, 1980*a* and *b*). According to Pêcheux, the subject that the text encounters is never a raw, unacculturated subject. Readers are

always already-formed, shaped into the subjects of specific forms
of consciousness, by the ideological discourses which have oper-
ated/operate/continue to operate upon them prior to, during
and subsequent to their immersion in the text in question. The
subject, Pêcheux argues, is formed in the *interdiscourse*, the meeting
place of the discourses which traverse the individual throughout
his/her history and it is in the space or interaction between any
given text and the discursive regimes which have already regulated
the thoughts and feelings of different individuals that the effects
of the former must be sought. The second consideration has to do
with the way in which the individual's access or exposure to different discursive regimes is structured by his or her position within
the social formation. Paul Willeman writes:

> The 'concrete experience' of the individual determined by his or
> her place in the relations of production, his or her place in the
> real, will determine in its turn to a large extent which institu-
> tions, what discursive regimes, etc., he or she will encounter and
> in what order. (1978, p. 67)

Putting these two considerations together, Morley has argued that
the question of reading 'is always a question of how social position
plus particular discourse positions produce specific readings;
readings which are structured because the structure of access to
different discourses is determined by social position' (1980*a*, p.
134). It is easy to see how, proceeding from this basis, a concrete
and empirically informed history of reading might be produced by
inserting the text within, and analysing its action in the light of its
articulation with, the different discursive formations which mediate between it and different categories of readers. Meaning is thus
regarded as the product of the interaction between text and reader
within a determinate discursive formation that is, in turn, structured by a determinate context. Viewed in this way, meaning is no
longer the property of the text; rather, the text is the site across
which the struggle for meaning is conducted:

> The analysis must aim to lay bare the structural factors which
> determine the relative power of different discursive formations
> in the struggle over the necessary multi-accentuality of the sign –
> for it is in this struggle over the construction and interpretation
> of signs that meaning . . . is produced (Morley, 1980*a*, p. 156).

It is this perspective, first outlined by Volosinov in his stress on 'the multi-accentuality of the sign' – on language as an arena of contestation over meaning as words are mobilised in different ways by 'differently orientated social interests within one and the same sign-community, i.e. by the class struggle' (Volosinov, 1973, p. 23) – that sounds the death-knell of the text. Not of the text as a material entity or as a set of discernible processes; but the subterfuge text within the text, the ideal text of bourgeois criticism.

III

'Text and history': normally, within marxist criticism, the connection between these has been made on the other, the production side of the literary process, viewing the text as a distillation of the determinations which condition the practice of writing. I have sought, in this essay, to outline those determinations – equally historical and material – which structure and condition the ways in which the text is consumed, and indeed, made available for consumption. It is through these that the connections between text and history are incessantly re-forged as the text is differentially mobilised politically, inserted within and articulated with different practices, critical and institutional, and written into different sets of reader-text relationships.

It should be stressed, however, that it is not sufficient merely to add these considerations on to the study of textual processes and structures. It is not a question of first distilling the text's meaning or analysing its structure *and then* considering the variable ways in which these are responded to, interpreted, used, put into effect or whatever. That way, the concept of the 'text itself', as a metaphysical entity which survives intact behind the surface detritus of such 'external' accretions, remains unchallenged. It is rather necessary to stress that the text only ever exists in the context of such determinations. There is no 'pure text' that is accessible behind or beyond the different forms in which its historical existence is modulated. To be sure, the specific constellation of determinations characterising the originating moment of a text's production may be regarded as of a unique significance. But these are in no sense ontologically privileged in relation to the subsequent determinations which bear upon the text's history; nor, from an analytical point of view, may they be allowed to override these. From the point of view of a thoroughgoing materialism, the text is a site on which varying meanings and effects may be produced according to the determinations within which the work is inscribed – determinations which are never single and given but plural and contested, locked in relations of struggle.

Clearly, in view of the work summarised in the preceding section of this essay and of other essays in the book, such considerations have been increasingly placed on the agenda for research in recent years so that it is now possible to define the parameters of what a materialist understanding of the connections between literary phenomena and social processes might look like. It is not merely the development of an adequate materialist *theory* of literature that is in question, however. There is also the question of the development of politically pertinent forms of *criticism*. This distinction between theory and criticism has been usefully summarised by Graham Pechey: the former, he argues, '*theorizes* the field that criticism practically *negotiates*' (Pechey, 1980, p. 77). The field which the critic has to negotiate, I have suggested, is more complexly structured than is usually thought. It is no longer enough, if ever it was, to stand in front of the text and deliver it of its truth. A politically motivated criticism, as feminist criticism has shown, must aim at making a strategic intervention within the determinations which modulate the text's existing modes of usage and consumption. It must aim to mobilise the text, to re-determine its connections with history by severing its existing articulations and forging new ones, actively politicising the process of reading. This requires, from a marxist standpoint, not the development of *a* criticism, validated by canons of theoretical correctness, but the development of a number of different critical practices aiming at politicising the process of reading differently in different contexts and for different categories of readers. It requires that the critic, too, must, as Brecht put it, think for whom (s)he writes and with what purposes in view. However, perhaps the first two of Walter Benjamin's theses on the critic's technique provide the most fitting epitaph with which to conclude. 'The critic', he wrote, 'is the strategist in the literary battle'; and: 'He who cannot take sides should keep silent' (Benjamin, 1979, p. 66).

236   Re-Reading English

References

Althusser, L. (1971), 'Ideology and ideological state apparatuses: notes toward an investigation' in *Lenin and Philosophy and Other Essays*, New Left Books.

Balibar, R. (1974), *Les Français Fictifs: le rapport des styles littéraires au français national*, Paris: Hachette.

—— (1978), 'An example of literary work in France: George Sand's "La Mare au Diable"/"The Devil's Pool" of 1846' in F. Barker *et al.* (eds), *1848: The Sociology of Literature*, Colchester: University of Essex Press.

—— and Laporte, D. (1974), *Le Français National: Politique et practique de la langue national sur la Révolution*, Paris: Hachette.

Benjamin, W. (1979), *One Way Street, and Other Writings*, New Left Books.

Bennett, T. (1979), *Formalism and Marxism*, Methuen.

Davies, T. (1978), 'Education, ideology and literature', *Red Letters*, 7.

Derrida, J. (1977), 'Signature event context' in *Glyph 1*, Baltimore and London: Johns Hopkins University Press.

Forster, E.M. (1927), *Aspects of the Novel*, Harmondsworth: Penguin, 1972.

Hall, S. (1980), 'Encoding/decoding' in Hall, Hobson, Lowe and Willis (eds), *Culture, Media, Language*, Hutchinson.

Iser, W. (1978), *The Act of Reading: A Theory of Aesthetic Response*, Routledge & Kegan Paul.

Laclau, E. (1977), *Politics and Ideology in Marxist Theory*, New Left Books.

Lovell, T. (1980), *Pictures of Reality: Aesthetics, Politics and Pleasure*, British Film Institute.

MacCabe, C. (1978), *James Joyce and the Revolution of the Word*, Macmillan.

Morley, D. (1980*a*), *The 'Nationwide' Audience*, British Film Institute.

—— (1980*b*), 'Texts, readers, subjects' in Hall, Hobson, Lowe and Willis (eds), op. cit.

Mouffe, C. (1979), 'Hegemony and ideology in Gramsci' in Mouffe (ed.), *Gramsci and Marxist Theory*, Routledge & Kegan Paul.

Pechey, G. (1980), 'Formalism and marxism', *Oxford Literary Review*, 4, 2.

Slatoff, W.J. (1970), *With Respect to Readers: Dimensions of Literary Response*, Ithaca and London: Cornell University Press.

Volosinov, V.N. (1973), *Marxism and the Philosophy of Language*, New York: Seminar Press.

Willeman, P. (1978), 'Notes on subjectivity', *Screen*, 19, 1 (Spring).

Consolidated bibliography

This alphabetical list contains the majority of works referred to in the course of *Re-Reading English* which are directly relevant to the issues the book raises.

At the end, there is a list of journals, mainly drawn from the references, which are or have been instrumental in furthering the debate about literary studies and education.

Althusser, Louis (1969), *For Marx*, Harmondsworth: Allen Lane.
—— (1971), *Lenin and Philosophy and Other Essays*, New Left Books.
—— and Balibar, Etienne (1970), *Reading Capital*, New Left Books.
Anderson, Perry (1964), 'Origins of the present crisis', *New Left Review*, 23. Reprinted in Anderson and Blackburn (eds), *Towards Socialism*, Fontana, 1965.
—— (1968), 'Components of the national culture', *New Left Review*, 50. Reprinted in Cockburn and Blackburn (eds), *Student Power*, Penguin, 1969.
—— (1976), *Considerations on Western Marxism*, New Left Books.
—— (1980), *Arguments within English Marxism*, New Left Books.
Bakhtin, M. (1968), *Rabelais and His World* (written 1940), Cambridge, Mass.: MIT Press.
Balibar, Renée (1974), *Les Français Fictifs, le rapport des styles littéraires au français national*, Paris: Hachette.
—— (1978), 'An example of literary work in France' in Francis Barker *et al.* (eds), *1848: The Sociology of Literature*, Colchester: University of Essex Press, pp. 27–46.
—— and Laporte, D. (1974), *Le Français National: Politique et practique de la langue national sur la Révolution*, Paris: Hachette.

Barker, Francis, *et al.* (eds) (1978), *1848: The Sociology of Literature*, Colchester: University of Essex Press.
—— (1979), *1936: The Sociology of Literature*, Colchester: University of Essex Press.
Barratt, M., *et al.* (eds) (1979), *Ideology and Cultural Production*, Croom Helm.
Barthes, Roland (1972), *Mythologies*, Jonathan Cape.
—— (1975), *S/Z*, Jonathan Cape.
Baxandall, Lee (ed.) (1973), *Marxism and Aesthetics*, New York: Humanities Press.
Belsey, Catherine (1980), *Critical Practice*, Methuen.
Bennett, Tony (1979), *Formalism and Marxism*, Methuen.
Bloch, Ernst, *et al.* (1977), *Aesthetics and Politics*, New Left Books.
Boulton, Marjorie (1980), *The Anatomy of Literary Studies*, Routledge & Kegan Paul.
Bourdieu, Pierre and Passeron, J.-C. (1979), *Reproduction in Education, Culture and Society*, Sage.
Bradbury, M. and Palmer, D. (eds) (1970), *Contemporary Criticism*, Edward Arnold.
Brown, C. and Olson, K. (eds) (1978), *Feminist Criticism: Essays in Theory, Poetry and Prose*, New Jersey: Scarecrow Press.
Centre for Contemporary Cultural Studies (1981), *Unpopular Education: Schooling and Social Democracy in England since 1944*, Hutchinson.
Clarke, Simon, *et al.* (eds) (1980), *One-Dimensional Marxism: Althusser and the Politics of Culture*, Allison & Busby.
Cornillon, S.K. (ed.) (1972), *Images of Women in Fiction: Feminist Perspectives*, Bowling Green, Ohio: University Popular Press.
Coward, Rosalind and Ellis, John (1977), *Language and Materialism*, Routledge & Kegan Paul.
Craig, David (ed.) (1975), *Marxists on Literature. An Anthology*, Harmondsworth: Penguin.
—— (1976), 'Marxism and popular culture', in C.W.E. Bigsby (ed.), *Approaches to Popular Culture*, Edward Arnold.
—— and Egan, Michael (1979), *Extreme Situations, Literature and Crisis from the Great War to the Atom Bomb*, Macmillan.
—— and Heinemann, Margot (eds) (1976), *Experiments in English Teaching*, Arnold.
Davies, Tony, 'Education, ideology and literature', *Red Letters*, 7 (n.d.), 4–15.
De Man, Paul (1979), *Allegories of Reading*, New Haven, Conn.: Yale University Press.
Derrida, Jacques (1973), *Speech and Phenomena*, Evanston: Northwestern University Press.
—— (1977), *Of Grammatology*, Baltimore: Johns Hopkins University Press.
—— (1977), 'Signature event context', *Glyph* I, Baltimore: Johns Hopkins University Press, 172–97.
—— (1978), *Writing and Difference*, Chicago: Chicago University Press.
Doyle, Brian, 'The tyranny of the past', *Red Letters*, 10 (n.d.), 23–33.
—— (1981), *Some Uses of English*, Birmingham: Centre for Contemporary Cultural Studies.

Eagleton, Terry (1976), *Marxism and Literary Criticism*, Methuen.
—— (1976), *Criticism and Ideology*, New Left Books.
—— (1977), 'Marxist literary criticism' in Hilda Schiff (ed.), *Contemporary Approaches to English Studies*, Heinemann.
—— (1979), 'Ideology, fiction, narrative', *Social Text*, 2, 62–80.
Ellis, John (ed.) (1977), *Screen Reader I, Camera/Ideology/Politics*, SEFT.
Fekete, John (1978), *The Critical Twilight: Explorations in the Ideology of Anglo-American Literary Theory from Eliot to McLuhan*, Routledge & Kegan Paul.
Firth, C.H. (1909), *The School of English Language and Literature*, Oxford: Blackwell.
Fiske, John and Hartley, John (1978), *Reading Television*, Methuen.
Foucault, Michel (1970), *Madness and Civilization*, Tavistock.
—— (1973), *The Birth of the Clinic*, New York and London: Pantheon and Tavistock.
—— (1973), *The Order of Things*, New York: Vintage.
—— (1974), *The Archaeology of Knowledge* (with Appendix, 'The Discourse on Language'), Tavistock.
—— (1977), *Discipline and Punish*, Harmondsworth: Allen Lane.
—— (1977), 'The political function of the intellectual', *Radical Philosophy*, 17, 12–14.
—— (1978), *Language, Counter-Memory, Practice* (ed. D.F. Bouchard), Oxford University Press.
—— (1979), *The History of Sexuality*, Harmondsworth: Allen Lane.
Fowler, R., *et al.* (eds) (1979), *Language and Control*, Routledge & Kegan Paul.
Frye, Northrop (1957), *Anatomy of Criticism*, Princeton: Princeton University Press.
Gilbert, Sandra and Gubar, Susan (1979), *The Madwoman in the Attic, the Woman Writer and the Nineteenth-century Literary Imagination*, New Haven, Conn.: Yale University Press.
Gramsci, Antonio (1971), *Selections from the Prison Notebooks*, Lawrence & Wishart.
Hall, S., *et al.* (eds) (1980), *Culture, Media, Language*, Hutchinson.
Harari, J.V. (ed.) (1979), *Textual Strategies: Perspectives in Post-Structuralist Criticism*, Ithaca: Cornell University Press; Methuen, 1980.
Hawkes, Terence (1979), *Structuralism and Semiotics*, Methuen.
Hoggart, Richard (1957), *The Uses of Literacy*, Harmondsworth: Penguin, 1958.
Holland, Ray (1977), *Self and Social Context*, Macmillan.
Iser, Wolfgang (1978), *The Act of Reading: A Theory of Aesthetic Response*, Routledge & Kegan Paul.
Jacobus, Mary (ed.) (1979), *Women Writing and Writing about Women*, Croom Helm.
Jakobson, Roman (1971), *Word and Language*, The Hague: Mouton.
Jameson, Fredric (1971), *Marxism and Form*, Princeton: Princeton University Press.
Johnson, Richard (1980), 'Cultural studies and educational practice', *Screen Education*, 34, 5–16.

240   Re-Reading English

Kristeva, Julia (1974), *La Révolution du langage poétique*, Paris: Seuil.

Lacan, Jacques (1977), *Ecrits: A Selection*, Tavistock.

—— (1977), *The Four Fundamental Concepts of Psycho-Analysis*, Hogarth Press.

Laclau, E. (1977), *Politics and Ideology in Marxist Theory*, New Left Books.

Lawford, Paul, 'Conservative empiricism in literary theory: a scrutiny of the work of F.R. Leavis', *Red Letters*, 1 (n.d.), 12–15; *Red Letters*, 2 (n.d.), 9–11.

Lawson, John and Silver, Harold (1973), *A Social History of Education in England*, Methuen.

Leavis, F.R. (1932), *New Bearings in English Poetry*, Harmondsworth: Penguin, 1963.

—— (1943), *Education and the University*, Cambridge: Cambridge University Press, 1979.

—— (1948), *The Great Tradition*, Harmondsworth: Penguin, 1962.

—— (1962), *The Common Pursuit*, Harmondsworth: Penguin.

Lefebvre, Henri (1971), *Au-delà du structuralisme*, Paris: Anthropos.

Lovell, Terry (1980), *Pictures of Reality: Aesthetics, Politics and Pleasure*, British Film Institute.

MacCabe, Colin (1978), *James Joyce and the Revolution of the Word*, Macmillan.

Macherey, Pierre (1966), *A Theory of Literary Production*, Routledge & Kegan Paul, 1978.

—— and Balibar, Etienne (1978), 'Literature as an ideological form', *Oxford Literary Review*, 3, 1, 4–12.

Marcuse, Herbert (1979), *The Aesthetic Dimension*, Macmillan.

Medvedev, P.N. and Bakhtin, M. (1928), *The Formal Method in Literary Scholarship*, Baltimore: Johns Hopkins University Press, 1978.

Mercer, Colin (1977), 'Culture and ideology in Gramsci', *Red Letters*, 8.

—— (1980), 'After Gramsci', *Screen Education*, 36, 5–15.

Morley, D. (1980), 'Texts, readers, subjects' in Hall *et al.*, *Culture, Media, Language*, Hutchinson.

Mulhern, Francis (1979), *The Moment of 'Scrutiny'*, New Left Books.

Newbolt Report (1921), *The Teaching of English in England* (Report of the Board of Education).

Newton, J.M. (1963), 'English literature at the university: a historical enquiry'. Unpublished thesis, University of Cambridge.

Palmer, D.J. (1965), *The Rise of English Studies*, Oxford University Press.

Plumb, J.H. (ed.) (1964), *Crisis in the Humanities*, Harmondsworth: Penguin.

Potter, Stephen (1937), *The Muse in Chains*, Jonathan Cape.

Richards, I.A. (1928), *Practical Criticism*, Routledge & Kegan Paul, 1970.

—— (1928), *The Principles of Literary Criticism*, Routledge & Kegan Paul, 1976.

Sampson, George (1921), *English for the English*, Cambridge: Cambridge University Press, 1970.

Schiff, Hilda (ed.) (1977), *Contemporary Approaches to English Studies*, Heinemann.

Showalter, Elaine (1978), *A Literature of Their Own*, Virago.

Slatoff, W.J. (1970), *With Respect to Readers: Dimensions of Literary Response*, Ithaca: Cornell University Press.

Steiner, George (1967), *Language and Silence*, Faber.

Sturrock, John (ed.) (1979), *Structuralism and Since*, Oxford University Press.

Thompson, E.P. (1955), *William Morris, Romantic to Revolutionary*, New York: Pantheon, 1978.

—— (1963), *The Making of the English Working Class*, Harmondsworth: Penguin, 1968.

—— (1978), *The Poverty of Theory and Other Essays*, Merlin Press.

Tillyard, E.M.W. (1958), *The Muse Unchained*, Bowes & Bowes.

Todorov, Tzvetan (1977), *The Poetics of Prose*, Oxford: Blackwell.

Vaneigem, Raoul (1967), *Traité de savoir-vivre à l' usage des jeunes générations*, Paris: Gallimard.

Volosinov, V.N. (1929), *Marxism and the Philosophy of Language*, New York: Seminar Press, 1973.

Watson, Garry (1977), *The Leavises, the 'Social' and the Left*, Swansea: Brynmill.

Williams, Raymond (1958), *Culture and Society*, Harmondsworth: Penguin, 1961.

—— (1961), *The Long Revolution*, Harmondsworth: Penguin, 1965.

—— (1974), *Television: Technology and Cultural Form*, Fontana.

—— (1976), *Keywords*, Fontana/Croom Helm.

—— (1977), 'Literature *in* society' in Hilda Schiff (ed.), *Contemporary Approaches to English Studies*, Heinemann.

—— (1977), *Marxism and Literature*, Oxford University Press.

—— (1979), *Politics and Letters*, New Left Books.

Wright, Iain (1979), 'F.R. Leavis, the *Scrutiny* Movement and the Crisis' in Clark, Heinemann, *et al.* (eds), *Culture and Crisis in Britain in the Thirties*, Lawrence & Wishart.

Zima, Pierre (1978), *Pour une sociologie du texte littéraire*, Paris: Union général d'éditions.

Some relevant journals

British Journal of Education

Centre for Contemporary Cultural Studies: *Working Papers in Cultural Studies*

Feminist Review	*Red Letters*
Literature and History	*Screen*
New Left Review	*Screen Education*
New Literary History	*Scrutiny*
Oxford Literary Review	*Social Text*
Radical Philosophy	*Studies in Higher Education*
Radical Teacher	*Use of English*

Index

This index refers only to the main text of the book, and not to the Notes, References or Consolidated bibliography.